P9-EDU-139

VARIATIONS
ON A THEME

SUNY Series, The Psychology of Women
Michele A. Paludi, Editor

VARIATIONS ON A THEME

Diversity and the Psychology of Women

edited by

JOAN C. CHRISLER
ALYCE HUSTON HEMSTREET

State University
of New York
Press

Published by
State University of New York Press, Albany

© 1995 State University of New York

All rights reserved

Production by Susan Geraghty
Marketing by Nancy Farrell

Printed in the United States of America

No part of this book may be used or reproduced
in any manner whatsoever without written permission.
No part of this book may be stored in a retrieval
system or transmitted in any form or by any means
including electronic, electrostatic, magnetic tape,
mechanical, photocopying, recording, or otherwise
without the prior permission in writing of the publisher.

For information, address State University of New York
Press, State University Plaza, Albany, N.Y., 12246

Library of Congress Cataloging-in-Publication Data

Variations on a theme : diversity and the psychology of women /
    [edited by] Joan C. Chrisler, Alyce Huston Hemstreet.
        p.   cm. — (SUNY series, the psychology of women)
    Based on papers presented at the 16th Annual Conference of the
Association for Women in Psychology, Hartford, Conn., March 1991.
    Includes bibliographical references and index.
    ISBN 0-7914-2435-9. — ISBN 0-7914-2436-7 (pbk.)
    1. Women—Psychology—Congresses. 2. Pluralism (Social sciences)-
-Congresses. I. Chrisler, Joan C. II. Hemstreet, Alyce Huston.
III. Association for Women in Psychology. National Conference (16th
: 1991 : Hartford, Conn.) IV. Series: SUNY Series in the psychology
of women.
HQ1206.V27 1995
155.3'33—dc20
                                                              94-26207
                                                                  CIP

10 9 8 7 6 5 4 3 2 1

CONTENTS

AUGUSTANA UNIVERSITY COLLEGE
LIBRARY

PREFACE

The inspiration for this volume was the 16th annual conference of the Association for Women in Psychology, which was held in Hartford, Connecticut, in March 1991. The theme of the conference was "Women in the '90s: Unified in Diversity." Organizing the conference was challenging and empowering, and attending it was intellectually exciting. This book was planned in order to share some of what we learned with a wider audience.

In keeping with the theme of the conference, the presentations explored the diversity and complexity of women's lives. The contributors to this volume were chosen from among the presenters at the conference and asked to expand their original presentations to better illustrate themes and variations in the psychology of women. In some cases women who had never worked together before were asked to collaborate in preparing chapters for this book, which resulted in unique challenges, rich scholarship, and new friendships.

The purpose of this book is to show clearly the unity and diversity, the themes and variations in women's lives. Rather than inviting separate chapters on ethnicity, sexual orientation, aging, and the like, each chapter weaves the variety of women's psychosocial experiences into a vivid tapestry. The topics (e.g, achievement, health, friendship, religion) that are covered in this book are familiar to all women, yet our personal experiences with them are different. Sharing experiences is the first step toward understanding each other, which is essential for an accurate psychology of women.

The editors are grateful to the members of the 1991 AWP Conference Committee—our friends and colleagues, who shared our vision, our joys and sorrows, our work, and our success. We also thank the attendees and presenters who inspired this volume, the authors who so generously contributed to it, our editor Lois Patton, and her staff at SUNY Press.

FOREWORD

Michele A. Paludi

At the celebration of my 40th birthday this year, I was with some relatives and developmental psychologists who seemed to think it was time for my life review!! I was asked about the various positions I've held and what, if anything, I miss about being in academia full time.

I remember saying without hesitation that I missed teaching the Psychology of Women course at Hunter College, for it was there I got spoiled. My friends and family thought it was a peculiar comment to make and wanted me to explain. I began my answer by noting that at Hunter 73 percent of its nineteen thousand students are women, and 54 percent of the student population are minorities, with the largest minority representation being African American non-Hispanic, with Hispanic and Asian or Pacific Islander next. I then went on to tell my guests how concerned I was when I went to Hunter in the fall of 1986, following my being at Kent State University: The text and readings I had ordered for the Psychology of Women course had nothing to do with the lives of the women who were sitting with me around the circle. These women, and the hundreds of women who participated in my Psychology of Women courses for six years at Hunter, taught me the real Psychology of Women.

They taught me to question paradigms in my own research on women's career development, especially sexual harassment, and to work with them to re-envision a diverse reality. As a requirement for the course, I would often ask students to write a term paper on an issue related to the diversity of women's experiences and then compile their papers into a textbook that was given to all students at the end of the semester. Many women students who had this "textbook" on the "real psychology of women" have written to me over the years to tell me how this collection of term papers has served as a resource guide, a "paper mentor," a help to them when they were going through various life stages and experiences, especially concerning their career development, relationships with women and with men, and changing relationships with their aging parents.

In my work as a consultant to businesses and campuses, I have been working on balancing policies, grievance procedures, and curricula for diversity. And, as a Legislative Advisor on Women's Issues to a member of the New York State Assembly, I try very hard to be vigilant in remembering all that the women minority students at Hunter taught me about race, class, and ethnicity when I share opinions, research findings, and theories of an issue related to a bill currently under debate.

Joan Chrisler and Alyce Hemstreet have provided us with a wonderful opportunity to rethink the psychology of women with their edited volume, *Variations on a Theme: Diversity and the Psychology of Women*. This text is written with caring and compassion for women that nurtures our spirit. It will serve as a useful guide for understanding similarities and valuing diversities, or as Johnetta Cole's book states in its title, "the ties that bind and the lines that divide." Chrisler and Hemstreet's text asks us to decenter from our own perspectives and life stages and recognize the needs and rights of all women. Their book brings us closer together, teaching and learning from each other in a cooperative process. This book represents what womanist education is all about.

I applaud Joan and Alyce and all contributors to this volume. I was especially honored to have been asked by them to co-author a chapter (with Darlene DeFour) for this volume. I am thrilled at their invitation to write this foreword. And, I am most pleased they decided to publish this book in the SUNY series on the Psychology of Women, of which I am the editor. This book enriches the series, and it will enrich all of our lives.

INTRODUCTION

Everywhere one goes these days the talk is about diversity—its value, its importance, its contribution to scholarship and academic life. Feminists are wondering, as Beverly Goodwin and Maureen McHugh put it, "Who is the woman in the psychology of women?" and are taking steps to broaden our perspectives. The addition of information about diverse populations should be done not just because we believe it's right (or politically correct) to do so, but because it is good science and essential for an accurate psychology of women.

How are we doing so far? Not very well, as you shall see. Each chapter in this volume reviews the literature in some area of importance to women's lives. The authors present an analysis of the state of the field and point out gaps in information or services. There are plenty of gaps, and, therefore, plenty of work for all of us to do!

We begin with a look at women's physical and mental health. Joan Chrisler and Alyce Huston Hemstreet examine selected issues in women's health to see whether the diversity of women's needs is being met. Unfortunately, the answer is no. There is almost nothing written about the health needs of Native American, Asian American, and poor, rural women. There is more, albeit insufficient, information available about black women, Latinas, lesbians, and elderly women, but the more we know, the more we realize how little we're doing to provide adequate health care for all women.

Martha Banks, Rosalie Ackerman, and Carolyn Corbett argue convincingly that women have not received proper treatment for brain injuries caused by accidents, rape, or other physical assaults. When women report neurological signs and symptoms, their complaints are often minimized by physicians who assume the women are hysterical or attention-seekers. The authors describe common neurological problems associated with various traumas, with a particular focus on rape-related injuries. They present the fascinating case of a deaf woman of color who has a seizure disorder and a history of abuse and neglect, and show how her communication problems and low tolerance for frustration make her a special challenge for psychotherapists.

In their chapter Geraldine Butts Stahly and Gwat-Yong Lie discuss the frequency and variety of domestic violence in women's lives, which has created a health crisis that physicians have been reluctant to confront. Battering relationships are found among both heterosexual and lesbian couples. Although there is a growing literature on both types of couples, Stahly and Lie point out that the literature has not been integrated, nor have the community services for battered women, which cater to the needs of women battered by men. With all we do know, we still lack a unified theory that can explain and predict domestic violence.

The next three chapters discuss topics all women have in common and consider the different ways we experience them. Suzanna Rose reviews the literature on women's friendships and describes the central role these relationships play in our lives. Friendships between women are different from those between men or between a woman and a man. Rose compares and contrasts friendship patterns and shows how women's friendships influence and are influenced by particular communities. Read this chapter with a friend.

Whether we've embraced religion or discarded it, we've all been influenced by the religious traditions of our society. Rachel Josefowitz Siegel, Sudha Choldin, and Jean Orost have long been interested in the effect of religion on women's psychosocial development. However, they had never met each other until the editors invited them to work together on their chapter. They developed a remarkable working relationship, and we think you will be fascinated by what they have to say about the impact of three of the world's great religions (Judaism, Hinduism, and Christianity) on women's lives.

Darlene DeFour and Michele Paludi have taken a comprehensive look at women's achievement needs and experiences that can enhance or block their fulfillment. How do women's achievement needs change with age? How do sexual harassment and mentoring affect women's careers? You will find the answer to these questions and more in this chapter.

Women's careers often get their start in college, and the two final chapters consider issues in higher education—first the needs of students, then those of faculty. Lillian Holcomb and Carol Giesen combine their expertise on women with disabilities and older women to argue for better services that will help these women cope with the challenges of higher education. They describe clearly the similarities and differences in the college experiences of older women and women with disabilities, and urge their readers not to think of these women as coming from discrete populations. After all, the older we are, the more likely we are to experience disabilities.

Although feminists agree on the necessity of adding diverse views to the psychology of women course, we may be confused about how to manage without the support of adequate textbooks. What's a professor to do? Ann Marie Orza and Jane Torrey share their combined forty years of experience teaching the psychology of women and provide many helpful suggestions. After a review of the development of the field, they describe pedagogical techniques they have used, and include a reading list of novels that can help students better understand the lives of women who are different from themselves. We bet you'll want to read every book on their list!

The Diversity of Women's Health Needs

Joan C. Chrisler
Alyce Huston Hemstreet

Health is both a psychosocial and a biomedical phenomenon. Researchers and practitioners must keep these two sets of factors in mind to adequately understand and provide care for the diversity of women's health needs. Women's health care needs differ from those of men in a number of important ways, but women differ among themselves as well. One might think of women's health needs as variations on a theme. Women may share the experience of chronic diseases, dysmenorrhea, premenstrual tension, and menopause, and yet be vulnerable to different types of disorders due to genetics or economics and experience similar situations differently due to sociocultural or religious backgrounds.

Byllye Avery (personal communication, March 8, 1991) has discussed the different responses she receives as she travels around the country speaking about women's health. White women expect her to talk about reproductive health; black women most want her to talk about diabetes and hypertension. Although these three topics are important for all women, it is clear that different communities have different priorities. Women's priorities vary by age, race, ethnicity, religion, physical ability, sexual orientation, and economic class.

It is these variations we kept in mind as we reviewed the literature on women's health. We found that there is almost nothing written about the health care needs of Native American and Asian American women. The needs of black women and Latinas have received better, albeit insufficient, attention. Little has been written about the needs of physically challenged women, lesbians, or poor, rural women. Most of the work on older women's health needs is on hormone replacement therapy, osteoporosis, and, most recently, coronary heart disease.

Mortality and Morbidity

On the average, women live about eight years longer than men and have lower rates for all of the major causes of death except breast cancer (Travis, 1988). The sex difference in mortality rate is so consistent that some have suggested that women are biologically advantaged over men (Strickland, 1988; Travis, 1988). Because women live longer than men, they are more likely to suffer from chronic illnesses, and they report more acute illnesses as well. Furthermore, gynecological operations are the most frequent category of surgical procedures (Strickland, 1988).

Women are more likely than men to suffer from hypertension and hypertensive heart disease, diabetes, anemia, rheumatoid arthritis, systemic lupus erythematosus, Alzheimer's disease, multiple sclerosis, and depression. Women are also more likely to be victims of sexual assault and battering and to be prescribed psychotropic medications (Strickland, 1988). Black women are more likely than white women to die of diabetes and cancer. They are three times more likely to have hypertension, and twice as likely to die from hypertensive heart disease. Black women are three times more likely to have lupus, twelve times more likely to contract AIDS, and four times more likely than white women to die of homicide. It has been estimated that most black women in the United States live in a state of chronic psychological stress (Davis, 1990).

Chronic conditions are exacerbated by the stresses of everyday living for poor, elderly, and disabled women, and by the continual struggles against racism, sexism, and homophobia. Behavioral changes also affect the incidence and progression of chronic diseases. Young women are the fastest growing group of smokers (Taylor, 1991), in large part due to nicotine's reputation as an appetite suppressant. Women are more likely now than in the past to use and abuse alcohol and other drugs. Alcohol and cigarettes are heavily advertised in urban minority neighborhoods, in women's magazines, and at women's sports events. Few substance abuse treatment programs specialize in meeting women's needs, and there is very little chance that pregnant substance abusers can find help despite the fact that they have been arrested and prosecuted in several states in recent years (Chrisler, 1993a).

Utilization of Services

Women utilize health care services more frequently than do men. Even when appointments for prenatal care are not counted, women still seek care more often than men do, and this seems to be the case in most countries (Cleary, Mechanic, & Greenley, 1982). It has been suggested that this difference may be due to the fact that women have better homeostatic mechanisms than men do; they experience temperature changes sooner, report pain earlier, and detect new smells more quickly, for example. Women may also be more sensitive to minor bodily dysfunctions and find it easier to express pain and discomfort than do men, who are expected to be tougher and stronger (Taylor, 1991). The very young and the elderly use medical services most frequently (Aday & Andersen, 1974), and members of the upper economic classes utilize services more often than those from the lower classes (Herman, 1972).

The attitudes of physicians directly affect the quality of care women receive as well as women's ability to make informed decisions about their health. The superior position of the physician as reflected in the use of the term "doctor-patient relationship" rather than "patient-doctor relationship" encourages passivity in women patients. The likelihood that the physician is a male further encourages women to adopt a traditional feminine role during their interactions. In fact, the role of the patient, especially in hospitals, closely resembles the stereotypical feminine role (Williams, 1977). The "good patient" is passive, cooperative, dependent, uncomplaining, and willing to "suffer in silence." Those who complain about their symptoms or treatment and ask a lot of questions are labeled demanding, "bad" patients, and may be punished by the medical staff by being made to wait for treatment or having their complaints dismissed as hysterical. Physicians equate trust in their judgment with being a "good" patient; therefore, patients who ask questions or seek second opinions are perceived as doubting their doctors' expertise and challenging their authority (Waitzkin & Waterman, 1974; Wright & Morgan, 1990).

There is evidence (Corea, 1977; Wallen, Waitzkin, & Stoekle, 1979; Weisman & Teitelbaum, 1985) that physicians do not take women's complaints as seriously as men's. Physicians tend to believe that women are more prone to minor ailments; that women are neurotic, difficult, emotional, and depressed; and that women often fail to understand medical explanations because of a tendency to "feel" rather than to "think" (Fidell, 1980; Fisher & Groce, 1985). Such biased assumptions not only hinder accurate diagnosis but also lead to the overprescription of psychotropic medications to women because of the belief that women's illnesses are psychologically rather than physiologically based (Cooperstock, 1971; Corea, 1977, Lack, 1982; Ogur, 1986; Wallen, Waitzkin, & Stoekle, 1979).

Impatience and a need to reassert control often lead physicians to cut off responses to their questions before the patients have conveyed information important for diagnosis (Waitzkin & Waterman, 1974; Wright & Morgan, 1990). Women, particularly those who are less well educated and not fluent in English, are most likely to be cut off by their physicians. Despite underestimating women's ability to understand medical information, physicians often use highly technical language when talking to their patients (Taylor, 1991). This compounds the problems of immigrant women, who must try to communicate during medical crises with physicians who not only do not understand their language and are impatient with their hesitant English, but who come from a different economic class and cultural background and do not understand the cultural assumptions of immigrant groups. After her medical training Michelle Harrison (1982) concluded that medical schools reinforce the idea that minority women are immature, irresponsible, and unlikely to return for follow-up care. Such bias is evident in Audre Lorde's (1990, p. 31) account of a conversation with an oncologist who told her, "If you do not do exactly what I tell you right now without questions, you are going to die a horrible death." There is some hope, however; several recent studies (Fisher & Groce, 1985; Maheux et al., 1989; Waller, 1988) have found that female physicians spend more time with their patients, and are more likely to listen, teach, practice preventive medicine, and involve their patients in decision making than are male physicians.

Heterosexist assumptions, homophobia, and outright hostility by health care providers have resulted in lesbians being concerned about their safety in traditional medical settings. Surveys (Randall, 1989; Stevens, 1992; Trippet & Bain, 1992; Young, 1988) of lesbians have revealed that disclosure of sexual orientation to health care providers has resulted in reactions of shock, pity, repulsion, embarrassment, fear, or overt hostility. Studies (Douglas, Kalman, & Kalman, 1985; Eliason & Randall, 1991; Randall, 1989; Young, 1988) find that many physicians and nurses are not only uncomfortable providing care for lesbian patients but also believe that lesbians are immoral, criminal, or mentally ill. Consequently, lesbians are faced with the conundrum of paying for unnecessary treatments (e.g., birth control or tests to rule out ectopic pregnancy as the cause of vaginal pain and bleeding) or running the risk of being pathologized and finding that their sexual orientation rather than their presenting complaints has become the focus of treatment (Reagan, 1981; Stevens, 1992). Many lesbians and celibate women delay seeking routine gynecological care or even treatment for serious symptoms because heterosexist assumptions lead practitioners to ask questions about heterosexual activity and contraceptive use, which the patients find annoying or embarrassing (Rosser, 1993). It is undoubtedly true that women's health care would be of better quality if lesbians felt free to disclose their sexual identity (Cochran & Mays, 1988; Rosser, 1993; Stevens & Hall, 1990).

Many women work in low-paying jobs that do not offer medical benefits or that require large deductibles and cost shares, often specifically excluding prenatal care and delivery, which make the insurance cheaper for the employers but nearly useless for the employees (Perales & Young, 1988). Women of color are overrepresented in occupations that pay low wages and carry high risks of occupational injuries that result from secondary exposure to chemicals (e.g., laundry workers, hairdressers) or repetitious movements (e.g., factory workers, word processors). Such injuries develop over time and so do not have the exact "date of injury" that is typical of men's industrial accidents and forms the usual criterion for coverage by workers' compensation (Stellman, 1988).

Although Medicaid is a federal welfare program designed to provide medical care for the poor or near poor, eligibility is determined by complex formulas that vary from state to state. The result of this complex web of qualifications is that almost half of the nation's poor do not qualify and, therefore, receive fragmented, episodic care or none at all (Perales & Young, 1988). Several states are currently attempting to pass laws to exclude illegal aliens from Medicaid coverage, which will have a devastating effect on immigrant women. Elderly women, who often suffer from multiple chronic conditions that require medication and monitoring by physicians, frequently fall into the poor or near poor category. Economically advantaged women may join the ranks of the near poor for many reasons as they grow older. For example, homemakers do not have pensions; low-paying jobs result in minimal social security payments; and Medicare, like many private insurance carriers, provides better coverage for conditions that predominantly affect men (Clancy & Massion, 1992; Sofaer & Abel, 1990). Furthermore, Medicare does not cover expenses for hearing aids, dentures, custodial home care, or preventive examinations, so many elderly women find that they cannot meet their health care needs (Clancy & Massion, 1992; Perales & Young, 1988; Woolhandler & Himmelstein, 1988). Thus, women of color, lesbians, the working poor, welfare recipients, elderly women, and women with physical or psychiatric disabilities often have difficulty obtaining adequate medical care as well as significant problems in being treated with respect (Christmas, 1983).

REPRODUCTIVE HEALTH

Obstetrics/gynecology, the only medical specialty exclusively focused on women, essentially defines women in terms of their traditional roles as wives and mothers. In fact, the centering of women's health in obstetrics and gynecology can be said to result in the defining of women's health care in terms of men's needs as reproduction becomes the major focus (Rosser, 1993). This has led to underfunding of and insufficient attention to other aspects of women's health, as well as the invisibility of the health needs of lesbian and celibate women (Rosser, 1993). The gynecologist is the primary care physician for most American women, and from puberty to menopause many women see no other medical health care provider on a regular basis (Ruzek, 1986).

Contraception

Most of the work on contraceptives has been conducted from a heterosexual, white, middle-class, educated, able-bodied perspective that assumes that "birth control is an accepted, desired given for all women of reproductive age" (Rosser, 1986, p. 53). In fact, women differ widely in their attitudes toward contraception in general and types of contraceptives in particular. Women's attitudes vary by age, race, ethnicity, religion, knowledge, experience, accessibility, needs, and pregnancy plans. These differences are not adequately taken into account by researchers or clinicians.

There are approximately 3 million unintended pregnancies per year in the United States (Hanrahan, 1990). About half of these pregnancies are the result of contraceptive failure; the rest occurred in women who were not using any form of birth control (Sweet, 1988). Although 95 percent of American women favor contraception (Forrest & Henshaw, 1983), many do not use it because of the expense, lack of information about how to obtain it, or fear of the possible or actually experienced side effects (Silverman, Torres, & Forrest, 1987). "There is no reversible method of contraception that is both highly efficacious in actual use and acceptable to most women" (Trussell & Kost, 1987, p. 275). Women's attitudes toward the various available methods of contraception have been reviewed elsewhere (Goodwin & Chrisler, 1990; Tanfer & Rosenbaum, 1986).

In 1987 66 percent of American women ages fifteen to forty-four were using some form of contraception; black women were less likely than white women to practice birth control. Oral contraceptives are the most popular method of birth control among young, single women, and sterilization is the most popular method among older, married women (Muller, 1990). Black women are less likely than white women to choose sterilization because of the history of sterilization abuse in this country. Puerto Rican women may regard birth control advocates with suspicion because of sterilization abuse or religious training, and because oral contraceptives were tested in Puerto Rico before they were considered safe for use in the mainland United States (Rosser, 1986). Many women of color are caught between the conflicting advice they receive about contraceptives from their ethnic liberation movements and from women's rights advocates (Rosser, 1986). Most lesbians are unconcerned about birth control except when their gynecologists attempt to prescribe it (Rosser, 1986). Disabled women may resent the availability of birth control and abortion because it seems to suggest that only perfect babies are wanted, or may be offended because their physicians do not ask them about contraceptive use because they assume that disabled patients are not sexually active.

Family planning clinics provide over one-third of birth control services. Teenagers and black women are the groups most likely to use clinic services and are therefore more vulnerable to fiscal constraints and politico-religious opposition to birth control and abortion (Muller, 1990). Oral contraceptives are the most frequently prescribed method at family planning clinics, and it is estimated that 60 percent of American women will use them at some point (Travis, 1988). Among the side effects of oral contraceptives are major vascular effects such as thromboembolism, cerebrovascular accidents, myocardial infarction, and hypertension (Travis, 1988). These effects are of particular importance to black women with sickle cell anemia or family histories of hypertension. Thus, their preferred and most readily available method of birth control may be too dangerous for them to use.

Abortion has become an important part of American women's reproductive health care as a backup for contraceptive failure and for various other reasons. Although the majority of the public is pro-choice, at least to some extent, the anti-choice movement in this country has been very successful in narrowing the availability of abortion services. For example, federal law prohibits the performing of abortions in hospitals that are financed by government money; this includes hospitals for the military and their dependents and hospitals that serve Native Americans who live on reservations. Because of harassment by hostile antiabortion groups, many gynecologists have refused to perform abortions. This is particularly problematic for rural women, who may live long distances from available services. Furthermore, since 1981 Medicaid funds for abortion have been restricted to cases when the woman's life is endangered, and virtually no payments have been made (Muller, 1990). Unless a poor woman who needs an abortion lives in a state that has agreed to make up for the loss of federal funds, she may find herself forced to risk her health or bear an unwanted child. As a result of these funding restrictions, abortions have been done at later gestational stages and with more complications (Muller, 1990).

It has been suggested that abortion has deleterious effects on women's mental health. Although many women report experiencing conflict or ambivalence over the decision to abort a pregnancy, negative feelings generally do not last long, and most women agree that their decision was the right one (Lemkau, 1988). The amount of conflict women experience depends on such factors as type of coping strategies employed (Major, Mueller, & Hildebrandt, 1985), whether the pregnancy was planned, and the stage of pregnancy in which the abortion was performed (Friedlander, Kaul, & Stimel, 1984). The types and extent of psychological responses to abortion have been reviewed elsewhere (Adler et al., 1990). Psychological studies generally conclude that the availability of abortion, which gives women greater control over their lives, enhances, rather than reduces, women's mental health.

The political and economic reasons why the development of new contraceptive and abortion technology is not a high priority in the United States have been detailed elsewhere (Djerassi, 1979; Goodwin & Chrisler, 1990). Nevertheless, researchers and women's health advocates must find ways to move women's contraceptive needs higher on the research agenda, lobby for better accessibility of abortion services, and demand the importation of RU-486. Scientists working on new contraceptive techniques need to consider women's attitudes about types of contraceptive methods and work in the planning stages directly with those who are likely to use them in order to provide the public with safe, effective, and acceptable options (Goodwin & Chrisler, 1990).

Sexually Transmitted Diseases

STDs are probably the women's health area in which the most research has been conducted on minority women. That's the good news. The bad news is that minority women have been treated with such concern because the turn-of-the-century division of women into the "good/clean" (those who can afford to visit private physicians) and the "bad/dirty" (the urban minority poor) still influences both physicians and scientists (Leonardo & Chrisler, 1992), who don't expect white, middle-class women to contract STDs. Medical personnel are more likely to screen routinely for STDs in clinic settings, which cater to urban populations of low socioeconomic status (Nettina & Kaufman, 1990). Most research conducted on STDs (except for AIDS) has been primarily concerned with the urban minority poor (Leonardo & Chrisler, 1992).

Penicillin was discovered to be an effective cure for both syphillis and gonorrhea in 1943; that discovery led to a dramatic decrease in the prevalence rates of STDs that lasted until the late 1950s. Since then, rates of STD infection have been steadily on the rise (Brandt, 1985). In 1986, for example, more than 4 million cases of chlamydia were reported to the Centers for Disease Control (Cates & Toomey, 1990); in 1987 more than 12 million cases of human papilloma virus (i.e., HPV or venereal warts) were reported (Stone, 1989). Comparison of ethnic populations is difficult because public clinics tend to be more thorough in their reporting than private physicians, who are widely believed to underreport (Goldsmith, 1989). Despite knowledge of this reporting bias, it is not uncommon for experts to conclude that "STDs occur disproportionately among lower socio-economic groups, primarily among Blacks and Hispanics" (Goldsmith, 1989, p. 3509).

The current campaign against STDs has been directed primarily at women, who are urged to limit the number of sexual partners, discuss STDs with their partners, and insist on condom use. The effectiveness of the campaign has been criticized elsewhere (Leonardo & Chrisler, 1992), both because it is not equally directed at men and women and because many women may be unable or unwilling to follow the advice. For example, Cochran and Mays (1989) and Worth (1989) have found that many women are more willing to risk infection than to risk ruining a relationship by discussing STDs or insisting on condom use. The simplistic advice offered does not address questions important to women. For example, many women have wondered how long they need to use a condom with their primary partner (Morokoff, 1991). Forever? If so, what do they do if they want to get pregnant?

Research on and advice to lesbians is virtually nonexistent. The emphasis on condom use may be interpreted as meaning that this is an issue about which lesbians need not concern themselves. Clearly, researchers need to diversify the populations they study to include lesbians, whites and Asians, and the middle and upper classes and to focus more on men taking responsibility for STD prevention. Health psychologists and public health officials need to work together to develop more effective ways to educate the public about STDs and to encourage less risky behavior.

Furthermore, to effectively meet women's health needs, the NIH budget for research on STDs needs to be increased and adjusted. In 1989 NIH allocated $60 million for research on STDs other than AIDS, which itself received $604 million. One-third of the budget was spent for research on herpes. Of the remaining $40 million, the largest amount was given to gonorrhea research; third on the list was chlamydia, followed by HPV. The most prevalent STD among women is chlamydia, which affects 15 percent to 20 percent of young women. Venereal warts (HPV) is the second most common STD among women and is believed to be a principal cause of genital cancers (Goldsmith, 1989). One cannot help but notice that NIH has targeted its available funds primarily toward those STDS that affect men more frequently than women (Leonardo & Chrisler, 1992).

Research on AIDS has concentrated on men to such an extent that much of the literature may be irrelevant to women (Shayne & Kaplan, 1991). "To date, women have received more attention for their potential role as infectors than for the problems they face as infectees" (Wofsy, 1987, p. 2075). It may take longer for women to be diagnosed as having AIDS. Many are not diagnosed until they have given birth to a child who develops AIDS (Shayne & Kaplan, 1991). HIV symptoms are vague, and physicians, who are influenced by scientific reports that deal only with male patients, may not be suspicious enough to correctly diagnose women (Wofsy, 1987). Most of the treatment studies have excluded women (Levine, 1990), although a study of survival rates found that black women who are intravenous drug users had a particularly poor prognosis (Rothenberg et al., 1987). Although blood banks routinely screen and test for HIV, sperm banks do not (Morokoff, 1991).

Until very recently minority heterosexuals were not properly alerted to their risk for AIDS (Shayne & Kaplan, 1991), and many remain unaware of the extent of the threat to their health. Popular press articles on heterosexuals and AIDS are typically illustrated with pictures of white couples, which convey the idea that AIDS is a white disease (Wofsy, 1987). Mays and Cochran (1988) have reported that 50 percent of the black adolescents they studied were not worried about AIDS and thought themselves less likely than their white peers to become infected. A survey of teenagers in San Francisco found that white adolescents were significantly more knowledgeable about the causes, transmission, and prevention of AIDS than were blacks who, in turn, were more knowledgeable than Latina/os (DiClemente, Boyer, & Morales, 1988). Such misconceptions increase the young people's risk of contracting AIDS.

Very little attention has been paid to lesbians with AIDS in part, no doubt, because lesbians represent the group at the lowest risk for contracting it. As of 1989 only two confirmed cases of woman-to-woman HIV transmission had been reported; however, there were seventy-nine known cases of lesbians with AIDS (Chu et al., 1990). They contracted AIDS primarily through intravenous drug use and contaminated blood products, but they may need specialized counseling not described in the literature. Bisexual women are at risk for AIDS, especially if they engage in intercourse with bisexual men.

Many basic research questions of importance to women remain unanswered (e.g., Does pregnancy accelerate the progression of HIV? How are women's attitudes toward childbearing—a primary goal of womanhood in many cultures—changed by the knowledge that they are HIV positive?, Where do women who become caretakers of AIDS patients find social support?). In addition, much applied work remains to be done. Most AIDS prevention and service programs don't meet women's needs

(Shayne & Kaplan, 1991) and must be redesigned in ways that make them culturally relevant and sensitive to the diversity of women's needs (Nyamathi, Shuler, & Porche, 1990; Shayne & Kaplan, 1990).

Routine Gynecological Care

The American woman's first pelvic exam is like a rite of passage to adulthood, yet few women have positive memories of the event (Hein, 1984). Many women hate the idea of pelvic exams, and "gynecological visits are dreaded, postponed, and can be emotionally as well as physically traumatizing" (Domar, 1986, p. 75). The experience of lack of personal control appears to be a major factor in women's negative attitudes toward pelvic exams, as many report feelings of vulnerability and helplessness (Domar, 1986). It's no wonder that women's health activists made cervical self-examination an early priority. The ability to examine oneself or, at least, to understand what the physician is doing should lead to an increased sense of personal control, as should specific coping instructions prior to examinations. Little has been done to test these hypotheses.

Several surveys (e.g., Debrovner & Shubin-Stein, 1975; Weiss & Meadow, 1979) have found that women wanted to spend time before and/or after the pelvic exam talking with their physicians to establish rapport and receive information and explanations about their exams. Talking while dressed in one's street clothes lessens embarrassment, enhances one's sense of control, and reduces the feeling that the physician is rushing from one patient to another. In recent years many gynecologists have reorganized their office routines in an attempt to incorporate these changes. It seems likely that private practitioners would find it easier to incorporate such changes than would clinic staff whose volume of patients is greater. Thus patients who are able to afford private care have more pleasant experiences and are more likely to make regular return visits.

Breast examination and the teaching of breast self-examination (BSE) are important aspects of routine gynecological care. Many physicians are poorly trained in breast examinations (Muller, 1990), and it is well known that most women do not practice BSE regularly. It is estimated that one in nine women will develop breast cancer, which is the second (after lung cancer) leading cause of cancer deaths among women (Strickland, 1988). Although fewer black women than white women suffer from breast cancer, black women are more likely to die from it (Davis, 1990), probably because their cancer is detected at a later stage.

Grady (1988) has reported that confidence in one's ability to perform BSE properly is the best predictor of BSE practice. Similarly, Trotta (1980) found that although pamphlets and physicians' descriptions were the most common sources of BSE training, those women who were taught by direct person-to-person instruction practiced BSE most frequently. Person-to-person instruction is time-consuming, but it is likely to be the best way to teach the technique and to increase women's confidence in their ability to perform it properly. Various reminder techniques have been used in an attempt to encourage BSE, but none has proved especially effective. Breast cancer detection and prevention is an obvious area for collaboration between researchers and clinicians; more work is needed, the sooner the better.

Because gynecologists are often the only physicians their patients see regularly, their role extends beyond cancer detection, pregnancy and infertility testing, prenatal care, birth control prescriptions, and abortion services. Alert gynecologists and their staff who are able to schedule time during office visits to ask patients if they are having any problems are in a unique position to refer patients to other medical specialists and to mental health services. But more than time to listen is necessary. In order to provide women with the best possible health care, medical and mental health practitioners must develop cultural sensitivity, tolerance for differences, and an awareness of the diversity of women's health needs.

CHRONIC DISORDERS

It is beyond the scope of this chapter to discuss all of the medical problems that affect women. We have chosen to concentrate on several chronic conditions that have a major impact on women's quality of life. It has been estimated that at least 50 percent of Americans have some chronic disorder that needs medical management, and because women live longer than men they are more likely to develop multiple chronic disorders (Taylor, 1991).

Coronary Heart Disease

Coronary heart disease (CHD) is the leading cause of death for both women and men (Sharpe, Clark, & Janz, 1991). However, over the past thirty years mortality has substantially decreased for men at the same time it has increased for women (Dittrich et al., 1988; Liao et al., 1992; Tobin et al., 1987). Erroneous beliefs (e.g., CHD is more severe in men; women's chest pains are due to anxiety; estrogens protect women from CHD; angina is more dangerous in men; women's smaller blood vessels make coronary artery surgery more dangerous for them) interfere with physicians' ability to properly diagnose and treat CHD in their women patients (Steingart et al., 1991; Tobin et al., 1987). The recent campaign for perimenopausal women to use hormone replacement therapy (HRT) to prevent CHD, which has been well communicated to women through the media (Chrisler, Torrey, & Matthes, 1991), may lead to the blaming of those who elect not to or cannot afford to use HRT for bringing the disease on themselves. Black and Hispanic women have a higher mortality rate from CHD than do white women (Liao et al., 1992).

The belief that CHD is more common or severe in men has resulted in ten times as many men as women undergoing such cardiac tests as radioactive heart scans, exercise/stress tests, and angiograms (Ayanian & Epstein, 1991; Tobin et al., 1987). Recent studies (Fiebach, Viscoli, & Horwitz, 1990; Steingart et al., 1991) have concluded that women's higher mortality rate during and after coronary bypass surgery is primarily due to the fact that women are on average seven years older than men at the time of the surgery and have more advanced CHD largely because their initial complaints were not taken as seriously as men's, and so they were "watched" for a longer period of time before surgery was scheduled. Men generally undergo cardiac surgery on an elective basis, but it is most often performed on an emergency basis for women, which further contributes to their higher mortality rate (Tobin et al., 1987).

Women are less likely than men to be referred to a cardiac rehabilitation program despite similar medical profiles and functional capacities at the time of discharge (Ades et al., 1992; Young & Kahana, 1993). After cardiac surgery men typically return to the workforce, usually secure in the knowledge that their wives will provide support in terms of household maintenance and preparing meals in accordance with their dietary rules, or they simply retire. The description "return to the workforce" is inapplicable to many women who were full-time homemakers before surgery. Furthermore, whether or not women work for pay they are still generally engaged in cooking, cleaning, and running their households as before, which can lead to fatigue, pain, and stress. In addition, complete remission of symptoms is less common in women than in men; women generally continue to complain of angina, shortness of breath, and other problems after surgery (Sharpe, Clark, & Janz, 1991; Vroman, 1983).

Finally, most studies of the causes and prevention of CHD have been done with male subjects, so it is unclear whether the findings and recommendations actually apply to women. Much more work is needed before women can receive appropriate diagnosis and treatment and enjoy better cardiovascular health.

Diabetes

Diabetes is one of the fastest growing health hazards for women, following CHD and cancer (Hartman-Stein & Reuter, 1988). Although it affects all populations, it is the third leading cause of death of black women, who are 50 percent more likely than white women to develop diabetes (Hartman-Stein & Reuter, 1988). Despite the high number of diabetic black women, very little research has specifically addressed their needs.

Poor black women are at significant risk for complications associated with diabetes, such as hypertension, atherosclerosis, peripheral vascular problems, retinopathy or blindness, stroke, and complications of pregnancy (Hartman-Stein & Reuter, 1988; Williams, 1990). Poor women are also at higher risk for delayed diagnosis because of the lack of routine medical care (Tallon & Block, 1988; Zambrana, 1988). In addition, the necessity of home glucose monitoring equipment, frequent physician visits, insulin, and a diabetic diet imposes a serious financial burden even on those with good health insurance, thus, the poor or near poor geriatric patient is in trouble (Hartman-Stein & Reuter, 1988). Many women either do without appropriate medical care or attend outpatient clinics where they may be seen by a different physician each time, which may decrease the probability of being properly taught to manage their medical condition.

Most diabetics are told by their physicians to lose weight and are scolded when they are unsuccessful. Weight loss and maintenance is rarely accomplished (cf. Chrisler, 1993b; Garner & Wooley, 1991), albeit much desired, especially by American women. Medical (Chrisler, 1994) and sociocultural (Rodin, Silberstein, & Striegel-Moore, 1985) directives to become thin and beautiful have led to dangerous practices among women with diabetes. Studies (Hilliard & Hilliard, 1984; LaGreca, Schwartz, & Satin, 1987) have found women who refused to take their insulin shots because of worries about unattractive scarring and those who, in an effort to lose weight, have adjusted their insulin dosage or taken up smoking, which decreases the absorption of insulin and may thus increase insulin requirements by as much as 20 percent. Physicians and therapists must be alert for these life-threatening behaviors in their diabetic patients. Furthermore, women with diabetes should be educated about how fluctuations in estrogen levels may affect insulin needs (Addanki, 1981; Toyoda, 1982).

Interstitial Cystitis

Interstitial cystitis (IC) is an inflammatory bladder condition, the cause of which is unknown; possible explanations of the etiology include genetic, allergic, autoimmune, toxic, infectious, viral, structural, vascular, psychosomatic, and iatrogenic (Webster, 1990). The symptoms, which mimic those of an acute urinary tract infection, include suprapubic pressure and pain (e.g., bladder spasms) and urinary urgency and frequency—patients may use the bathroom as much as sixty times per day (Ratner, 1987; Ratner, Slade, & Whitmore, 1992). IC was once thought to be a rare disorder found only in postmenopausal women; however, it has become apparent through more advanced diagnostic procedures and increased physician awareness that it is far more prevalent than previously thought and can affect women at any age (Meares, 1987; Ratner, Slade, & Whitmore, 1992).

Ninety percent of IC patients are women (Meares, 1987). The disorder is chronic, difficult to treat, and often misdiagnosed. The chronic pain and frequent need to urinate seriously disrupt the lives of IC patients, who often report sleep disruption, painful sexual intercourse, depression, and worries about leaving home (Ratner, Slade, & Whitmore, 1992). Typically women with IC have waited four to seven years for diagnosis, been seen by several physicians, received various diagnoses (e.g., endometriosis, urethral syndrome, bacterial cystitis), and been told that their problems are psychological and prescribed psychotropic medication (Messing, 1987; Sant & Meares, 1990).

There is no cure for IC. Treatments, which usually include medication and repeated dilation of the bladder under anesthesia, are expensive, painful, and time-consuming. Comprehensive diagnosis and some treatment options are available only through hospitalization. Those who can afford it are taking a drug that is widely marketed in Europe but considered "investigational" in the United States and so is not covered by insurance. The second author of this chapter, who has IC, was told by her urologist that this appears to be a disease that disproportionately affects professional women and must therefore be stress-related. He has clearly missed the point that only educated women with financial and emotional resources are able to persist until an accurate diagnosis is made.

Most of the medical research on IC has been financed by the Foundation for Interstitial Cystitis, a privately funded organization. NIH has not identified IC as a priority. Nor have epidemiologists or health psychologists turned their attention to this disorder, despite the obvious need for behavioral medicine interventions.

Autoimmune Disorders

Autoimmune disorders occur when the body fails to discriminate between self and nonself and thus attacks its own cells. Many inflammatory (e.g., rheumatoid arthritis, systemic lupus erythematosus) and degenerative (e.g., multiple sclerosis) disorders have been attributed to probable autoimmune reactions. Women are much more likely than men to experience an autoimmune disorder; they are two to three times more likely to experience rheumatoid arthritis (RA) and five to ten times more likely to experience systemic lupus erythematosus (SLE) (Carr, 1986; Lawrence et al., 1989). Furthermore, autoimmune disorders are more common in some ethnic groups than in others. Black women are three times more likely than white women to have SLE (Carr, 1986; Davis, 1990), and RA is more common in some Native Americans (e.g., Chippewa and Yakima) than in the general population (Weiner, 1991). Black women tend to experience earlier onset and more severe manifestations of SLE than whites, and they tend to die sooner, probably because of lower socioeconomic status and lack of quality health care (Liang et al., 1991). Women are also more likely than men to experience multiple sclerosis (MS), which occurs five times more frequently in people who were raised in temperate, as opposed to tropical, climates (*Merck Manual*, 1992).

Autoimmune disorders vary considerably in the way they affect different individuals, and they also vary within individuals. They present unique coping challenges because periods of active disease, which may last for weeks, months, or even years, alternate with spontaneous improvement or even remission of symptoms. Flare-ups may be relatively mild or quite severe, and it is difficult to plan one's activities around them (Chrisler & Parrett, in press).

The onset of autoimmune disorders is usually insidious, and the symptoms vague and transient. This makes them difficult to diagnose. The symptoms of SLE resemble those of more than twenty other diseases, which has led to its nickname "the great imposter" (Carr, 1986). The first signs of MS often appear months or even years before it can be diagnosed, which has led some to call it "the malignant uncertainty" (Weeks, 1980). Even RA, whose symptoms are clearly characteristic of the disorder, may take some time to diagnose because a number of other diseases (e.g., SLE, Lyme disease, Sjogren's syndrome, gout) have symptoms that overlap with it (*Merck Manual*, 1992).

There is much for health psychology to contribute to the understanding and treatment of individuals with autoimmune disorders. The severity of the symptoms is affected by stress, and patients must learn to cope with chronic pain, disability, changes in quality of life, body image issues, and the unpredictability of living with a chronic autoimmune illness (Chrisler & Parrett, in press). Disease flare-ups strain family relations and friendships and create a need for specialized social support. Women with MS experience a higher divorce rate than do men with MS (Russell, 1989). This higher divorce rate is also true for women with cancer (Stahly, 1992), and probably for women with other chronic diseases as well. Despite such a clear need for psychosocial interventions, researchers and clinicians have focused their attention on cancer, coronary heart disease, and hypertension, and done little to improve the lives of women with autoimmune disorders.

CONCLUSION

Obviously, there is much more to be said about the diversity of women's health needs than can be discussed here. Sexism, heterosexism, racism, ageism, and classism have had major effects on women's health. They have influenced what researchers deem important, what government agencies fund, what attracts practitioners' attention, and the type of advice patients receive. Gender-role stereotypes, too, have had an influence on women's health by creating dynamics in the patient-doctor relationship that lead physicians to dismiss women's complaints.

In order to improve health care for women, the following are necessary: (1) better education for medical students and other health care practitioners, including sensitivity training and attention to multicultural, gender, and other diversity issues in coursework; (2) additional funding and broadening of the topics covered by the Women's Health Initiative (NIH) and higher priorities for women's health issues at all granting agencies and foundations; (3) lobbying by citizens to change Medicare and Medicaid funding restrictions, insurance regulations, and workers' compensation rules to better meet women's needs; (4) more attention to women's health needs by medical and behavioral researchers and practitioners; (5) better funding of clinics to provide quality health care to poor and near poor urban and rural women; (6) reviewing programs for preventive medicine, AIDS, substance abuse, and the like to see that they are culturally sensitive and gender fair. Such things, at a minimum, are essential to improving women's quality of life.

REFERENCES

Aday, L. A., & Andersen, R. (1974). A framework for the study of access to medical care. *Health Services Research, 9,* 208-220.

Addanki, S. (1981). Roles of nutrition, obesity, and estrogen in diabetes mellitus: Human leads to an experimental approach to prevention. *Preventive Medicine, 10,* 577-589.

Ades, P. A., Waldmann, M. L., Polk, D. M., & Coflesky, J. T. (1992). Referral patterns and exercise response in the rehabilitation of female coronary patients aged 62 years or over. *American Journal of Cardiology, 69,* 1422-1425.

Adler, N. F., David, H. P., Major, B. N., Roth, S. H., Russo, N. F., & Wyatt, G. E. (1990). Psychological responses after abortion. *Science, 248,* 41-44.

Ayanian, J. Z., & Epstein, A. M. (1991). Differences in the use of procedures between women and men hospitalized for coronary heart disease. *New England Journal of Medicine, 325,* 221-225.

Brandt, A. (1985). *No magic bullet: A social history of venereal disease in the United States since 1880.* New York: Oxford University Press.

Carr, R. (1986). *Lupus erythematosus: A handbook for physicians, patients and their families.* Rockville, Md.: Lupus Foundation of America.

Cates, W., & Toomey, K. E. (1990). Sexually transmitted diseases: Overview of the situation. *Primary Care, 17,* 1-27.

Chrisler, J. C. (1993a). Whose body is it anyway? Psychological effects of fetal protection policies. In R. Muraskin & T. Alleman (Eds.), *It's a crime: Women and justice* (pp. 263-268). Englewood Cliffs, N.J.: Regents/Prentice Hall.

Chrisler, J. C. (1993b). Feminist perspectives on weight loss therapy. *Journal of Training and Practice in Professional Psychology, 7*(1), 35-48.

Chrisler, J. C. (1994). Reframing women's weight: Does thin equal healthy? In A. Dan (Ed.), *Reframing women's health: Multidisciplinary research and practice* (pp. 330-338). Newbury Park, Calif.: Sage.

Chrisler, J. C., & Parrett, K. L. (in press). Women and autoimmune disorders. In A. L. Stanton & S. J. Gallant (Eds.), *Women's health: An introduction.* Washington, D.C.: American Psychological Association.

Chrisler, J. C., Torrey, J. W., & Matthes, M. (1991). Brittle bones and sagging breasts, loss of femininity and loss of sanity: The media describe the menopause. In A. M. Voda & R. Conover (Eds.), *Proceedings of the 8th Conference of the Society for Menstrual Cycle Research* (pp. 13-22). Scottsdale, Ariz.: Society for Menstrual Cycle Research.

Christmas, J. J. (1983). Sexism and racism in health policy. In M. Fooden, S. Gordon, & B. Hughley (Eds.), *Genes and gender IV: The second X and women's health* (pp. 205-215). New York: Gordian Press.

Chu, S. Y., Buehler, J. W., Fleming, P. L., & Berkelman, R. L. (1990). Epidemiology of reported cases of AIDS in lesbians, United States 1980-1989. *American Journal of Public Health, 80,* 1380-1381.

Clancy, C. M., & Massion, C. T. (1992). American women's health care: A patchwork with gaps. *Journal of the American Medical Association, 268,* 1918-1920.

Cleary, P. D., Mechanic. D., & Greenley, J. R. (1982). Sex differences in medical care utilization: An empirical investigation. *Journal of Health and Social Behavior, 23,* 106-119.

Cochran, S. D., & Mays, V. M. (1988). Disclosure of sexual preference to physicians by black lesbian and bisexual women. *Western Journal of Medicine, 149,* 616-619.

Cochran, S. D., & Mays, V. M. (1989). Women and AIDS-related concerns: Roles for psychologists in helping the worried get well. *American Psychologist, 44,* 529-535.

Cooperstock, R. A. (1971). A review of women's psychotropic drug use. *Canadian Journal of Psychiatry, 24,* 29-34.

Corea, G. (1977). *The hidden malpractice: How American medicine treats women as patients and professionals.* New York: William Morrow.

Davis, A. Y. (1990). Sick and tired of being sick and tired: The politics of black women's health. In E. C. White (Ed.), *The black women's health book: Speaking for ourselves* (pp. 18-26). Seattle: Seal Press.

Debrovner, C., & Shubin-Stein, R. (1975). Psychological aspects of vaginal examinations. *Medical Aspects of Human Sexuality, 9,* 163-164.

DiClemente, R. J., Boyer, C. B., & Morales, E. S. (1988). Minorities and AIDS: Knowledge, attitudes, and misconceptions among black and Latino adolescents. *American Journal of Public Health, 78,* 55-57.

Dittrich, H., Gilpin, E., Nicod, P., Cali, G., Henning, H., & Ross, J. (1988). Acute myocardial infarction in women: Influence of gender on mortality and prognostic variables. *American Journal of Cardiology, 62,* 1-7.

Djerassi, C. (1979). *The politics of contraception.* New York: Freeman.

Domar, A. D. (1986). Psychological aspects of the pelvic exam: Individual needs and physician involvement. *Women & Health, 10*(4), 75-90.

Douglas, C. J., Kalman, C. M., & Kalman, P. T. (1985). Homophobia among physicians and nurses: An empirical study. *Hospital and Community Psychiatry, 36,* 1309-1311.

Eliason, M. J., & Randall, C. E. (1991). Lesbian phobia in nursing students. *Western Journal of Nursing Research, 13,* 363-374.

Fidell, L. S. (1980). Sex role stereotypes and the American physician. *Psychology of Women Quarterly, 4,* 313-330.

Fiebach, N. H., Viscoli, C. M., & Horwitz, R. I. (1990). Differences between women and men in survival after myocardial infarction. *Journal of the American Medical Association, 263,* 1092-1096.

Fisher, S., & Groce, S. (1985). Doctor-patient negotiation of cultural assumptions. *Sociology of Health and Illness, 7,* 342-374.

Forrest, J. D., & Henshaw, S. K. (1983). What U.S. women think and do about contraception. *Family Planning Perspectives, 15,* 157-166.

Friedlander, M. L., Kaul, T. J., & Stimel, C. A. (1984). Abortion: Predicting the complexity of the decision-making process. *Women & Health, 9*(1), 43-54.

Garner, D. M., & Wooley, S. C. (1991). Confronting the failure of behavioral and dietary treatments for obesity. *Clinical Psychology Review, 11,* 729-780.

Goldsmith, M. (1989). "Silent epidemic" of "social disease" makes STD experts raise their voices. *Journal of the American Medical Association, 261,* 3509-3510.

Goodwin, C. C., & Chrisler, J. C. (1990). *Contraceptive technology in the U.S.: Why so few safe, effective options?* Unpublished manuscript.

Grady, K. E. (1988). Older women and the practice of breast self-examination. *Psychology of Women Quarterly, 12,* 473-487.

Hanrahan, W. (1990, May 24). Birth control research in the U.S. at a standstill. *New Haven Register, 178,* 7.

Harrison, M. (1982). *A woman in residence.* New York: Random House.

Hartman-Stein, P., & Reuter, J. M. (1988). Developmental issues in the treatment of diabetic women. *Psychology of Women Quarterly, 12,* 417-428.

Hein, K. (1984). The first pelvic examination and common gynecological problems in adolescent girls. In S. Golub (Ed.), *Health care of the female adolescent* (pp. 47-63). New York: Haworth Press.

Herman, M. (1972). The poor: Their medical needs and the health services available to them. *Annals of the American Academy of Political and Social Science, 399,* 12-21.

Hilliard, J. R., & Hilliard, P. J. (1984). Bulimia, anorexia nervosa, and diabetes: Deadly combinations. *Psychiatric Clinics of North America, 7,* 367-379.

Lack, D. Z. (1982). Women and pain: Another feminist issue. *Women & Therapy, 1*(1), 55-64.

LaGreca, A. M., Schwarz, L. T., & Satin, W. (1987). Eating patterns in young women with IDDM: Another look. *Diabetes Care, 10,* 657-660.

Lawrence, R. C., Hochberg, M. C., Kelsey, J. L., McDuffie, F. C., Medsger, T. A., Felts, W. R., & Shulman, L. E. (1989). Estimates of the prevalence of selected arthritic and musculoskeletal diseases in the United States. *Journal of Rheumatology, 16,* 427-441.

Lemkau, J. P. (1988). Emotional sequelae of abortion: Implications for clinical practice. *Psychology of Women Quarterly, 12,* 461-472.

Leonardo, C., & Chrisler, J. C. (1992). Women and sexually transmitted diseases. *Women & Health, 18*(4), 1-15.

Levine, C. (1990). Women and HIV/AIDS research: The barriers to equity. *Evaluation Review, 14,* 447-463.

Liang, M., Partridge, A., Daltroy, L., Straaton, K., Galper, S., & Holman, H. (1991). Strategies for reducing excess morbidity and mortality in blacks with systemic lupus erythematosus. *Arthritis and Rheumatism, 34,* 1187-1196.

Liao, Y., Cooper, R. S., Ghali, J. K., & Szocka, A. (1992). Survival rates with coronary artery disease for black women compared with black men. *Journal of the American Medical Association, 268,* 1867-1871.

Lorde, A. (1990). Living with cancer. In E. C. White (Ed.), *The black women's health book: Speaking for ourselves* (pp. 27-37). Seattle: Seal Press.

Maheux, B., Pineault, R., Lambert, J., Beland, F., & Berthiaume, M. (1989). Factors influencing physicians' preventive practices. *American Journal of Preventive Medicine, 5*(4), 201-206.

Major, B., Mueller, P., & Hildebrandt, K. (1985). Attributions, expectations, and coping with abortion. *Journal of Personality and Social Psychology, 48,* 585-599.

Mays, V. M., & Cochran, S. D. (1988). Issues in the perception of AIDS risk and risk reduction activities by black and Hispanic/Latina women. *American Psychologist, 43,* 949-957.

Meares, E. M. (1987). Interstitial cystitis. *Urology, 29*(Suppl. 4), 46-48.

Merck Research Laboratories. (1992). *The Merck manual of diagnosis and therapy* (16th ed.). Rahway, N.J.: Merck & Co., Inc.

Messing, E. M. (1987). The diagnosis of interstitial cystitis. *Urology, 29*(Suppl. 4), 4-7.

Morokoff, P. J. (1991, August). *AIDS: Special issues for prevention in women.* Paper presented at the meeting of the American Psychological Association, San Francisco, Calif.

Muller, C. F. (1990). *Health care and gender.* New York: Russell Sage Foundation.

Nettina, S. L., & Kaufman, F. H. (1990). Diagnosis and treatment of sexually transmitted genital lesions. *Nursing Practitioner, 15*(1), 20-39.

Nyamathi, A., Shuler, P., & Porche, M. (1990). AIDS educational program for minority women at risk. *Family and Community Health, 13*(2), 54-64.

Ogur, B. (1986). Long day's journey into night: Women and prescription drug abuse. *Women & Health, 11*(1), 99-115.

Perales, C. A., & Young, L. S. (Eds.). (1988). *Too little, too late: Dealing with the health needs of women in poverty.* New York: Harrington Park Press.

Randall, C. E. (1989). Lesbian phobia among BSN educators: A survey. *Journal of Nursing Education, 28,* 302-306.

Ratner, V. (1987). Rediscovering a "rare" disease: A patient's perspective on interstitial cystitis. *Urology, 29*(Suppl. 4), 44-45.

Ratner, V., Slade, D., & Whitmore, K. E. (1992). Interstitial cystitis: A bladder disease finds legitimacy. *Journal of Women's Health, 1,* 63-68.

Reagan, P. (1981). The interaction of health professionals and their lesbian clients. *Patient Counseling and Health Education, 3,* 21-25.

Rodin, J., Silberstein, L., & Striegel-Moore, R. (1985). Women and weight: A normative discontent. In T. B. Sonderegger (Ed.), *Nebraska Symposium on Motivation: Psychology and gender* (pp. 267-304). Lincoln, Nebr.: University of Nebraska Press.

Rosser, S. V. (1986). *Teaching science and health from a feminist perspective.* New York: Pergamon Press.

Rosser, S. V. (1993). Ignored, overlooked, or subsumed: Research on lesbian health and health care. *NWSA Journal, 5,* 183-203.

Rothenberg, R., Woelfel, M., Stoneburner, R., Milberg, J., Parker, R., & Truman, B. (1987). Survival with the acquired immunodeficiency syndrome: Experience with 5,833 cases in New York City. *New England Journal of Medicine, 317,* 1297-1302.

Russell, S. (1989). From disability to handicap: An inevitable response to social constraints? *Canadian Review of Sociology and Anthropology, 26,* 276-293.

Ruzek, S. (1986). Feminist visions of health: An international perspective. In J. Mitchell & A. Oakley (Eds.), *What is feminism?* (pp. 184-207). New York: Pantheon.

Sant, R., & Meares, E. M. (1990, Jan./Feb.). Interstitial cystitis: Pathogenesis, diagnosis, and treatment. *Infections in Urology,* pp. 24-30.

Sharpe, P. A., Clark, N. M., & Janz, N. K. (1991). Differences in the impact and management of heart disease between older women and men. *Women & Health, 17*(2), 25-43.

Shayne, V. T., & Kaplan, B. J. (1991). Double victims: Poor women and AIDS. *Women & Health, 17*(1), 21-37.

Silverman, J., Torres, A., & Forrest, J. (1987). Barriers to contraceptive services. *Family Planning Perspectives, 19,* 94-102.

Sofaer, S., & Abel, E. (1990). Older women's health and financial vulnerability: Implications of the Medicare benefit structure. *Women & Health, 16*(3/4), 47-67.

Stahly, G. B. (1992). Cancer and stigma: Problems of seriously ill women. In J. C. Chrisler & D. Howard (Eds.), *New directions in feminist psychology: Practice, theory, and research* (pp. 141-153). New York: Springer.

Steingart, R. M., Packer, M., Hamm, P., Coglianese, M. E., Gersh, B., Geltman, E. M., Sollano, J., Katz, S., & Moye, L. (1991). Sex differences in the management of coronary artery disease. *New England Journal of Medicine, 325,* 226-230.

Stellman, J. M. (1988). The working environment of the working poor: An analysis based on workers' compensation claims, census data, and known risk factors. In C. A. Perales & L. S. Young (Eds.), *Too little, too late: Dealing with the health needs of women in poverty* (pp. 83-101). New York: Harrington Park Press.

Stevens, P. E. (1992). Lesbian health care research: A review of the literature from 1970 to 1990. *Health Care for Women International, 13,* 91-120.

Stevens, P. E., & Hall, J. M. (1990). Abusive health care interactions experienced by lesbians: A case of institutional violence in the treatment of women. *Response: To the Victimization of Women and Children, 13*(3), 23-27.

Stone, K. M. (1989). Epidemiological aspects of genital HPV infection. *Clinical Obstetrics and Gynecology, 32,* 112-116.

Strickland, B. R. (1988). Sex-related differences in health and illness. *Psychology of Women Quarterly, 12,* 381-399.

Sweet, E. (1988, March). A failed revolution. *Ms., 16,* 75-79.

Tallon, J. R., & Block, R. (1988). Changing patterns of health insurance coverage: Special concerns for women. In C. A. Perales & L. S. Young (Eds.), *Too little, too late: Dealing with the health needs of women in poverty* (pp. 119-136). New York: Harrington Park Press.

Tanfer, K., & Rosenbaum, E. (1986). Contraceptive perceptions and method choice among young single women in the U.S. *Family Planning Perspectives, 17,* 169-177.

Taylor, S. E. (1991). *Health psychology* (2nd ed.). New York: McGraw-Hill.

Tobin, J. N., Wassertheil-Smoller, S., Wexler, J. P., Steingart, R. M., Budner, N., Lense, L., & Wachpress, J. (1987). Sex bias in considering coronary bypass surgery. *Annals of Internal Medicine, 107,* 19-25.

Toyoda, N. (1982). Insulin receptors on erythrocytes in normal and obese pregnant women: Comparisons to those in non-pregnant women during the follicular and luteal phases. *American Journal of Obstetrics and Gynecology, 144,* 679.

Travis, C. B. (1988). *Women and health psychology: Biomedical issues.* Hillsdale, N.J.: Lawrence Erlbaum.

Trippet, S. E., & Bain, J. (1992). Reasons American lesbians fail to seek traditional health care. *Health Care for Women International, 13,* 145-154.

Trotta, P. (1980). Breast self-examination: Factors influencing compliance. *Oncology Nursing Forum, 7*(3), 13-17.

Trussell, J., & Kost, K. (1987). Contraceptive failure in the United States: A critical review of the literature. *Studies in Family Planning, 18,* 237-283.

Vroman, G. M. (1983). The health of older women in our society. In M. Fooden, S. Gordon, & B. Hughley (Eds.), *Genes & gender IV: The second X and women's health* (pp. 185-204). New York: Gordian Press.

Waitzkin, H. B., & Waterman, B. (1974). *The exploitation of illness in capitalist society.* Indianapolis: Bobbs-Merrill.

Wallen, J., Waitzkin, H., & Stoekle, J. (1979). Physician stereotypes about female health and illness: A study of patient's sex and the informative process during medical interviews. *Women & Health, 4*(2), 135-146.

Waller, K. (1988). Women doctors for women patients? *British Journal of Medical Psychology, 61,* 125-135.

Webster, D. (1990). Comparing patients' and nurses' views of interstitial cystitis: A pilot study. *Urologic Nursing, 10*(3), 10-15.

Weeks, C. C. (1980). MS: The malignant uncertainty. *American Journal of Nursing, 80,* 298-299.

Weiner, H. (1991). Social and psychobiological factors in autoimmune disease. In R. Ader, D. Felten, & N. Cohen (Eds.), *Psychoneuroimmunology* (pp. 955-1011). New York: Academic Press.

Weisman, C. S., & Teitelbaum, M. A. (1985). Physician gender and the physician-patient relationship: Recent evidence and relevant questions. *Social Science and Medicine, 20,* 1119-1127.

Weiss, L., & Meadow, R. (1979). Women's attitudes toward gynecological practices. *Obstetrics and Gynecology, 54,* 110-114.

Williams, J. H. (1977). *Psychology of women: Behavior in a biosocial context.* New York: Norton.

Williams, K. M. (1990). The best foot forward: A black woman deals with diabetes. In E. C. White (Ed.), *The black women's health book: Speaking for ourselves* (pp. 167-171). Seattle: Seal Press.

Wofsy, C. B. (1987). Human immunodeficiency virus infection in women. *Journal of the American Medical Association, 257,* 2074-2076.

Woolhandler, S., & Himmelstein, D. U. (1988). Reverse targeting of preventive services due to lack of health insurance. *Journal of the American Medical Association, 259,* 2872-2874.

Worth, D. (1989). Sexual decision-making and AIDS: Why condom promotion among vulnerable women is likely to fail. *Studies in Family Planning, 20,* 297-307.

Wright, A. L., & Morgan, W. J. (1990). On the creation of "problem" patients. *Social Science and Medicine, 30,* 951-959.

Young, E. W. (1988). Nurses' attitudes toward homosexuality: Analysis of change in AIDS workshops. *Journal of Continuing Education in Nursing, 19*(1), 9-12.

Young, R. F., & Kahana, E. (1993). Gender, recovery from late life heart attack, and medical care. *Women & Health, 20*(1), 11-31.

Zambrana, R. E. (1988). A research agenda on issues affecting poor and minority women: A model for understanding their health needs. In C. A. Perales & L. S. Young (Eds.), *Too little, too late: Dealing with the health needs of women in poverty* (pp. 137-160). New York: Harrington Park Press.

AUTHOR NOTE

An earlier version of this chapter was presented at the North American Congress on Women's Health Issues in Phoenix, Arizona, in September 1991.

Feminist Neuropsychology: Issues for Physically Challenged Women

Martha E. Banks
Rosalie J. Ackerman
Carolyn A. Corbett

Brain injury is often unacknowledged and seldom medically investigated in women who have experienced accidents, illnesses, and physical assaults; this is particularly the case when the brain injury is mild. Neurological injuries or difficulties in women are often minimized and discounted by medical professionals as hysterical complaints, somatic disorders, nervousness, or attention-seeking behaviors. As a result, brain injury is perceived by many people as a problem faced primarily by men and boys. This stereotyping of victims is reflected in the neurological and neuropsychological literature; most of the examples of people suffering from and/or treated for brain dysfunction are portrayed as male. Neurological and physical injuries have been ignored in women, both clinically and in research studies. This phenomenon is particularly evident for women who have been raped.

Sexual assault is the fastest growing violent crime in the United States (Hochbaum, 1987). Recent investigators have found that 8 percent to 67 percent of victims show evidence of external trauma, usually on mouth, throat, wrists, breasts, and thighs (Beebe, 1991; Cartwright & Sexual Assault Study Group, 1987; Tintinalli & Hoelzer, 1985). Marchbanks, Lui, and Mercy (1990) described physical injuries of living rape victims sustained through physical resistance to rape. They noted that no records are kept of the fatalities due to such struggles nor of the number of suspicious injuries not reported as a consequence of rape. These authors also reported on specific injuries: black eyes and swelling (82%); bites, physical restraints or bindings, burns, and scaldings (25%); internal injuries and unconsciousness (19%); broken bones or teeth (8%); and knife or gunshot wounds (2%). Golding (1994) reported on the prevalence of physical symptoms in a randomly selected population. Especially prominent were neurological problems. Such injuries in men often lead to neuropsychological evaluations, but this does not appear to be the case for women (Ackerman & Banks, 1990).

Discriminatory attributions of "inability" on the basis of gender have led to serious psychological, social, and economic consequences for women. Physically challenged women seeking appropriate treatment and the many women who face the overwhelming task of caring for survivors of brain injury deal with most of the same issues. A first step in consciousness-raising is the unification of the diverse groups of brain-injured women and caretaking women as advocates for appropriate assessment, treatment, and support. This chapter describes some of the issues faced by these women, with an emphasis on physical aspects of brain injury and barriers to appropriate diagnosis and treatment. Although not every rape has sequelae of brain injury, we have chosen to focus on multiple consequences of rape, as examples of sources of *potential* brain injury and the problems women face in the pursuit of health care. Considerations of the ethics in feminist models of neuropsychology will be illustrated by a clinical case example involving a number of symptoms.

SOURCES AND DESCRIPTIONS OF NEUROPSYCHOLOGICAL DYSFUNCTION— FOCUS ON RAPE

Psychological problems arise when women experience difficulties and are repeatedly dismissed as having "unspecified somatic complaints" or "hysteria." Even physical manifestations of psychological problems are sometimes treated as if they were specific to people of one gender or the other (Horton, 1984). Of particular concern is the treatment approach taken to rape victims. The literature reflects attempts to define rape syndromes with a focus on psychological sequelae of rape (e.g., Burge, 1988; Burgess & Holmstrom, 1974; DiVasto, 1985; Kilpatrick, Resick, & Verenon, 1981; McCarthy, 1986; Mezey & Taylor, 1988; Resick, 1983; Spiegel, 1989) or mythology-based minimization and victim-blaming (Mayr & Price, 1989). Perhaps the most dangerous research in the area of consequences of rape is the recent focus on sociobiology, which attempts to explain rape as a "natural phenomenon," thereby implying that there are no negative consequences (Crawford & Galdikas, 1986; Thornhill & Thornhill, 1990a, 1990b, 1990c). Many of the problems with sociobiological approaches have been articulated by Ackerman (1991) and Sunday and Tobach (1985).

Some of the concerns, however, about lack of progress during psychological treatment ignore possible physical/neurological explanations for the victims' behavior in therapy. Koss, Koss, and Woodruff (1991, p. 342), in their examination of women as health care consumers, found support for their hypotheses that "emotional responses to crime might be perceived by the patient as physical disease. Second, preexisting symptoms could be exacerbated, or the tolerance for them lowered, by crime-induced stress. Third, resistance might be taxed by the stress of crime victimization, thereby inducing disease." Similar conclusions have been reached by others (Bloom, 1985; Kiecolt-Glaser & Glaser,1987; Waigandt et al., 1990). Koss, Koss, and Woodruff (1991) advise primary physicians to consider abuse and sexual assault as the causes of presenting physical problems, such as painful menses, pain with frequent urination, and vaginal discharge (see Waigandt et al., 1990). Ende, Gertner, and Socha (1990) described long-term hormonal changes in rape victims, which could be due to extreme stress or injury to the central nervous and endocrine systems. Depression can also be a consequence of such chronic, externally induced hormonal imbalance. Beebe (1991) recommended that family physicians and emergency room staff adopt a more extensive protocol, including careful physical examination, collection of legal evidence, prompt treatment of physical injuries, psychological support, arrangements for follow-up counseling during the post-trauma stages, evaluation of behavioral correlates of rape trauma syndrome (after Burgess & Holmstrom, 1974), and assessment of the emotional consequences of rape.

Recent research with neuropsychological assessment has revealed previously undiagnosed brain damage in survivors of physical abuse, diseases, and accidents such as falls or whiplash injuries. Such survivors are often assessed and treated only for cuts, bruises, and broken bones (Beebe, 1991; Cartwright et al., 1986; Cartwright & Sexual Assault Study Group, 1987; Harlow, 1989). We recommend that, for women with physical injuries, *especially* about the head and upper torso, a neuropsychological evaluation also be administered. This recommendation applies to women who are victims of both sexual and other physical assaults. Although it is clear that many women appear to recover "fully" from assaults, appropriate assessments are necessary as a first step toward treatment for people who need it (Golding, 1994).

A modal percentage of physician-documented nongenital injury in all age groups that are reported in a hospital setting is 40 percent to 50 percent (Beebe, 1991; Cartwright & Sexual Assault Study Group, 1987). Harlow (1989) interpreted 80 percent of these physical injuries to be "minor," and he noted that of the 39 percent of the U.S. group of women sustaining physical injury from the rape trauma, only 54 percent received medical treatment for their physical injuries. All of the above professionals agreed that this is a gross underestimate due to the hesitancy of many rape victims to report their injuries. Physical injury does appear to provide some impetus for rape victims to seek physician care, though it is not always the case with women of color. Fear of public humiliation, social stigma, and social retribution also prevent women from reporting this crime and seeking medical care (Beebe, 1991; Davis, 1983).

Lesh and Marshall (1984, p. 21) commented on the "lack of professional literature on the subject of women with disabilities . . . and a paucity of systematically acquired, research based knowledge regarding this group." Most of the case examples and/or research results in the literature on neuropsychology and cognitive rehabilitation of brain-injured patients are not identified with respect to gender, age, and/or ethnicity (e.g., Goldstein & Ruthven, 1983; Lam, Priddy, & Johnson, 1991; Niemann, Ruff, & Baser, 1990). Studies are primarily limited to young European-American men (e.g., Gianutsos & Matheson, 1987; Helm-Estabrook, Fitzpatrick, & Baressi, 1982; Posner & Rafal, 1987;

Sparks, Helm, & Albert, 1974; Webster & Scott, 1983), and this difference in gender rehabilitation is reflected in hospital censuses (Ackerman & Banks, 1990, 1992; Fine & Asch, 1988; Mudrick, 1987).

"Analysis of the receipt of rehabilitation services by men and women has shown that, although men and women report receiving rehabilitation services with nearly equal frequency, women are less likely than men to be offered services that facilitate employment" (Mudrick, 1989, p. 321). "Young white men receive a disproportionately large amount of computerized cognitive treatment . . . for brain injuries" (Ackerman & Banks, 1990, p. 87).

Lesbians and women of color are particularly at risk for not having their neurological complaints taken seriously (Cartwright & Sexual Assault Study Group et al., 1991; Thompson & Andrzejewski, 1988). Such women are often severely stigmatized and penalized by misdiagnosis and withholding of assessment and treatment. Cartwright and his colleagues described (1987, p. 46) "a belief in black women that it is useless to report being raped by a white man because the authorities and courts will not take her claim seriously."

Sexually Transmitted Diseases

One important side effect of rape is the acquisition of sexually transmitted diseases (McGregor, 1985). During the 1980s and 1990s we have become aware of the fatal acquired immune deficiency syndrome (AIDS), which develops from infection with the human immunodeficiency virus (HIV). Amaro (1988) noted that Hispanic women were particularly at high risk for contracting HIV, due in large part to minimal contact with educational programs in the gynecological health system. Early reports by the Centers for Disease Control stated that 93 percent of AIDS patients were male; as a result, there were relatively few gender comparative research studies (Des Jarlais & Friedman, 1988). Des Jarlais and Friedman's (1988) work indicated that the course of AIDS in New York intravenous drug users appears to be gender-specific, with women being underrepresented and men being overrepresented, and they cited the 1987 work of Rothenberg et al., who observed that "females survive for a shorter time after a diagnosis of AIDS than do males" (p. 162). Des Jarlais and Friedman (1988, p. 162) interpreted that to "suggest differences in the time period from initial infection to the seeking of treatment as a possible unifying hypothesis for many of the observed gender differences." Women, especially those of color, are not getting medical diagnosis or treatment early in the course of HIV infection.

Much of the focus of research on AIDS has been on physical symptoms and the terminal aspects of the disease. Here, however, we are reviewing the neuropsychological aspects of AIDS. Bridge (1988) noted that there is a specific and progressive neuropsychological dementia syndrome that is manifested in people with AIDS. In the early stages of AIDS, patients exhibit

> forgetfulness, poor concentration, confusion, slowed thinking, loss of balance, poor handwriting, leg weakness, depression, fatigue, paranoia, hallucinations, and anergy. Early signs include impaired cognition, moderate to severe psychomotor retardation, ataxia, tremor, paresis, pyramidal tract signs, as well as behavioral signs (apathy, dysphoria, psychosis, and regression). In the latter course of the illness, frank dementia is apparent with mutism, ataxia, hypertonia, moderate to severe paresis, incontinence, tremor, facial release signs, myclonus, seizures, and psychosis (Navia, Jordan, & Price, 1986, as cited in Bridge, 1988, p. 2).

It is important to note that several of the early symptoms of dementia—specifically depression, hallucinations, psychosis, tremor, psychomotor slowness, weakness, dyscoordination, short-term memory loss, apathy, dysphoria, and regression—are all sequelae of both brain injury and dementia (Bridge, 1988; Mirsky, 1988; Sohlberg & Mateer, 1989) and rape (Burge, 1988; Burgess & Holmstrom, 1974; Cohen & Roth, 1987; DiVasto, 1985; Felitti, 1991; Ruch et al., 1991).

Rubinow et al. (1988, p. 111) reported that "organic mental syndromes have been reported both in association with CNS lymphoma and opportunistic infections and as part of an HIV-induced subacute encephalitis." They supported that statement with results of neuropsychological screening tests, and suggested that neuroscientists need to become more involved in the study of the neuropsychological impact of AIDS. Mirsky (1988, p. 117) points out that the cognitive changes documented in AIDS patients present "dangers for the patients themselves and for those with the responsibility of dealing with them or for planning their care." Given the concern about late diagnosis of HIV infection in women, it is likely that many infected women experience difficulties with problem solving, language, and memory, which seriously impair their ability to seek treatment. Poor judgment, an early sign of AIDS-related dementia, can lead to promiscuity with unsafe sexual practices, resulting in acceleration of the course of the disease.

Social Consequences of Brain Injury

In addition to the neuropsychological symptoms and sexually transmitted diseases, there are several social problems victims of rape and other brain injured women face. These include misdiagnosis (Fine, 1983-84), inappropriate treatment, multiple role changes with unrealistic expectations, and employment problems.

In girls and young women, learning disabilities are often overlooked and mistakenly considered to be "feminine attributes" such as math anxiety, inability to think logically, and poor reading comprehension. Categorized as "attributes," learning disabilities are not assessed or treated, thereby causing many women to be stigmatized and, at the worst, institutionalized due to misdiagnosis. Furthermore, learning disabilities are often sequelae of brain dysfunction (Browder, 1991).

Social problems include the refusal of families to tolerate complaints of pain or difficulty more than two weeks after a known physical insult. Families unrealistically expect a quick return to premorbid functioning, but such recovery is rare (Ackerman & Banks, 1992; Banks, Ackerman, & Clark, 1987).

In many instances, women without nursing or medical preparation are providing more than full-time care for survivors of brain injury. When such caregivers describe the behavioral problems of brain-injured patients, their descriptions are perceived as "complaints" and ignored. Guidelines must be developed to assist health professionals in acknowledging and providing appropriate support for the management of numerous physical and behavioral problems (Ackerman & Banks, 1992; Anderson & Parente, 1985; Banks, Ackerman, & Clark, 1987; Brody, 1990).

Economic considerations result from the tendency to fire women who are unable to produce at a consistent rate on their jobs, even though there might be medical reasons for changes in performance. It is too soon to predict how the 1992 Americans with Disabilities Act might change this trend for women. Gouvier et al. (1991) found that people with neuropsychological disabilities, such as strokes and head injuries, were rated lower in employability by college students. These authors related the results to continuing discrimination practices based on stereotypes about attractiveness and misattributions about brain injury.

In the absence of medical attribution for low productivity, women are given pejorative labels, which can lead to unwarranted institutionalization. If diagnoses are made, women are seldom given the opportunity for light duty, reassignment, or other adaptive strategies used to assist injured men in maintaining their jobs. One example of this is the difference in management of repetitive injury strains in the United States and Australia. Hopkins (1990) identified repetitive strain injury among computer and postal workers who had keyboard entry tasks with high level of work load, coincident with increased work pressures (Bammer, 1987). The repetitive movement injury was recognized as an occupational hazard in Australia and compensated under workmens' compensation; it decreased in prevalence as the workplace was designed ecologically to prevent the occurrence of repetitive strain injury (RSI). There is recognition of injuries such as RSI, carpal tunnel syndrome, tendonitis, bursitis, and tenosynvitis by the Australian government, disability reimbursement agencies, and the public. Most of the Australian clientele are blue-collar workers, and most of them are women. In the United States, there is a *lack* of medical, governmental, or social recognition of repetitive motion injuries being initiated at the workplace due to poor design of equipment and working conditions. Much money would be needed to compensate workers for RSI, and the Occupational Safety and Health Administration has been reluctant to acknowledge that such injuries occur. Because of the distribution of the labor force in computer fields in the United States, much of the compensation for RSI would be paid to women of color (Banks & Ackerman, 1990), who are heavily represented in keyboard entry jobs.

"Women with prior labor force experience are less likely than equally experienced men to be employed after rehabilitation" (Mudrick, 1989, p. 321). In 1983 Mudrick found that married and unmarried women employed outside of the home are less likely to be disabled than women who do not work outside of the home. Mudrick (1983) found that marriage is negatively correlated with disability; married men are less likely to report disability than their unmarried counterparts (Mudrick, 1989). She attributed this to commitment to family responsibilities and/or maintaining the breadwinner role.

Mudrick (1989, p. 323) also noted that "When disabled men and women under age 65 are asked their main activity in the prior week, men are likely to describe themselves as retired rather than disabled. In contrast, disabled women report that they are keeping house. Retirement is an age-related status; homemaking is not. Perhaps impaired men are more likely to report themselves as being disabled as they approach the normative retirement age range." Age is a significant demographic variable for disabled men, but not for disabled women; women's work of homemaking is never done. Reisine and Fifield (1988) raised several questions about the disabling impact of the home working environment for women with rheumatoid arthritis; they recognized that deeply entrenched social roles interfere with perceptions of disability in women with chronic disease.

Belgrave and Walker (1991) found that African Americans with disabilities were more likely to be employed than unemployed if they had accessible transportation and social support. Their future research will focus on clarification of the useful types of social support, and their research model can be extended to physically challenged women of all ethnic groups. If women are provided with the appropriate supports, they can adapt to their disabilities.

We would like to illustrate some of the neuropsychological implications in a differently abled woman of color. Treatment planning for such women must address a variety of presenting and underlying problems. The case example illustrates the multidimensional facets of assessing and treating differently abled women. The goal of this example is to underscore the importance of assessing multiple sociocultural factors, which must be considered in comprehensive evaluations. Although there are unusual characteristics in this case, such aspects need to be evaluated. In this case, issues of communication limitations, dual diagnoses of seizures and depression, abuse history, sexuality, and legal competence will be addressed.

*Case Example**

A twenty-year-old deaf woman of color was referred to a university counseling center through the office of residence. She had arrived at the university six weeks prior to a program designed to teach sign language to new students. During this program, she had difficulty interacting with peers and had a physical altercation with her roommate. At the time of referral, she was experiencing further difficulties with her peers during freshman orientation week, and reported having some suicidal ideation. Due to the severity of her difficulties, it was decided that a multidisciplinary, interdepartmental treatment staff meeting (staffing) would be held to address the multiple problems and find the best possible options for the student.

Communication limitations.   Language is essential to daily interaction and is a complex comprehension task. Neuropathology and psychopathology may have negative impact on an individual's ability to remember and follow through with what is being communicated. In order to fully understand the implications of the current case study, it is important to examine some background variables about the deaf population.

In deaf individuals, several points might be raised about the role of language in their daily lives. Many deaf individuals do not rely on speech for communication with others. The native language of the deaf community is American Sign Language (ASL; Benderly, 1980; Marcowicz, 1977; Padden & Humphries, 1988). ASL has its origins in French Sign Language and is not based on English morphology or syntax (Marcowicz, 1977). Thus, many deaf individuals are not skilled users of the English language and have difficulties with reading and writing. The average reading level for deaf adults in the United States is fifth grade (Benderly, 1980).

The controversy over whether to use signs or speech with hearing impaired people has led to a long history of difficulty in the education of deaf individuals. Very few deaf students continue into higher educational programs. Those who do attend college are usually older than the average hearing college stu-

---

*Identifying information of the case example has been altered in order to maintain confidentiality.

dent. English language proficiency continues to be a significant problem in college-age deaf students, and the need for remedial work is quite common. A recent investigation found that the average student at Gallaudet worked six years in order to obtain a bachelor's degree. Minority students tended to stay for seven years to complete the degree (Corbett, 1992).

The acquisition of communication skills enables the person to become socially integrated. Proficiency in ASL determines degree of social acceptance in the deaf community (Trybus, 1980). Deaf individuals who are not fluent in sign language tend to be self-isolating and rejected by their peers. Brinton and Fujiki (1989) and Kretschmer and Kretschmer (1988) provide a variety of techniques for assessing the linguistic fluency of children with language and hearing impairments.

Johnson, Liddell, and Erting (1989) proposed that in order for a deaf individual to become proficient in English, she or he must be proficient in ASL, or vice versa. However, for many deaf individuals, language delays occur when they are not proficient in either English or ASL. In the current case study, the student was not fluent in either language. Thus, she experienced both educational and social difficulties.

Assessment of sign language ability is important in the diagnosis of psychopathology in deaf clients. Ideally, the therapist should be fluent in American Sign Language and able to evaluate the type of signing the client is using. There are a variety of sign languages, and it is important to establish whether the client is using visual-gestural communication, English-based sign language, pidgin signed English (PSE), or ASL. Poor use of sign language or peculiarities in syntax can be indicative of psychopathology.

When the therapist is not able to sign, it is not unusual to use a certified sign language interpreter to facilitate communication. However, the use of an interpreter raises several issues in the evaluation process (Goetz, Guess, & Stremel-Campbell, 1987; Veltri, 1993; Williams, 1993). For example, peculiarities in language could become lost in the translation and the evaluator might miss important information. Transference that the client usually directs toward the therapist might be directed toward the interpreter instead. In addition, the interpreter's countertransference to material presented during the assessment and treatment interviews might influence her or his interpreting style (e.g., facial expression and body language).

In the current case, the client had minimal ability to generate American Sign Language. Her English language skills were at a primary school level. Her ability to produce and understand language was severely impaired. Thus, for this client, daily interaction with others was fraught with miscommunication. This severe lack of daily language skill led to several frustrating episodes on a daily basis and frequent negative interactions with peers. Educationally, this student had a history of private individualized special instruction and had limited opportunities to interact with peers during her formative years. She also had many language difficulties in her community. Simple sentences were difficult for the student to comprehend, which creates a predicament in the inquiry process of the evaluation and the communication of remediation and rehabilitation tasks.

Explosive emotional outbursts are often observed in clients who have impaired communication (Goetz, Guess, & Stremel-Campbell, 1987). For the current client, the frequent negative interactions also led to depression and suicidal risk.

Seizure disorder.   The student had a lifelong history of seizure disorder. She had had two brain surgeries within the preceding six years to reduce seizure activity and had been maintained on appropriate antiseizure medication. The student's medical status was monitored by campus health services.

The two recent invasive surgical procedures to alleviate the severity of seizures might have had a significant impact on the client's functioning. It is not clear whether her difficulties with language and communication existed premorbidly or if her functioning in these areas worsened after the surgeries. It is expected that a procedure involving surgery to the brain would result in some loss of functioning. The student needed concrete instructions and written lists in order to follow through on tasks.

Frustration tolerance and suicidal ideation.   During the two years that this student was in college, she had seen four counselors and a psychiatrist. She usually came to the center on an emergency basis. At times, the emergency was related to depression and suicidal ideation. Behaviorally, there was evidence to suggest poor impulse control, as she had engaged in self-mutilation and striking out at others. At other times, the emergency involved case management issues in which the counselor had to explain how a checking account works or the meaning of official letters the client had received.

Attempts at establishing an ongoing psychotherapy relationship proved to be quite difficult. The student tended to storm out of the counselor's office at the slightest disagreement. During the two years of therapy, she continued to report occasional suicidal ideation and had one brief psychiatric hospitalization.

Given the severity of the client's difficulties, the level of frustration she encountered daily should not be underestimated. Her ability to cope with frustration in an appropriate manner was compromised as she had a paucity of "feeling words," which made it difficult for her to discuss her experiences with the counselor. Although attempts were made to provide concrete, educational approaches with this client, her comprehension level was not adequate. She had difficulty retaining information given by counselors. Memory problems led to several other difficulties. In addition, the client rarely could follow through on issues discussed in therapy. Judgment, insight, and evaluation of consequences were lacking in this brain-injured patient.

One option was to use a written contract to limit self-mutilation, hitting other students, and suicidal obsessions. The contract involved having the student seek help at the counseling center if she felt like hurting herself or others. Due to her language difficulties, the final draft of the contract was written at the primary school reading level.

Age and legal competence.   Although this client was over eighteen years of age, she was not functioning at the maturity level of the average college student. Campus professionals were doubtful about the appropriateness of her remaining on campus given her limitations. However, fear of legal reprisal from her parents prevented formal dismissal of this student.

The student's parents were aware of her difficulties, yet preferred that she stay at the university. The university accepts some responsibility for students while they are residents on the campus (*in loco parentis*). However, due to her poor judgment, she often placed herself in high-risk situations and was in danger of being hurt by individuals outside of the university. Although this student was legally an adult, she was not able to take care of herself adequately for independent living. It is doubtful that she would ever be able to manage in an unsupervised living arrangement; hence, placement assistance will be necessary after completion of college.

History of abuse/neglect.   The nature of the student's emotional and learning difficulties raises the question of a history of possible abuse and/or neglect. There are several excellent educational facilities for deaf individuals, which accept children from ages two years and older for language training. The fact that this student had neither English nor ASL fluency at age twenty raises a suspicion of neglect on the part of the parents or inappropriate referral on the part of the local school system in the early education of this student.

Her parents knew that she had severe emotional problems, but wanted her to have a chance to interact with other university students and engage in age-appropriate activities. Once the student was dropped off at school, the parents maintained only superficial contact with her. The "dumping" of this student at the university with minimal support from home might also be interpreted as neglect.

Emotionally, her explosiveness and combativeness might be indicative of past physical abuse. Her involvement with an older, hearing man with no knowledge of sign language reflected the poor judgment sometimes noted in victims of childhood sexual abuse (Felitti, 1991).

Sexuality.   This student was involved with an older, homeless man with whom communication was absolutely minimal. It was unclear whether a sexual relationship developed, however. Due to the student's severe communication problems, it was extremely difficult to teach her about basic sex and birth control, and virtually impossible to explain the importance of safe sex with relationship to AIDS. She was especially at risk for sexual assault, as she lacked the social skills for self-protection and the comprehension skills to evaluate consequences of her sexual behaviors. Differently abled women are particularly vulnerable to recently incarcerated sex offenders, who easily recognize that victims are unable to report the crime (Longo & Gochenour, 1981).

This student's limited social experiences led to poor relationships with other students since she had come to the campus. Finally, poor judgment made this student vulnerable to individuals who might take advantage of her.

SUMMARY AND RECOMMENDATIONS

In summary, the goal of this chapter is to challenge the assumptions made about the diverse groups of differently abled women who have neuropsychological problems and enhance the awareness of feminist psychologists and other health professionals of the clinical relevance of brain injury to groups of battered, physically abused, raped, and disease-afflicted women who are being overlooked in diagnosis and access to treatment. Brain dysfunction can result from abuse as well as many disorders and diseases. As A. H. Hemstreet (personal communication, July 27, 1993) noted, rape is "a far more common causative factor to brain injury in women than currently acknowledged." We recommend that any woman who has physical injuries from sexual assault, *especially* about the head and upper torso, have a neuropsychological evaluation, pursue treatment, and return to the labor force. In our case example, we have demonstrated the need for differently abled women to be treated in the context of their impairments. Psychologists are aware of the need for appropriate, nonstereotypical, culturally relevant contexts in the assessment and treatment of patients; it is important to acknowledge that culture includes the nature and impact of disability as well as age, gender, and ethnicity.

REFERENCES

Ackerman, R. J. (1991). *Sociobiology: Issues of ethnicity and gender.* Manuscript submitted for publication.

Ackerman, R. J., & Banks, M. E. (1990). Computers and ethical treatment for brain-injured patients. *Social Science Computer Review, 8,* 83-95.

Ackerman, R. J., & Banks, M. E. (1992). Family therapy for caregivers of brain injured patients. In J. Chrisler & D. Howard (Eds.), *New directions in feminist psychology: Practice, theory, and research* (pp. 66-84). New York: Springer.

Amaro, H. (1988). Considerations for prevention of HIV infection among Hispanic women. *Psychology of Women Quarterly, 12,* 429-443.

Anderson, J. K., & Parente, F. J. (1985). Training family members to work with the head-injured patient. *Cognitive Rehabilitation, 4*(1), 12-15.

Bammer, G. (1987). How technological change can increase the risk of repetitive motion injuries. *Seminars in Occupational Medicine. 2,* 25-30.

Banks, M. E., & Ackerman, R. J. (1990). Ethnic and gender computer employment status. *Social Science Computer Review, 8,* 75-82.

Banks, M. E., Ackerman, R. J., & Clark, E. (1987). Elderly women in family therapy. In D. Howard (Ed.), *Dynamics of feminist therapy* (pp. 107-116). New York: Haworth Press.

Beebe, D. K. (1991). Emergency management of the adult female rape victim. *American Journal of Emergency Medicine,. 43,* 2041-2046.

Belgrave, F. Z., & Walker, S. (1991). Predictors of employment outcome of black persons with disabilities. *Rehabilitation Psychology, 36,* 111-120.

Benderly, B. L. (1980). *Dancing without music: Deafness in America.* New York: Anchor Press/Doubleday.

Bloom, B. L. (1985). *Stressful life event theory and research: Implications for primary prevention* (DHHS Publication No. ADM 85-1385). Washington, D.C.: U.S. Government Printing Office.

Bridge, T. P. (1988). AIDS and HIV CNS disease: A neuropsychiatric disorder. In T. P. Bridge, A. F. Mirsky, & F. K. Goodwin (Eds.), *Psychological, neuropsychiatric, and substance abuse aspects of AIDS.* (Vol. 44, *Advances in Biochemical Psychopharmacology*) (pp. 1-13). New York: Raven Press.

Brinton, B., & Fujiki, M. (1989). *Conversational management with language-impaired children.* Rockville, Md.: Aspen Publishers.

Brody, E. M. (1990). *Women in the middle: Their parent-care years.* New York: Springer.

Browder, D. M. (1991). *Assessment of individuals with severe disabilities: An applied behavior approach to life skills management.* Baltimore: Paul H. Brookes.

Burge, S. K. (1988). Post-traumatic stress disorder in victims of rape. Special issue: Progress in traumatic stress research. *Journal of Traumatic Stress, 1,* 193-210.

Burgess, A. W., & Holmstrom, L. L. (1974). Rape trauma syndrome. *American Journal of Psychiatry, 131*, 981-986.

Cartwright, P. S., Moore, R. A., Anderson, J. R., & Brown, D. H. (1986). Genital injury and implied consent to alleged rape. *Journal of Reproductive Medicine, 31*, 1043-1044.

Cartwright, P. S., & Sexual Assault Study Group. (1987). Factors that correlate with injury sustained by survivors of sexual assault. *Obstetrics & Gynecology, 70*, 44-46.

Cohen, L. J., & Roth, S. (1987). The psychological aftermath of rape: Long-term effects and individual differences in recovery. *Journal of Social and Clinical Psychology, 5*, 525-534.

Corbett, C. A. (1992). *Dual minority status and college adjustment: An examination of social and academic adjustment in black deaf college students.* (Doctoral dissertation, The Pennsylvania State University, 1991). *Dissertation Abstracts International, 53*, 2055B.

Crawford, C., & Galdikas, B. (1986). Rape in nonhuman animals: An evolutionary perspective. *Canadian Psychology, 27*, 215-230.

Davis, A. (1983). *Women, race, and class.* New York: Vintage.

Des Jarlais, D. C., & Friedman, S. R. (1988). Gender differences in response to HIV infection. In T. P. Bridge, A. F. Mirsky, & F. K. Goodwin (Eds.), *Psychological, neuropsychiatric, and substance abuse aspects of AIDS.* (Vol. 44, *Advances in Biochemical Psychopharmacology*) (pp. 159-163). New York: Raven Press.

DiVasto, P. (1985). Measuring the aftermath of rape. *Journal of Psychosocial Nursing, 23*, 33-35.

Ende, N., Gertner, S. B., & Socha, B. (1990). Unexpected changes in urinary catecholamines and vanillymandelic acid following rape assault. *Hormones and Behavior, 24*, 62-70.

Felitti, V. J. (1991). Long-term medical consequences of incest, rape, and molestation. *Southern Medical Journal, 84*, 328-331.

Fine, M. (1983-84). Coping with rape: Critical perspectives on consciousness. *Imagination, Cognition and Personality, 3*, 249-267.

Fine, M., & Asch, A. (Eds.) (1988). *Women with disabilities: Essays in psychology, culture and politics.* Philadelphia: Temple University Press.

Gianutsos, R., & Matheson, P. (1987). The rehabilitation of visual perceptual disorders attributable to brain injury. In M. Meier, A. Benton, & L. Diller, (Eds.) *Neuropsychological Rehabilitation* (pp. 202-241). New York: Guilford Press.

Goetz, L., Guess, D., & Stremel-Campbell, K. (1987). *Innovative program design for individuals with dual sensory impairments.* Baltimore: Paul H. Brookes.

Golding, J. M. (1994). Sexual assault history and physical health in randomly selected Los Angeles women. *Health Psychology, 13*, 130-138.

Goldstein, G., & Ruthven, L. (1983). *Rehabilitation of the brain injured adult*. New York: Plenum.

Gouvier, W. D., Steiner, D. D., Jackson, W. T., Schlater, D., & Rain, J. S. (1991). Employment discrimination against handicapped job candidates: An analog study of the effects of neurological causation, visibility of handicap, and public contact. *Rehabilitation Psychology, 36*, 121-129.

Grisso, J. A., Wishner, A. R., Schwarz, D. F., Weene, B. A., Holmes, J. H., & Sutton, R. L. (1991) . A population-based study of injuries of inner-city women. *American Journal of Epidemiology, 134*, 59-68.

Harlow, C. W. (1989). *Injuries from crime*. Washington, D.C.: Department of Justice, Bureau of Justice Statistics.

Helm-Estabrook, N., Fitzpatrick, P., & Baressi, B. (1982). Visual action therapy for global aphasia. *Journal of Speech and Hearing Disorders, 47*, 385-389.

Hochbaum, S. R. (1987). The evaluation and treatment of the sexually assaulted patient. *Emergency Medical Clinics in North America, 5*, 601-622.

Hopkins, A. (1990). The social recognition of repetition strain injuries: An Australian/American comparison. *Social Science and Medicine, 30*, 365-372.

Horton, C. F. (1984). Women have headaches, men have backaches: Patterns of illness in an Appalachian community. *Social Science and Medicine, 19*, 647-654.

Johnson, R. E., Liddell, S. K., & Erting, C. (1989). *Unlocking the curriculum: Principles for achieving access in deaf education* (Working Paper 89-3). Washington, D.C.: Gallaudet University, Department of Linguistics and Interpreting and The Gallaudet Research Institute.

Kiecolt-Glaser, J. K., & Glaser, R. (1987). Psychosocial moderators of immune function. *Annals of Behavioral Medicine, 9*, 16-20.

Kilpatrick, D. G., Resick, P. A., & Verenon, L. J. (1981). Effects of rape experience: A longitudinal study. *Journal of Social Issues, 37*, 105-122.

Koss, M. P., Koss, P. G., & Woodruff, W. J. (1991). Deleterious effects of criminal victimization on women's health and medical utilization. *Archives of Internal Medicine, 151*, 342-347.

Kretschmer, R. R., & Kretschmer, L. W. (Eds.) (1988). Communication assessment of hearing-impaired children: From conversation to classroom. *Journal of the Academy of Rehabilitative Audiology, 23* (Monograph Supplement).

Lam, C. S., Priddy, D. A., & Johnson, P. (1991). Neuropsychological indicators of employability following traumatic brain injury. *Rehabilitation Counseling Bulletin, 35*, 68-74.

Lesh, K., & Marshall, C. (1984). Rehabilitation: Focus on disabled women as a special population. *Journal of Applied Rehabilitation Counseling, 15,* 18-21.

Longo, R. E., & Gochenour, C. (1981). Sexual assault of handicapped individuals. *Journal of Rehabilitation, 47,* 24-27.

McCarthy, B. W. (1986). A cognitive-behavioral approach to understanding and treating sexual trauma. *Journal of Sex and Marital Therapy, 12,* 322-329.

McGregor, J. A. (1985). Risk of STD in female victims of sexual assault. *Medical Aspects of Human Sexuality, 19,* 30-42.

Marchbanks, P. A., Lui, K-J., & Mercy, J. A. (1990). Risk of injury from resisting rape. *American Journal of Epidemiology, 132,* 540-549.

Marcowicz, H. (1977). *American Sign Language: Fact and fancy.* Washington, D.C.: Gallaudet College.

Mayr, S., & Price, J. L. (1989). The lo syndrome: Symptom formation in victims of sexual abuse. *Perspectives in Psychiatric Care, 25,* 36-39.

Mezey, G. C., & Taylor, P. J. (1988). Psychological reactions of women who have been raped: A descriptive and comparative study. *British Journal of Psychiatry, 152,* 330-339.

Mirsky, A. F. (1988). Neuropsychological manifestations and predictors of HIV disease in vulnerable persons. In T. P. Bridge, A. F. Mirsky, & F. K. Goodwin (Eds.), *Psychological, neuropsychiatric, and substance abuse aspects of AIDS.* (Vol. 44, *Advances in Biochemical Psychopharmacology*) (pp. 117-123). New York: Raven Press.

Mudrick, N. R. (1983). Disabled women. *Society, 20,* 51-55.

Mudrick, N. R. (1987). Differences in receipt of rehabilitation by impaired midlife men and women. *Rehabilitation Psychology, 32,* 17-28.

Mudrick, N. R. (1989). The association of roles and attitudes with disability among midlife women and men. *Journal of Aging and Health, 1,* 306-326.

Niemann, H., Ruff, R. M., & Baser, C. A. (1990). Computer-assisted attention retraining in head-injured individuals: A controlled efficacy study of an outpatient program. *Journal of Consulting and Clinical Psychology, 58,* 811-817.

Padden, C., & Humphries, T. (1988). *Deaf in America: Voices from a culture.* Cambridge, Mass.: Harvard University Press.

Posner, M., & Rafal, R. (1987). Cognitive theories of attention and the rehabilitation of attentional deficits. In M. Meier, A. Benton, & L. Diller, (Eds.), *Neuropsychological Rehabilitation* (pp. 182-201). New York: Guilford Press.

Reisine, S. T., & Fifield, J. (1988). Defining disability for women and the problem of unpaid work. *Psychology of Women Quarterly, 12,* 401-415.

Resick, P. A. (1983). The rape reaction: Research findings and implications for intervention. *Behavioral Therapy, 6,* 129-132.

Rubinow, D. R., Joffe, R. T., Brouwers, P., Squillance, K., Lane, H. C., & Mirsky, A. F. (1988). Neuropsychiatric impairment in patients with AIDS. In T. P. Bridge, A. F. Mirsky, & F. K. Goodwin (Eds.), *Psychological, neuropsychiatric, and substance abuse aspects of AIDS*. (Vol. 44, *Advances in Biochemical Psychopharmacology*) (pp. 111-115). New York: Raven Press.

Ruch, L. O., Amadeo, S. R., Leon, J. J., & Gartrell, J. W. (1991). Repeated sexual victimization and trauma change during the acute phase of the sexual assault trauma syndrome. *Women & Health, 17*, 1-19.

Sohlberg, McK. M., & Mateer, C. A. (1989). *Introduction to cognitive rehabilitation: Theory and practice.* New York: Guilford Press.

Sparks, R., Helm, N., & Albert, M. (1974). Aphasic rehabilitation resulting from melodic intonation therapy, *Cortex, 10*, 303-312.

Spiegel, D. (1989). Hypnosis in the treatment of victims of sexual abuse. *Psychiatric Clinics of North America, 12*, 295-305.

Sunday, S. R., & Tobach, E. B. (1985). *Violence against women: A critique of the sociobiology of rape.* New York: Gordian Press.

Thompson, K., & Andrzejewski, J. (1988). *Why can't Sharon Kowalski come home?* San Francisco: Spinsters/Aunt Lute.

Thornhill, N. W., & Thornhill, R. (1990a). An evolutionary analysis of psychological pain following rape I: Effects of victim's age and marital status. *Ethology & Sociobiology, 11*, 155-176.

Thornhill, N. W., & Thornhill, R. (1990b). An evolutionary analysis of psychological pain following rape II: Effects of stranger, friend, and family-member offenders. *Ethology & Sociobiology, 11*, 177-193.

Thornhill, N. W., & Thornhill, R. (1990c). An evolutionary analysis of psychological pain following rape III: Effects of force and violence. *Aggressive Behavior, 16*, 297-320.

Tintinalli, J. E., & Hoelzer, M. (1985). Clinical findings and legal resolution in sexual assault. *Annals of Emergency Medicine, 14*, 447-453.

Trybus, R. (1980). Sign language, power and mental health. In C. Baker & R. Battison (Eds.), *Sign language and the deaf community: Essays in honor of William C. Stokoe* (pp. 201-220). Silver Spring, Md.: National Association of the Deaf.

Veltri, D. (1993). What makes the mental health setting different? TRANSFERENCE! *RID Views, 10*, pp. 1, 7, 12.

Waigandt, A., Wallace, D. L., Phelps, L., & Miller, D. A. (1990). The impact of sexual assault on physical health status. *Journal of Traumatic Stress, 3*, 93-102.

Webster, J., & Scott, R. (1983). The effects of self-instructional training on attentional deficits. *Clinical Neuropsychology, 4*, 69-74.

Williams, R. (1993). What is mental health interpreting? *RID Views, 10*, 1-2.

AUTHORS' NOTES

Portions of this paper were delivered at the annual meeting of the Association for Women in Psychology, Hartford, Conn., March 1991, and The First International Conference on Women in Africa and the African Diaspora: Bridges across Activism and the Academy, in Nsukka, Nigeria, July 1992.

Women and Violence: A Comparison of Lesbian and Heterosexual Battering Relationships

Geraldine Butts Stahly
Gwat-Yong Lie

Aggression appears to be a nearly universal human behavior and is cited in the earliest records of human interactions. As such, the study of aggression has played a key role in theory and research in the social sciences and has been an important topic in psychology since its inception. However, like society in general, psychology appeared to discover family violence, and in particular woman battering, only in the past two decades. This discovery was concurrent with the rise of feminist consciousness and women's demand for equality and safety.

HETEROSEXUAL BATTERING RELATIONSHIPS

Crime statistics have long indicated that women are most often victims of their male partners. FBI crime statistics from the 1950s through the 1986 Unified Crime Report consistently concluded that one-third of murdered women are such victims (Federal Bureau of Investigation, 1984; U.S. Department of Justice, 1986a, 1986b). However, the immense problem of woman battering was virtually ignored until women's rights activists of the 1970s brought it forcefully to public attention (Martin, 1976; Pizzey, 1977; Roy, 1977; Walker, 1979). The first national survey of spousal violence in 1975 estimated, based on a probability sample, that over 2 million women had experienced at least one severe beating in the previous year, and over 1.7 million women had been attacked by a male partner with a gun or a knife (Straus, Gelles, & Steinmetz, 1980). A replication of the survey in 1985 found a similarly high rate of spousal violence, and estimated that approximately 25 percent of all married women are battered and that 15 percent experience frequent and severe physical abuse (Straus & Gelles, 1986).

The U.S. Justice Department's National Crime Survey findings (1986a) support the high rate of occurrence of woman battering, estimating that 2.1 million women are victims of domestic violence in an average year. Not only are fewer than half of these incidents reported to law enforcement agencies, but once a woman has experienced battering, there is a very high probability that the violence will continue. Furthermore, leaving the batterer apparently provides little protection because 70 percent of the reported incidents of partner violence occurred after the woman separated from her abuser (U.S. Department of Justice, Uniform Crime Reports, 1986b).

While few empirical studies existed before the late 1970s (Stahly, 1977-78), during the past decade the effects of battering on women have been extensively documented. The battered woman suffers serious physical, emotional, and social consequences. Psychologically, the battered woman has been described as anxious, depressed, passive, dependent, low in self-esteem, self-blaming, experiencing learned helplessness, and frequently as suffering from post-traumatic stress disorder (e.g., Ferraro, 1983; Gellen et al., 1984; Rosewater, 1985; Walker, 1977-78, 1979, 1984, 1985, 1989, 1991; Wetzel & Ross, 1983). Physically, the battered woman exhibits the full range of stress-related disorders, including sleeping and eating disturbances, migraine headaches, neuromuscular, skeletal, and gynecological disorders, and higher rates of obstetrical complications including miscarriage (Mandel & Marcotte, 1983; Stark, Flitcraft, & Frazier, 1979). Socially, the battered woman is isolated by the jealousy and domination of her batterer, and by the feelings of guilt, shame, and stigma that result from the attitudes of the larger society (Coley & Beckett, 1988; Star, 1981; Walker, 1981, 1984, 1989). Despite the high level of danger, the woman is often ashamed to confide in friends or family and may lack the material and psychological resources necessary to leave. The battered woman often suffers alone without social support, effective intervention from a social network, or the helping services of the larger society (Pagelow, 1984; Kurtz, 1989; Walker, 1989).

Social scientists have been slow to recognize the widespread occurrence and serious individual and social consequences of battering, and only recently have theoretical explanations of human aggression included family violence as an important phenomenon. Sociologists were the first to explore the roots of violence as originating in the family experience. There have been a number of sociological theories that attempt to explain violence in a social-structural context, with a focus on family relationships. An early conceptualization of the sociology of violence is the subculture of violence hypothesis (Wolfgang, 1958; Wolfgang & Ferracutti, 1967). According to this hypothesis, rather than being deviant, a violent act may be a response to subcultural values, attitudes, and rituals that define violent behavior as normative.

Wolfgang (1958) observed that individuals adjudicated for acts of violence were disproportionately male, black or Hispanic, and poor. He theorized that acts of violence were normative in subcultures of poor minorities who, cut off from the paths to dominance available to white middle-class men, were left to define their masculinity in large part by dominating others through aggression. In this subculture, women and children, as well as other men, were considered appropriate targets of male aggression. Wolfgang further suggested that aggression was not a normative feminine gender-role expectation even in a culture of poverty (although a woman might use violence to dominate her children in her parental role), and that, when a woman was violent, it was generally a reaction to male assault. No data existed at the time regarding the high frequency of partner battering by white middle-class males, and Wolfgang's hypothesis tended to support the prevailing myth that family violence was primarily a behavior of poor, minority men.

This theory has never been well supported by empirical data. A Harris poll of a representative sample of 1,176 American adults (Stark & McEvoy, 1970) indicated that 20 percent of the sample approved of slapping one's spouse, and that approval of this behavior actually increased with income and education. In addition, both in terms of attitudes about violence and reported participation in violence, either as the perpetrator or victim, neither members of lower socioeconomic nor ethnic/racial minority groups differed statistically from the rest of the sample.

Broadening the perspective of violence as a problem beyond the culture of poverty, Goode (1969, 1971) presented a theoretical perspective on the occurrence of "violence between intimates" as part of a staff report to the National Commission on the Causes and Prevention of Violence. Citing statistics that one-half to three-fourths of all homicide victims are murdered by someone with whom they are acquainted, Goode's theoretical framework differentiates social-structural and interpersonal process variables in violence between intimates. The social-structural variables are based on the underlying structure of force inherent in hierarchical social institutions and unequal social relationships. Such hierarchical structures are suffused with force and control, and the power of the dominant individual may rest, ultimately, on the use of violence as an instrument of social control.

The child learns this instrumental violence and the socially sanctioned uses of force in early family experiences. The young boy learns from observing his own parents that males are physically stronger than females and that they may use violence to assert dominance and elicit compliance when other power strategies fail. Even if he observes no battering, he may observe (even in a middle-class household) that his mother is frightened when his father is angry (Goode, 1969). Likewise, the girl learns the limits of female power, and the necessity of deference to male force and dominance. Parents and teachers may tell children to be nonviolent, while demonstrating an opposite and much more powerful lesson in instrumental violence by using physical punishment or its threat as a penalty when the child fails to heed their injunctions.

Parents warn, "Don't hit," and then hit the child for hitting. This paradoxical message to the child is ambivalent at best. The child may receive a message that nonviolence is a rule only for the weak and for those in inferior positions of social power, whereas the powerful individuals may legitimately enforce their will with aggression toward their perceived subordinates. Male children are more likely to be labeled as violent and may be encouraged to play out that role through the development of a self-image as tough or bad-tempered. Conversely, the female child may be encouraged to be dependent on others for her physical protection and rewarded for submissive and docile behavior, even in the face of aggression from others. Gender-role stereotypes thus come to embody different views of personal power and the appropriateness of the use of aggression to establish social power and control (Goode, 1969, 1971).

Straus (1973) was the first to develop a systems theory approach to family violence. He suggested that the variables that determine violence can be conceptualized over time as antecedent, precipitation, and consequent variables. Antecedent variables are essential risk factors for violence (family structure differences such as authoritarian versus egalitarian, individual differences of family members such as temperament and past experience with violence, rigid gender-role expectations, substance abuse, socioeconomic status of the family, etc.). Precipitating variables are defined as degrees of environmental or other stressors on the family members. Consequent variables include all that happens as a result of the violent episode.

The relationship among the sets of variables creates a feedback process that then results in either an upward spiral (increasing frequency and severity of violent episodes) or an opposite, dampening effect on the occurrence of violence in the family (Straus, 1973). Among the critical variables that either increase or decrease the probability of further violence are: whether the violent act is consistent with the actor's and system's goals; whether labeling and reinforcement are present; what conditions are present to cause internalization of the self-image of "violent" in the perpetrator; whether the violence fits role expectations of the perpetrator and victim; whether alternate behavior is available and known to the perpetrator; whether the alternatives to violence are acceptable to the perpetrator and victim; and whether the level of violence within the system is acceptable to the members of the family.

Although they acknowledge that gender-role expectations, the hierarchical structure of the family and society, and male expectation of privilege and power are at the root of family violence, some sociologists manage nevertheless to blame the woman. Battering has been attributed to the rise of women's expectations and demands for equality and increased role status, and to men's perceptions of lost power as they find inconsistency between their ascribed status (male superiority over women in general) and their achieved status (equality or less with a women in a specific relationship) (Whitehurst, 1974).

In a study comparing level of violence as a function of the husbands' versus the wives' achieved status (level of income and education), findings indicate that the better educated or higher-earning wives are more likely to be the victims of violence (O'Brien, 1971). Further support for status inconsistency as the cause of wife battering is found in a study of decision making by married couples (Blood & Wolfe, 1960). The highest violence occurred in couples in which either the husband or wife dominated decision making, and the lowest violence where decision making was shared. The authors considered these findings unequivocal support for status inconsistency theory, in spite of the high violence found in the couples where women had low power, the largest group in the sample.

Psychological theories of aggression have historically ignored family violence. The earliest theories were intrapsychic and clinical, and both Freudians and Neo-Freudians view aggression as acts of individual deviancy, failing completely to consider the social context (e.g., Freud, 1924/1960). The intrapsychic explanation of aggression emphasizes the biological origin of sexual and aggressive motives, as well as the role of the ego and superego in repressing and redirecting such behaviors. Freud's psychosexual developmental theory posits a gender difference in aggression, with sadism an inevitable aspect of male development and masochism of female development (Freud, 1925/1974). Whereas the sadism of males was not emphasized, the masochism of females became a defining feature of femininity and has been used extensively by psychiatry to blame women victims of male physical and sexual aggression (Masson, 1984). The view of the battering relationship as rooted in female masochism is alive and well, as illustrated in the attempt of some members of the American Psychiatric Association to include survivors of battery in a diagnostic category labeled the "Masochistic Personality Syndrome" (Herman, 1992).

Learning theory has contributed the frustration-aggression hypothesis (Dollard et al., 1939), which posits a biological/evolutionary link between states of frustration and aggressive responses. Later formulations of this theory (e.g., Berkowitz, Lepinski, & Angulo, 1969) postulate violent behavior as just one of the repertoire of possible behavioral responses whenever goal-directed activity is blocked, but no explanation is offered for gender differences in aggression.

Social learning theory denies the biological inevitability of violent behavior and treats it as just another learned response. Violence, like all behavior, is learned through reinforcement (direct or vicarious) and cued by appropriate situational stimuli (Bandura, Ross, & Ross, 1961). This hypothesis predicts violence in relationships of individuals from families where assaultive behavior is observed and positively reinforced. This theory fits well with the sociological theories previously discussed, which locate violence within a social context.

Social learning theory suggests mechanisms that facilitate an upward spiral of violence. If instrumental violence is observed in childhood and experienced as a legitimate and successful means of imposing the will of the stronger on the weaker, violence becomes a behavioral alternative to be tried later when other variables, such as frustration or stress, are present. The spiral of violence results from the laws of reinforcement: any behavior positively rewarded will occur with greater probability in the future. Violence, if successful, is expected to increase; however, why the physical violence is accompanied by increasing psychological violence and why the victim of the violence tolerates the increasing pain and fear is not explained well by learning theory.

More recent psychological theory attempts to explain the role of the victim in a violent relationship by hypothesizing the family as a system in which all members play a role in maintaining a status quo (homeostasis), however violent or destructive. These family system theorists generally see the victim as fully participating in the cycle of violence, if not actually instigating violent episodes (Hoffman, 1981; Lawson, 1989; Schecter, 1982; Wardell, Gillespie, & Leffler, 1983; Weitzman & Dreen, 1982). Related to these theories is the concept of "codependency," a perspective that attempts to explain victimization almost entirely from the intrapsychic dynamics of the victim. In the most extreme formulation, the codependency model suggests, in fact, that the perpetrator of violence and his motives are largely irrelevant; because the code-pendent woman is "addicted" to violent relationships, she always "finds" another abuser (Brown, 1990). This perspective has much in common with Freud's formulation of feminine masochism (Freud, 1925/1974), although the etiology and intervention modalities are different.

Although psychologists and sociologists with a feminist per-spective come from a variety of theoretical backgrounds and may use parts of the theories discussed above, the aspect that best characterizes feminist analysis is the recognition of gender and power as the fundamental issues in the explanation of vio-lence within relationships (Bograd, 1990; Dobash & Dobash, 1979; Kurtz, 1989; Pagelow, 1984; Taubman, 1986; Walker, 1979, 1984, 1989). Relationships between women and men are based on a value structure that assumes an unequal distribution of power. Males form a dominant class, with greater access to resources and social power (Bograd, 1984). Women are deval-ued, masculinity is defined as superior and "not feminine," and the male is normative. Males share a sense of entitlement to respect and service from women based on the superiority of their gender alone. Feminist theories view violence against women as first and foremost political, an act of terrorism designed to maintain the privileges and power of men and the structure of patriarchy at whatever cost to women and child vic-tims (Bograd, 1982, 1984; Brownmiller, 1975; Taubman, 1986; Yllo & Bograd, 1988).

Social institutions, including most religions, and the crimi-nal justice and mental health establishments function within the rules and assumptions of patriarchy. These institutions, like mar-riage itself, generally support the right of the man to dominate the woman in a relationship, ignore or trivialize violence against the woman, and blame the victim (APA Task Force, 1975; Cali-fornia Judicial Council, 1991; Jackson & Rushton, 1982; McNeely & Robinson-Simpson, 1987; Saunders, 1988; Ullrich, 1986). The feminist approach to woman battering is predicated on the need for basic changes in sexual inequality, gender-role conditioning, and the social institutions that support and perpetuate male dom-inance.

Feminist theories of battering are consistent with the theo-retical formulations of psychology and sociology to the extent that violence is conceptualized as predominately male and related to male dominance and privilege within the larger structure of patriarchy. However, none of these theories have prepared us to acknowledge and understand the violence that occurs in intimate relationships between women. Just as the traditions of patriarchy led to the ignoring and trivializing of heterosexual battering, the belief of feminist theorists and the lesbian community in the basically egalitarian and mutually supportive nature of lesbian relationships has made it difficult to acknowledge and explore the violence that occurs in them.

LESBIAN BATTERING RELATIONSHIPS

Compared to the wealth of information and data available on spouse/partner abuse in heterosexual relationships, research and analysis of the dynamics of abuse in lesbian relationships are still in the formative stages. Hart (1986) described the phenomenon as "lesbian battering," and defined it as "that pattern of violent and coercive behaviors whereby a lesbian seeks to control the thoughts, beliefs or conduct of her intimate partner or to punish the intimate for resisting the partner's control over her" (p. 173). The range of behaviors implicated in lesbian battering are similar to those found in heterosexual battering and include threats, emotional or psychological abuse, physical violence, sexual abuse, property theft and damage, and economic control (Hammond, 1989; Hart, 1986).

The distinction is also made between the phenomenon of battering and incidents of violence (Morrow & Hawxhurst, 1989; Hart, 1986), the critical difference being, as in heterosexual battering relationships, the power dynamics and the cyclic and progressive characteristics: "The danger in battering (as opposed to isolated incidents of violence) is that it becomes progressively worse and more dangerous to the victim" (Morrow & Hawxhurst, 1989, p. 59).

Knowledge about the prevalence and incidence of lesbian battering appears to be about a decade behind the work on heterosexual violence. Because studies on lesbian battering are comparatively few and recent, and may be less known than the voluminous work on heterosexual violence, these works will be reviewed in some detail.

AUGUSTANA UNIVERSITY COLLEGE
LIBRARY

Sources of information on lesbian battering include anecdotal and clinical observations (e.g., Hammond, 1989; Leeder, 1988; Lobel 1986), and, more recently, several empirical studies (e.g., Brand & Kidd, 1986; Bologna, Waterman, & Dawson, 1987; Kelly & Warshafsky, 1987; Lie & Gentlewarrior, 1991; Lie et al., 1991; Renzetti, 1988; Waterman, Dawson, & Bologna, 1989). The generalizability of these collective research findings, however, is severely limited by the research and methodological characteristics of the studies themselves. Sampling issues—in particular, the use of nonprobability samples and/or lack of control groups—render the findings subject to the critique that the documented results are unique to the sample being studied.

Despite the lack of methodological rigor, the studies all substantiate the occurrence of battering in the lesbian community. However, the proportion of lesbians who reported battering by a partner varies widely by study. The variation in the results appears to be a function of: (1) different research focus; (2) differences in the definition of what constitutes abuse, or the lack of any definition at all; and (3) varying methods of recruitment and sampling of participants used in each study.

Bologna, Waterman, and Dawson (1987) have focused on violence in both gay and lesbian relationships. They are also interested in the use of violence by a partner in a past relationship and by a current or most recent partner. Among their lesbian subsample, they found that 64 percent report violence by a past partner as compared to 40 percent who say that they have experienced violence by a current or most recent partner.

Lie and her colleagues (1991) made similar differentiations of battering by past and current partners, and have also investigated the different forms of battering. Their findings show that 59.8 percent of members of the study sample reported having experienced at least one form of physical violence by a partner, 80.5 percent reported verbal/psychological abuse, and 26.4 percent experienced sexual abuse. In addition, 51.5 percent of all participants have been battered by a past partner and 26.0 percent by a current partner. In another study of 1,099 lesbians, 51.5 percent reported that they had been battered by a female partner (Lie & Gentlewarrior, 1991). The authors also noted that the most common form of battering is a combination of physical violence and emotional/psychological abuse.

In the case of the Renzetti study sample (1988, 1989), all one hundred lesbian participants were recruited only if they identified themselves as victims of battering. The author noted that the most common forms of physical violence were pushing and shoving; hitting with fists or open hands; scratching or hitting the face, breasts, or genitals; and throwing things. In general, psychological abuse is more frequently reported than physical violence. Renzetti (1988) further noted that battering is "not an isolated or one-time event in a relationship" (p. 398).

Brand and Kidd (1986) examined the frequency with which a sample of heterosexual and homosexual women reported physical violence and rape in a committed relationship. The proportion of lesbians reporting violence by a partner is 25 percent and rape by another "female whom you were dating" is 29 percent. These rates are comparable to those reported for violence in heterosexual relationships (Straus, Gelles, & Steinmetz, 1980) as well as for heterosexual date rape (Struckman-Johnson, 1988; Worth, Mathews, & Coleman, 1990).

Waterman, Dawson, and Bologna (1989) investigated the prevalence and correlates of coercive sex in gay and lesbian relationships. They reported that 31 percent of lesbians in their sample indicated that they were victims of forced sex by their current or most recent partners. In the Lie et al. (1991) study, 56.8 percent of lesbians in the sample reported having been sexually victimized by a past partner, whereas only 8.9 percent reported sexual victimization by a current partner. In this study, sexual victimization refers to a range of acts from sexual name calling and unwanted touching to intercourse and oral sex.

Lie and Gentlewarrior (1991) noted that 17 percent of the participants in their study reported combinations of sexual-physical, sexual-psychological, and sexual-physical-psychological abuse. Consistent with this rate of occurrence, Loulan's (1987) survey of 1,566 lesbians revealed that 17 percent had been sexually abused by a female mate or female lover/friend.

Few studies differentiate among sample members who have battered a partner, those who have been battered by a partner, and those who have both battered and been battered. Kelly and Warshafsky (1987), for example, examined the use of aggressive and violent conflict tactics by one or both partners in a sample of gay and lesbian couples. The study does not offer separate findings for gay and lesbian couples. The authors report that "When one crosstabulates the respondents' and partners' physical aggression scores, only 26 percent were mismatched on aggression. It was significant that the rest of the subjects were either both aggressive or both not aggressive. . . . Only 40 percent of the couples experienced no physical aggression in their relationships" (p. 5).

In the Lie and Gentlewarrior (1991) study, 26.3 percent of lesbians in the sample reported both battering and being battered by a lover/partner, whereas 24.7 percent said that they had experienced battery by a partner, but had never battered a partner. In addition, 44.6 percent of the sample indicated that they had never abused nor been abused by a partner/lover, whereas 3.8 percent claimed to have battered a partner/lover but never been victimized themselves.

In another study, Lie et al. (1991) reported that 29.4 percent of lesbian participants who had been in a heterosexual relationship had not only experienced battery, but also had battered their male partners. Of the participants reporting previous lesbian relationships, 68 percent described having been involved in an abusive relationship where they battered and were themselves battered. Current relationships appeared to be less abusive, although 19.9 percent claimed to have battered and been battered. On this phenomenon of reciprocal battering, which appears to be more commonly reported in lesbian than heterosexual violence, Walker (1986, p. 76) observed that "the only difference that I have ever seen in the interpersonal dynamics and perpetration of battering in lesbian couples is that lesbian women report physically fighting back more often than women who are battered by men." Based on her clinical experience, Walker (1986) hypothesized that reciprocal violence is more common in woman-to-woman abuse and cited several factors that may account for this difference, including the smaller size and weight differential between same-sex partners, fewer normative restraints on "fighting back," and tacit permission to talk about "fighting back." A problem with this analysis is the failure to make clear distinctions between mutual combat and self-defense, a conceptually challenging and politically sensitive area in research on lesbian battering.

An important similarity between explanations for lesbian and heterosexual battering is the reference to the power motive that may underlie the violence. According to Hart (1986), lesbians who batter "seek to achieve, maintain and demonstrate power over their partners in order to maximize the ready accomplishment of their own needs and desires" (p. 174). She goes on to explain that, like everyone else, lesbians have been socialized to designate the family unit as the context for the operationalization of power and control. Even within a lesbian family unit, a hierarchy of privilege, power, and ultimate authority may be established, with each family member being assigned a slot. Lesbians, like nonlesbians, "often desire control over the resources and decisions in family life that power brings" (p. 175). Within this situation, violence may become the chosen means of control. Lesbians have also learned that violence achieves compliance. Thus, lesbian battering is "the pattern of intimidation, coercion, terrorism or violence, the sum of all past acts of violence and the promises of future violence, that achieves enhanced power and control for the perpetrator over her partner" (Hart, 1986, p. 174). This analysis mirrors the feminist construction of heterosexual battering.

Renzetti's (1989) theoretical analysis is similar to Hart's (1986) with respect to her thesis on the dynamics of power between intimates. At the same time, her analysis differs from Hart's in her examination of the role of dependency. Drawing on empirical findings, she posits that the difficulty of balancing each partner's need for attachment and intimacy with the need for autonomy and independence is particularly acute for lesbian as compared to heterosexual couples. Because of the lack of social validation that lesbian relationships receive outside of the lesbian community, lesbian couples may nurture their relationships as closed systems.

Although such a system "fosters emotional intensity and closeness," it also "generates insecurity by disallowing separateness or autonomy" (p. 158). At the same time, dependency on one's partner is regarded as reprehensible. One manifestation of this fear or hatred of perceived dependency is self-destructive behavior; another may be violence against one's partner. Renzetti (1989) posits that the greater a batterer's dependency on her partner and the greater a victim's desire to be independent, the more likely the batterer is to inflict more types of abuse with greater frequency. Furthermore, this conflict surrounding dependency-autonomy is also related to the balance of power in lesbian relationships, with power imbalance being related to violent relationships.

This analysis has disturbing similarities to the family systems analysis and attachment theories of heterosexual battering (Bograd, 1984; Bowlby, 1984; Weitzman & Dreen, 1982). In such a framework, the overt violence against the partner is "understood" in terms of the perpetrator's neediness and vulnerability, and the victim's "willingness"—through her availability and nurturance—to foster that dependency, or, conversely, her "unwillingness"—through demands for autonomy and independence. In either case, the victim becomes the focus of the perpetrator's internal conflicts, and, by this analysis, the victim has complicity in "maintaining" the violence within the family system. Feminist theorists have labeled such analyses as a double-bind that blames the victim, reduces the perpetrator's responsibility, and trivializes the real helplessness and pain the victim experiences (Bograd, 1984; Hare-Mustin, 1991; Yllo, 1990).

Correlates of battering in lesbian relationships appear in several important areas to mirror well-established findings regarding heterosexual violence.

Power

As discussed previously, power and its relationship to gender-role stereotypes and the assumption of male dominance is a central feature of the feminist analysis of heterosexual battering. Several researchers studying lesbian violence have also looked at the role of power and its association with battering. Bologna, Waterman, and Dawson (1987) found that for some lesbian couples, perceived power is directly related to being a perpetrator of violence in both current and past relationships, and, for others, it is related to being a victim of violence in current relationships.

Kelly and Warshafsky (1987) operationalized the concept of power in their study as decision making with respect to various household activities. They found that decision making in regard to certain household activities is significantly correlated with being abused. Similarly, Renzetti (1988) reported significant correlations between violence and some indicators of power imbalance (e.g., social class differences and differences in intelligence).

In contrast, Waterman, Dawson, and Bologna (1989) found no significant correlations between perceived power and forced sex, or sexual victimization.

Renzetti's (1988) study showed that batterers tend to be decision makers in the relationship. An unequal distribution of household labor is evident in abusive relationships. However, unlike the findings regarding heterosexual battering relationships where the woman is at a clear disadvantage in regard to role functions and the distribution of resources (Hornung, 1981; Straus, 1976; Wetzel & Ross, 1983), it was not clear whether the distribution favored victims or batterers in lesbian relationships. Money was also a major source of conflict or strain in almost half of the relationships. Renzetti (1988) also found that particular indices of power imbalances were strongly associated with some of the most severe forms of physical and psychological abuse.

Substance Use

The research on the relationship between alcohol and/or substance use and lesbian battering appears to suggest that alcohol use is correlated with battering, as has been the consistent finding in heterosexual violence (Coleman, Weinman, & Hsi, 1983; Eberle, 1982; Miller & Potter-Efron, 1989; Miller, Downs, & Gondoli, 1989; Telch & Lindquist, 1984). For example, Kelly and Warshafsky (1987) reported that 33 percent of participants in their sample indicated the use of alcohol or some sort of substance during altercations with their partners. Brand and Kidd (1986) found that aggressors are influenced by alcohol in 33 percent of the violent episodes reported. However, it remains unclear as to what proportion of the 33 percent cited were lesbian aggressors.

Schilit, Lie, and Montagne (1990) noted that the number and kinds of abusive acts that participants reported committing against their partners was significantly correlated with the frequency of alcohol use. In addition, frequency of partner's drinking was related to incidents of battering, and the frequency of participants' drinking is significantly correlated with partner's use of drugs and/or alcohol prior to, or during, incidents of battering. However, insofar as the frequency of drug use is concerned, no significant correlations are found between it and battering.

Exposure to Violence

The intergenerational nature of family violence is well established for heterosexual families (Caesar, 1988; Carroll, 1980; Coleman, Weinman, & Hsi, 1983; Kalmuss, 1984; Waldo, 1987). There is compelling empirical evidence that this relationship holds for lesbian violence as well; exposure to battering, whether as the target of and/or witness to battering in the family of origin, and/or past intimate relationships, is a correlate of battering.

Specifically, Lie et al. (1991) found that participants who have witnessed the battering of another family member, and/or have been victimized themselves in the family of origin, are at risk of subsequent abusive adult relationships. These findings are consistent with those offered by Kanuha (1986), who found that 47 percent of lesbian victims and 68 percent of abusers reported the presence of physical abuse in their families of origin.

Lie et al. (1991) also reported that individuals who have been victimized in a past relationship with a male partner are also likely to be victims, batterers, or both, in a current lesbian relationship. Those who have battered and been battered by a past female partner are also likely to have battered and been battered in the current relationship. Bologna, Waterman, and Dawson (1987) offered similar findings. They noted that being a perpetrator of violence in a current relationship is positively correlated with being a victim of violence in that relationship. Also, their findings indicated that perpetrating violence in current relationships is positively correlated with perpetrating violence in past relationships. Although the recidivism of lesbian perpetrators appears to be consistent with data regarding battering men, the recidivism of lesbian victims is not consistent with reports by battered heterosexual women (Pagelow, 1984; Walker, 1979, 1984). Reciprocity of violence in heterosexual relationships is a topic of intense debate; empirical findings are inconsistent, and feminist theorists have generally disputed data that seem to indicate high levels of violence by the woman (Bush, 1990; McNeely & Robinson-Simpson, 1987; Saunders, 1988).

Length of Time in the Relationship

Renzetti (1989) found that the first abusive incident occurred less than six months after the relationship began for 77 percent of women in the sample. Sixty-five percent of lesbians in her sample maintained their relationships with their batterers for one to five years; 14 percent maintained the relationship for more than five years.

Although early research on heterosexual violence suggested that violence often happens after a relationship is well established and formalized (it has been suggested that the marriage license becomes a hitting license) (Dobash & Dobash, 1979; Fagan et al., 1983; Martin, 1976; Russell, 1983; Schechter, 1982), more recent studies suggest that at least some episodes of violence generally happen early in a relationship, often during the dating, phase (Levy, 1991; Roscoe & Benaske, 1985; Rouse, 1988; Worth, Mathews, & Coleman, 1990).

The heterosexual literature describes a number of other correlates to violence, including perpetrator variables such as history of criminal and impulsive behavior (Ganley, 1981; Roberts, 1987), perpetrators' occupation and employment status (Fitch & Papantonio, 1983; Nichols, 1982; Roberts, 1987; Wasileski, Callaghan-Chaffee, & Chaffee, 1982), perpetrators' irrational beliefs including those regarding male dominance (Coleman, Weinman, & Hsi, 1980; Lohr, Hamberger, & Bonge, 1988; Stahly, 1987; Wetzel & Ross, 1983), perpetrators' personality characteristics (Hamberger & Hastings, 1984), and perpetrators' mental health status (Mullen, 1986; Watson, Rosenber, & Petrik, 1982). Victim variables have included socialization to rigid gender-role stereotypes and consequent low self-esteem, passivity, dependence (Strube & Barbour, 1983; Walker, 1979, 1985, 1989), mental health status (Back, Post, & Darcy, 1982; Gellen et al., 1984), physical handicap or chronic illness (Egley, 1982), and subcultural and family structure variables such as economic stress, geographic dislocation, social isolation, and/or sparcity of social support networks (Gelles, 1985; Hornung, 1981; Kalmuss, 1984; Straus, Gelles, & Steinmetz, 1980), and traditional values and ideology regarding male dominance (Telch & Lindquest, 1984; Wetzel & Ross, 1983).

A significant difference between the heterosexual and lesbian victim is the availability of mainstream helping resources. Both Renzetti (1988) and Lie and Gentlewarrior (1991) noted that many mainstream sources of help are not perceived by lesbian victims to be sources of help that *they* would utilize. In Renzetti's (1988) study, participants reported that official help providers (e.g., shelter workers, physicians, police officers, and attorneys) are of little or no help to them. Slightly more than one-third have sought help from relatives; for the majority, relatives are not available because family members are not aware of their homosexuality. Even if they are aware, many are critical and disapproving of their lesbian orientation. Although battered heterosexual women may choose informal helping networks over public services (Dobash & Dobash, 1979), and a number of barriers may still exist in using existing institutions, some services are at least available in most localities. Lesbian victims, on the other hand, are generally denied the choice of public services because most agencies that serve battered women are ill-equipped and/or unwilling to provide appropriate and culturally sensitive services to lesbian women. Services with a feminist orientation are more likely to be aware of the problem of homophobia as an impediment to helping lesbian victims, and many such programs have undertaken to educate their staff and provide advocacy and outreach to lesbians.

Lesbian victims most often turn to counselors and friends for assistance (Renzetti, 1988). About 54 percent of the women in the Lie and Gentlewarrior (1991) study indicated that they were most likely to turn to a counselor/therapist in private practice for help. In response to the question, "What services would you like to see available to you?" one-quarter suggested peer counseling, and roughly 18 percent asked for a center for lesbian survivors that would offer a full range of services including shelter and counseling.

FUTURE DIRECTIONS FOR RESEARCH

The first priority in research on violence against women in intimate relationships must be to address not only the continuing sexism that exists in the study of heterosexual violence, but also the homophobia that has made the problem of lesbian violence largely invisible. Research and service delivery to battered women that has been developed over the past fifteen years has almost entirely overlooked battered lesbians. It is especially incumbent on feminist researchers and activists to conscientiously and sensitively include the lesbian community and samples of lesbian couples in all relevant research, education, and intervention activities. Women of color and women from under-represented ethnic and cultural groups have also been largely ignored in the current literature on family violence. It is a moral and empirical imperative not only to include all of these diverse groups, but to do so in a way that respects and preserves the unique aspects of each woman's experiences.

In addition to the general need to bring diversity to existing research, there are several important and problematic areas in considering current findings and future research on lesbian battering.

First, the rate of occurrence of lesbian battering appears to be higher than well-established findings in heterosexual violence. These findings are inconsistent with the entire body of psychological, sociological, and anthropological theory and research that has consistently found males to be more violent than females. It is important to improve methodology and prevent the sampling bias that may account for these surprising discrepancies (Rosenbaum, 1988). It is also important to explore gender differences in defining and reporting violence. Women appear to report higher levels of violence, whether they are reporting themselves to be victims or perpetrators, than men do (Gully, Pepping, & Dengerink, 1982), and this may be introducing a systematic self-report bias in the comparison of levels of violence in lesbian versus heterosexual relationships. Related to this is the sensitive issue of victim recidivism that is being addressed in research on lesbian battering, but has been largely ignored by feminist researchers of heterosexual battering, and is problematic in the literature of family systems and codependency (Yllo, 1990). Battered heterosexual women were much less likely to report multiple battering relationships in studies that did address the issue (Walker, 1979; Pagelow, 1984) than is indicated in the research cited above on lesbians.

Second, although the response of the criminal justice system to family violence has been the focus of extensive research and activism, there is little or no work to date on the response of this system to the battered lesbian. Likewise, forensic psychologists have developed successful strategies for defending the heterosexual woman who kills her abuser. The effects of homophobia on the criminal justice system's handling of both the perpetrators and victims of lesbian battering is still largely unknown and untested.

Third, theoretical formulations of the causes and correlates of violence against heterosexual women are well grounded in gender-role theory and the understanding of the contributions of male dominance and patriarchy. The applicability of these theories, including feminist analyses, to lesbian violence needs to be carefully examined and revised. New theories may be needed that explain violence from a nonsexist, nonhomophobic, and non-Eurocentric perspective.

Finally, an important consideration in comparing lesbian and heterosexual violence must be the psychological and social meaning of violence within a relationship. That women can be aggressors is evident in the phenomenon of lesbian battering, but has been evidenced, as well, in the homicide statistics concerning heterosexual partners and is suggested by reports of battered men in heterosexual relationships (McNeely & Robinson-Simpson, 1987; Steinmetz, 1977); however, these data have been questioned by feminist critics (Saunders, 1988; Pleck et al., 1977-78). The fact that a woman may engage in an act of violence does not necessarily mean that women's violence is the equivalent of men's use of violence to control, intimidate, and terrorize. A woman who slaps a man in an argument is conveying a different psychological message than a man who slaps a woman; the slapping of a man by a woman seldom conveys a message of terror and threat of escalation, nor is it calculated to control and subdue by an appeal to fear and vulnerability. Even when a woman kills her partner, she is much more likely than a male perpetrator to be acting defensively (Goetting, 1989; Wolfgang, 1958).

The notion of a heterosexual battering relationship as mutual, with power exercised equally by man and woman, is nearly inconceivable from a feminist perspective. The question that remains unanswered is the applicability of this analysis to lesbian battering. Specifically, does there exist such a thing as mutual violence between a lesbian couple, or does lesbian battering always include the same power inequity and control issues present in heterosexual relationship violence?

Early in the women's movement, those of us who participated in consciousness-raising groups agreed to heed the injunction not to compare oppression, for to do so distracts us from our common experience as women in a sexist, racist, and homophobic society. It is important for feminist researchers and activists, lesbian and heterosexual, to reaffirm this injunction as we continue the vital work of understanding and combating every form of violence against women.

REFERENCES

APA Task Force (1975). Report of the task force on sex bias and sex role stereotyping in psychotherapeutic practice. *American Psychologist, 30,* 1169-1175.

Back, S. M., Post, R. D., & Darcy, G. (1982) . A study of battered women in a psychiatric setting. *Women & Therapy, 1*(2), 13-26.

Bandura, A., Ross, D., & Ross, S. (1961) . Transmission of aggression through imitation of aggressive models. *Journal of Abnormal and Social Psychology, 63,* 575-582.

Berkowitz, L., Lepinski, J. P., & Angulo, E. J. (1969) . Awareness of own anger level and subsequent aggression. *Journal of Personality and Social Psychology, 11,* 293-300.

Blood, R. O., & Wolfe, D. M. (1960). *Husbands and wives: Dynamics of married living.* New York: Free Press.

Bograd, M. B. (1982). Battered women, cultural myths and clinical interventions: A feminist analysis. In New England Association for Women in Psychology (Eds.), *Current feminist issues in psychotherapy.* New York: Haworth Press.

Bograd, M. B. (1984). Family systems approaches to wife battering: A feminist critique. *American Journal of Orthopsychiatry, 54*(4), 558-568.

Bograd, M. B. (1990). Why we need gender to understand human violence. *Journal of Interpersonal Violence, 5*(1), 132-135.

Bologna, M. J., Waterman, C. K., & Dawson, L. J. (1987, July). *Violence in gay male and lesbian relationships: Implications for practitioners and policy makers.* Paper presented at the Third National Conference for Family Violence Researchers, Durham, N.H.

Bowlby, J. (1984). Violence in the family as a disorder of the attachment and caregiving systems. *American Journal of Psychoanalysis, 44*(1), 9-27.

Brand, P. A., & Kidd, A. H. (1986) . Frequency of physical aggression in heterosexual and female homosexual dyads. *Psychological Reports, 59,* 1307-1313.

Brown, L. (1990). What's addiction got to do with it: A feminist critique of co-dependency. *Psychology of Women Newsletter,* Winter, *17*(1), 1-4.

Brownmiller, W. (1975). *Against our will: Men, women, and rape.* New York: Simon & Schuster.

Bush, L. D. (1990). Violent acts and injurious outcomes in married couples: Methodological issues in the national survey of families and households. *Gender and Society, 4*(1), 56-67.

Caesar, P. L. (1988). Exposure to violence in the families-of-origin among wife-abusers and maritally nonviolent men. *Violence and Victims, 3*(1), 49-63.

California Judicial Council (1991). *Gender bias in the courts*. Sacramento, Calif.: State of California.

Carroll, J. C. (1980). The intergenerational transmission of family violence: The long-term effects of aggressive behavior. *Advances in Family Psychiatry, 2*, 171-181.

Coleman, K. H. (1980). Conjugal violence: What 33 men report. *Journal of Marital and Family Therapy, 6*, 207-214.

Coleman, K. H., Weinman, M. L., & Hsi, B. P. (1983) Factors affecting conjugal violence. *Journal of Counseling Psychology, 105*(2), 197-202.

Coley, S. M., & Beckett, J. O. (1988). Black battered women: A review of empirical literature. *Journal of Counseling and Development, 66*(6), 266-270.

Dobash, R. E., & Dobash, R. P. (1979). *Violence against wives*. New York: Free Press.

Dollard, J., Doob, L. W., Miller, N. E., Mowrer, 0. H., & Sears, R. R. (1939). *Frustration and aggression*. New Haven: Yale University Press.

Eberle, P. A. (1982). Alcohol abusers and non-users: A discriminant analysis of differences between two subgroups of batterers. *Journal of Health and Social Behavior, 23*(3), 260-271.

Egley, L. C. (1982). Domestic violence and deaf people: One community's response. *Victimology: An International Journal, 7*(1-4), 24-34.

Fagan, J. A., Stewart, D. K. & Hansen, K. B. (1983). Violent men or violent husbands? Background factors and situational correlates. In J. Finkelhor, R. Gelles, J. Hotelling, & M. Strauss (Eds.), *The dark side of families* (pp. 49-67). Beverly Hills, Calif.: Sage.

Federal Bureau of Investigation (1984). *Uniform crime reports, 1984*. Washington, D.C.: U.S. Government Printing Office.

Ferraro, K. J. (1983). How women experience battering: The process of victimization. *Social Problems, 39*(3), 325-339.

Fitch, F. J., & Papantonio, A. (1983). Men who batter: Some pertinent characteristics. *Journal of Nervous and Mental Disease, 171*, 190-192.

Freud, S. (1924/1960). *A general introduction to psychoanalysis* (Riviere, Trans.). New York: Washington Square Press.

Freud, S. (1925/1974). Some psychical consequences of the anatomical distinction between the sexes. In *The standard edition of the complete psychological works of Sigmund Freud* (Vol. 19). London: Hogarth Press and the Institute of Psycho-Analysis.

Ganley, A. (1981). *Court-mandated counseling for men who batter: A three-day workshop for mental health professionals*. Washington, D.C.: Center for Women's Policy Studies.

Gellen, M., Hoffman, R., Jones, M., & Stone, M. (1984). Abused and non-abused women: MMPI profile differences. *Personnel and Guidance Journal, 61*, 601-604.

Gelles, R. (1985). Family violence. *Annual Review of Sociology, 11*, 347-367.

Goetting, A. (1989). Patterns of marital homicide: A comparison of husbands and wives. *Journal of Comparative Family Studies, 20*(3), 341-354.

Goode, W. J. (1969). Violence among intimates. In D. Mulvihill & M. Tumin (Eds.), *Crimes of violence*. Washington, D.C.: U.S. Government Printing Office.

Goode, W. J. (1971). Force and violence in the family. *Journal of Marriage and the Family, 33*, 624-636.

Gully, K. J., Pepping, M., & Dengerink, H. A. (1982). Gender differences in third-party reports of violence. *Journal of Marriage and the Family, 44*(2), 497-498.

Hamberger, L. K., & Hastings, J. E. (1984) . Personality correlates of men who abuse their partners: A cross-validation study. *Journal of Family Violence, 1*(4), 323-341.

Hammond, N. (1989). Lesbian victims of relationship violence. In E. D. Rothblum & E. Cole (Eds.), *Loving boldly: Issues facing lesbians* (pp. 89-105). Binghamton, N.Y.: Harrington Park Press.

Hare-Mustin, R. T. (1991). Sex, lies and headaches: The problem is power. *Journal of Feminist Family Therapy, 3*(1/2), 39-41.

Hart, B. (1986). Lesbian battering: An examination. In K. Lobel (Ed.), *Naming the violence: Speaking out about lesbian battering* (pp. 173-189). Seattle: Seal Press.

Herman, J. L. (1992). *Trauma and recovery*. New York: Basic Books.

Hoffman, L. (1981). *Foundations of family therapy*. New York: Basic Books.

Hornung, C. A. (1981). Status relationships in marriage: Risk factors in spouse abuse. *Journal of Marriage and the Family, 43*(3), 675-692.

Jackson, S., & Rushton, R. (1982). Victims and villains: Images of women in accounts of family violence. *Women's Studies International Forum, 5*(1), 17-28.

Kalmuss, D. (1984). The intergenerational transmission of marital aggression. *Journal of Marriage and the Family, 46*(1), 11-19.

Kanuha, V. (1986). *Violence in intimate lesbian relationships*. Unpublished manuscript.

Kelly, E. E., & Warshafsky, L. (1987, July). *Partner abuse in gay male and lesbian couples*. Paper presented at the Third National Conference for Family Violence Researchers, Durham, N.H.

Kuhl, A. F. (1987). Personality traits of abused women: Masochism myth refuted. *Victimology: An International Journal, 9*(3/4), 450-463.

Kurtz, L. (1989). Social science perspective on wife abuse: Current debates and future directions. *Gender and Society, 3*(4), 489-505.

Lawson, D. M. (1989). A family systems perspective on wife battering. *Journal of Mental Health Counseling, 11*(4), 359-374.

Leeder, E. (1988). Enmeshed in pain: Counseling the lesbian battering couple. *Women & Therapy, 7,* 81-99.

Levy, B. (1991) *Dating violence: Young women in danger.* Seattle: Seal Press.

Lie, G. Y., & Gentlewarrior, S. (1991). Intimate violence in lesbian relationships: Discussion of survey findings and practice implications. *Journal of Social Service Research, 15*(1/2), 41-59.

Lie, G. Y., Schilit, R., Bush, J., Montagne, M., & Reyes, L. (1991). Lesbians in currently aggressive relationships: How frequently do they report aggressive past relationships? *Violence and Victims, 6*(2), 121-135.

Lobel, K. (Ed.) (1986). *Naming the violence: Speaking out about lesbian battering.* Seattle: Seal Press.

Lohr, J. M., Hamberger, L. K., & Bonge, D. (1988). The nature of irrational beliefs in different personality clusters of spouse abusers. *Journal of Rational Emotive and Cognitive Behavioral Therapies, 6*(4), 273-285.

Loulan, J. (1987). *Lesbian passion.* San Francisco: Spinsters/Aunt Lute Book Company.

McNeely, R., & Robinson-Simpson, G. (1987). The truth about domestic violence: A falsely framed issue. *Social Welfare, 32*(6), 485-490.

Mandel, J. B., & Marcotte, D. B. (1983). Teaching family practice residents to identify and treat battered women. *Journal of Family Practice, 17*(4), 708-716.

Martin, D. (1976). *Battered wives.* San Francisco: Glide Publications.

Masson, J. (1984). *The assault on truth: Freud's suppression of the seduction theory.* New York: Farrar, Straus & Giroux.

Miller, B. A., Downs, W. R., & Gondoli, D. M. (1989). Spousal violence among alcoholic women as compared to a random household sample of women. *Journal of Studies on Alcohol, 50*(6), 533-540.

Miller, M. M., & Potter-Efron, R. T. (1989). Aggression and violence associated with substance abuse. *Journal of Chemical Dependency Treatment, 3*(1), 1-36.

Morrow, S. L., & Hawxhurst, D. M. (1989). Lesbian partner abuse: Implications for therapists. *Journal of Counseling and Development, 68*(1), 58-62.

Mullen, P. E. (1986). The risk of violence in psychotics: Commentary. *Integrative Psychiatry, 4*(2), 136-138.

Nichols, C. (1982). The military installation: How the company town deals with rape, spouse abuse and child abuse. *Victimology: An International Journal, 7*(1-4), 242-251.

O'Brien, J. E. (1971). Violence in divorce prone families. *Journal of Marriage and Family, 33*(4), 692-698.

Pagelow, M. D. (1984) *Family violence.* Westport, Conn.: Praeger.

Pizzey, E. (1977). *Scream quietly or the neighbors will hear.* Short Hills, N.J.: Ridley Enslow.

Pleck, E., Pleck, J. H., Grossman, M., & Bart, P. B. (1977-78). The battered data syndrome: A comment on Steinmetz. *Victimology: An International Journal, 2*(3/4), 680-683.

Renzetti, C. M. (1988). Violence in lesbian relationships: A preliminary analysis of causal factors. *Journal of Interpersonal Violence, 3*(4), 381-399.

Renzetti, C. M. (1989). Building a second closet: Third party responses to victims of lesbian partner abuse. *Family Relations, 38,* 157-163.

Roberts, A. R. (1987). Psychosocial characteristics of batterers: A study of 234 men charged with domestic violence offenses. *Journal of Family Violence, 2*(1), 81-93.

Roscoe, B., & Benaske, N. (1985). Courtship violence experienced by abused wives: Similarities in pattern of abuse. *Family Relations Journal of Applied Family and Child Studies, 34*(4), 419-424.

Rosenbaum, A. (1988). Methodological issues in marital violence research. *Journal of Family Violence, 3*(2), 91-104.

Rosewater, L. B. (1985). Schizophrenia or battered? A feminist interpretation of tests. In L. B. Rosewater & L. E. A. Walker (Eds.), *Handbook on feminist therapy* (pp. 215-225). New York: Springer.

Rouse, L. P. (1988). Abuse in dating relationships: A comparison of black, whites and Hispanics. *Journal of College Student Development, 29*(4), 312-319.

Roy, M. (Ed.) (1977). *Battered women: A psychosociological study of domestic violence.* New York: Van Nostrand-Reinhold.

Russell, E. (1983). *Rape in marriage.* New York: Macmillan.

Saunders, D. G. (1988). Other "truths" about domestic violence: A reply to McNeely and Robinson-Simpson. *Social Welfare, 33*(2), 179-183.

Schechter, S. (1982). *Women and male violence: The visions and struggles of the battered women's movement.* Boston: South End

Schilit, R., Lie, G. Y., Bush, J., Montagne, M.,& Reyes, L. (1990). Substance use as a correlate of violence in intimate lesbian relationships. *Journal of Homosexuality, 19*(3), 51-65.

Stahly, G. B. (1977-78). A review of the select literature of spousal violence. *Victimology: An International Journal, 2*(3/4), 591-607.

Stahly, G. B. (1987, March). *Roots of misogyny: Long-term effects of family violence on children's attitudes.* Paper presented at the meeting of the Association for Women in Psychology, Denver, Colo.

Star, B. (1981). The impact of violence on families. *Conciliation Courts Review, 19*(2), 33-40.

Stark, E., Flitcraft, A., & Frazier, W. (1979). Medicine and patriarchal violence: The social construction of a "private" event. *International Journal of Health Service, 9*, 461-492.

Stark, R., & McEvoy, J. III. (1970, November). Middle class violence. *Psychology Today*, 30-31.

Steinmetz, S. (1977). Wife beating, husband beating: A comparison of the use of physical violence between spouses to resolve marital fights. In M. Roy (Ed.), *Battered women: A psychosocial study of domestic violence* (pp. 63-67). New York: Van Nostrand-Reinhold.

Steinmetz, S. (1977-78). The battered man. *Victimology: An International Journal, 2*(3/4), 499-509.

Straus, M. A. (1973). A general systems theory approach to a theory of violence between family members. *Social Science Information, 12*(3), 105-125.

Straus, M. A. (1976). Sexual inequality, cultural norms, and wife-beating. *Victimology, 1*(1), 54-70.

Straus, M. A., & Gelles, R. J. (1986). Societal change and change in family violence from 1975 to 1985 as revealed by two national surveys. *Journal of Marriage and the Family, 48*(3), 465-480.

Straus, M. A., Gelles, R. J., & Steinmetz, S. K. (1980). Physical violence in a nationally representative sample of American families. In J. Trost (Ed.), *The family in change* (pp. 149-165). Vasteras, Sweden: International Library.

Strube, M. J., & Barbour, L. S. (1983). The decision to leave an abusive relationship: Economic dependence and psychological commitment. *Journal of Marriage and the Family, 45*(4), 785-793.

Struckman-Johnson, C. (1988). Forced sex on dates: It happens to men, too. *Journal of Sex Research, 24*, 234-241.

Taubman, S. (1986). Beyond the bravado: Sex roles and the exploitive male. *Social Work, 31*(1), 12-18.

Telch, C. F., & Linquist, C. U. (1984). Violent versus nonviolent couples: A comparison of patterns. *Psychotherapy, 21*(2), 242-248.

Ullrich, V. H. (1986). Equal but not equal—A feminist perspective on family law. *Women's Studies International Forum, 9*(1), 41-48.

U.S. Department of Justice, Bureau of Justice Statistics (1986a). *Preventing domestic violence against women: Special report.* Washington, D.C.: U.S. Government Printing Office.

U.S. Department of Justice, Bureau of Justice Statistics (1986b). *National Crime Survey.* Washington, D.C.: U.S. Government Printing Office.

Waldo, M. (1987). Also victims: Understanding and treating men arrested for spouse abuse. *Journal of Counseling and Development, 65*(7), 385-388.

Walker, L. (1977-78). Battered women and learned helplessness. *Victimology: An International Journal, 3*(3), 525-533.

Walker, L. (1979). *The battered woman.* New York: Harper & Row.

Walker, L. (1981). Battered women: Sex roles and clinical issues. *Professional Psychology: Research and Practice, 12*(1), 84-94.

Walker, L. (1984). *The battered woman syndrome.* New York: Springer.

Walker, L. (1985). Psychological impact of the criminalization of domestic violence on victims. *Victimology: An International Journal, 10*(14), 281-300.

Walker, L. (1986). Battered women's shelters and work with battered lesbians. In K. Lobel (Ed.), *Naming the violence: Speaking out about lesbian battering* (pp. 73-76). Seattle: Seal Press.

Walker, L. (1989). Psychology and violence against women. *American Psychologist, 44*(4), 695-702.

Walker, L. (1991). Post-traumatic stress disorder in women: Diagnosis and treatment of battered woman syndrome. *Psychotherapy, 28,* 21-29.

Wardell, L., Gillespie, D., & Leffler, A. (1983). Science and violence against wives. In D. Finkelhor, R. J. Gelles, G. T. Hotaling, & M. A. Straus (Eds.), *The dark side of families: Current family violence research.* Beverly Hills, Calif.: Sage.

Wasileski, M., Callaghan-Chaffee, M. E., & Chaffee, R. B. (1982). Spousal violence in military homes: An initial survey. *Military Medicine, 147*(9), 761-765.

Waterman, C. K., Dawson, L. J., & Bologna, M. J. (1989). Sexual coercion in gay male and lesbian relationships: Predictors and implications for support services. *Journal of Sex Research, 26,* 118-124.

Watson, C. G., Rosenber, A. M., & Petrik, N. (1982). Incident of wife-battering in male psychiatric hospital patients: Are special treatment programs necessary? *Psychological Reports, 51*(2), 563-566.

Weitzman, J., & Dreen, K. (1982). Wife beating: A view of the marital dyad. *Social Casework, 63,* 259-265.

Wetzel, L., & Ross, M. (1983). Psychological and social ramifications of battering: Observations leading to a counseling methodology. *Personnel and Guidance Journal, 61*(7), 423-428.

Whitehurst, R. N. (1974). Violence in husband-wife interactions. In S. Steinmetz & M. Straus (Eds.), *Violence in the family* (pp. 75-82). New York: Harper & Row.

Wolfgang, M. E. (1958). *Patterns of criminal homicide.* Philadelphia: University of Pennsylvania Press.

Wolfgang, M. E., & Ferracutti, F. (1967). *The subculture of violence: Toward an integrated theory of criminology.* New York: Tavistock Publications.

Worth, D. M., Mathews, P. A., & Coleman, W. R. (1990). Sex role, group affiliation, family background, and courtship violence in college students. *Journal of College Student Development, 31*(3), 250-254.

Yllo, K. (1990, March). *Feminist reformulations: A critique of conjoint treatment for violent couples.* Paper presented at the Harvard Medical School Conference on Abuse and Victimization, Boston, Mass.

Yllo, K., & Bograd, M. (Eds.) (1988). *Feminist perspectives on wife abuse.* Newbury Park, Calif.: Sage.

Women's Friendships

Suzanna Rose

Two women, long lost friends, were deeply engrossed in a conversation in a bar when a man walked over and said to one woman, disregarding the friend, "Well, I see you're all alone. Do you mind if I buy you a drink?" Almost every woman who has tried to socialize with a friend in a public setting has experienced a similar situation. Its commonness reflects the widely held view that women's friendships are relatively unimportant and easily relinquished in favor of male companionship. Historically, women have been portrayed as unable to bond with other women; our capacity to commit to each other has been regarded as inferior to both woman-to-man and man-to-man relationships. However, negative views of women's friendships recently have been challenged. New research has revealed a long tradition of female friendships throughout history and established their significance for the modern woman. The supposed superiority of men's friendships has been disputed by evidence showing that women's friendships are deeper and more intimate. The focus in this chapter will be on the large body of work now available that reveals the rich texture of women's friendships; explores their variety across social class, race, sexual orientation, and gender roles; and examines their broader social context and impact.

THE NATURE OF FRIENDSHIP

Friendship has been exalted and celebrated throughout the ages. "No one would choose to live without friends," proclaimed Aristotle over two thousand years ago (trans. 1962). In 1792 Mary Wollstonecraft (1967) declared, "Friendship is the most holy bond of society" and "the most sublime of all affections." Friendship has been described as "the most universal and noblest form of communication" (Lepp, 1966), a form of love (Sadler, 1970), and one of the most fundamental human values (Rake, 1970). In some cultures, friendships are considered of such importance to the individual and society that formal rights and responsibilities are associated with them. For instance, among the Bangwa of the Cameroon, a lifelong best friendship often is arranged by parents for their children, much like marriage is (Brain, 1974).

In Western culture, friendships typically are relationships of "voluntary interdependence" (Wright, 1974). Friendship is willingly undertaken, is self-managed, and has as its only motive the preservation and enjoyment of the relationship. The voluntariness of friendship contributes to its attractiveness, but also to its fragility (Wiseman, 1986). A change in the quality or quantity of companionship, belongingness, stimulation, or emotional support provided by the friendship can place it in jeopardy. Unlike kin and work relationships, friendships have no formal bonds to induce the pair to salvage the relationship.

Friendships exist in many forms. Some are emotionally close, committed, and long-term; others are based solely on shared tasks or leisure activities. Generally, best, close, or true friendships are regarded as those that are based on an appreciation of the friend's uniqueness and a sincere wish for the other's well-being. In contrast, superficial friendships are ones established for personal gain or pleasure (Wright, 1974). The distinction between true and superficial friendships parallels one Clark and Mills (1979) have made between communal and exchange relationships. In communal relationships, partners are motivated to fulfill the needs of the other without concern for who gives and who gets. In exchange relationships, whatever is given is expected to be returned.

True friendships have five basic elements, according to Sadler (1970). First, they provide joy. Friends delight in each others' company, they introduce each other to new ideas and activities, and their liking and acceptance give pleasure. Friendships also involve communion. Friends build a common life by playing or working together and talking openly and intimately. Freedom is the third quality. Friends must be free to enhance their personal development. The friend's loyalty and forgiveness encourage this growth. The fourth element is truth. Truthfulness enables friends to develop a genuinely intimate relationship; both strengths and limitations are revealed and understood. Last, friendships require sacrifice. Responding to a friend in need requires that important plans or activities be set aside. Some friendships will require greater effort and commitment to maintain than others.

A degree of equality between people along key dimensions such as age and social class often is reported as a precondition for friendship. Equality is significant because it is a widely held belief that friendship involves a reciprocal "give and take" (Argyle & Henderson, 1984). Friends also tend to be similar in terms of sex, race, intelligence, and marital status, which may ensure equality as well.

The potential benefits of friendship are numerous. Friendships provide emotional resources, including intimacy, support, acceptance, belongingness, self-esteem, and status. They also offer material resources, such as help with tasks or tangible goods, and cognitive ones, like stimulation, social comparison, and information. They contribute to happiness and life satisfaction and improve one's ability to cope with stress as well. People with friends are less lonely and depressed and more stable than those who have no friends (e.g., Ferraro, Mutran, & Barresi, 1984). As Cicero observed, "A friend multiplies our joys and divides our sorrows."

Friendships are believed to be lasting; the loss of a friend is often painful. To be an ex-friend is a negative role, not a neutral one (Bell, 1981). External forces, such as a move, marriage, or death, can drive friends apart, but friendships ultimately are broken from the inside. Anger, resentment, or disappointment in the friend leading to unresolved conflict or avoidance can spur the demise. However, actively dissolving a friendship is a drastic step. Many people prefer just to let them "drift apart" gracefully (Rose & Serafica, 1986).

WOMEN'S FRIENDSHIPS

Women's friendships began to receive positive attention with the advent of the women's movement in the 1960s. Feminism promoted an ideology of sisterhood that encouraged friendships between women, both to help them identify common forms of oppression and as rewards for their own sake (Seiden & Bart, 1975). Prior to this, historians and anthropologists regarded women as incapable of true friendship, as described earlier, or their relationships as secondary and inferior to male-female bonds. For example, "abnormal" impulses once were attributed to women who regularly sought out one another socially, and "normal" ones to women who preferred the company of men (Taylor & Lasch, 1963).

Current evidence suggests that women's friendships are deep and abiding, in contrast to previous negative portrayals. Diaries and private letters written by women reveal that close emotional ties between women friends have occurred since the sixteenth century (Faderman, 1981). "Dear darling Sarah!" wrote a twenty-nine-year-old woman to her friend in 1864. "You are the joy of my life. . . . I cannot tell you how much happiness you gave me . . . [and] . . . how I long for the time when I shall see you" (Smith-Rosenberg, 1975, p. 4). These passionate romantic friendships were a widely recognized and accepted social institution. Women were expected to seek and form strong bonds with friends, apart from marriage and family. Friendships provided help and companionship, survived marriages and geographic separation, and played a central emotional role in women's lives.

Intimacy in particular is very highly valued in contemporary women's friendships (Reisman, 1990). An ideal woman friend provides a trusting ear for sharing confidences and is accepting, affectionate, and dependable. Ease and comfort with and respect for the friend are of less concern. Actual friendships reflect these ideals. Women's friendships tend to be "face-to-face." They are affectively rich, communal, reciprocal, and empathic (Wright, 1988).

Talking is central to most women's friendships, even if the relationship is oriented around shared activities or work. The conversational content of women's friendship is geared toward disclosure. For instance, Johnson and Aries (1983) found that young women college students discussed family activities and problems, personal problems, doubts and fears, intimate relationships, secrets about the past, sexual concerns, daily life, shared activities, and reminiscences with their friends in depth and often. Talking also serves to entertain. "A friend, like a storyteller, builds a solid knowledge of the characters, setting the plot by piling detail on detail, adding touches of humor and pathos . . . [and] . . . interpreting along the way" (Gouldner & Strong, 1987, p. 67).

Women tend to seek "all purpose" friends to whom they can relate in many different areas, as opposed to developing different friends to meet different needs (Barth & Kinder, 1988). Young women usually have more friends than women in their forties and fifties, who in turn have more frequent, specialized interactions with fewer friends (Shulman, 1975). However, not every woman has a friend. Anywhere from 7 percent to 57 percent of women report not having a close or best friend at some point in their lives (Ratcliff & Bodgan, 1988; Goodenow & Gaier, 1990).

The characteristics of women's friendship appear to be established in childhood. Girls prefer to have a few close relationships rather than a "gang" of less intimate friends and to enjoy exploring interpersonal issues with them (Sharabany, Gershoni, & Hofman, 1981). Yet difficulties are not unknown to female friendship. Young girls demonstrate a friendship pattern that alternates between intimacy and repudiation (Bardwick, 1979). Close relationships between "best friends" often are broken by a third girl, and the triad reassembles in a different configuration soon after. This pattern may be one basis for mistrust of other females. Adolescent friendships are particularly intense, with girls relying very much on friends for emotional support, but the nature of friendship changes once dating begins. They become more playful, and sometimes, competitive. Relationships with boys may become more significant and ones with girls denigrated.

Establishing a heterosexual relationship often has a negative impact on women's friendships. Women more often than men report that dating or marriage precipitates the loss of a friendship (Rose, 1984; Rose & Serafica, 1986). Among married couples, the typical pattern is for the husband's friends to become the couple's friends (Fischer & Oliker, 1983). This is even the case when both the man and woman work and have no children and when, presumably, both would have equal access to work-based friendships. Several structural factors have been used to explain men's advantage in selecting and maintaining the couple's friends (Fischer & Oliker, 1983). First, women have less income and social status relative to husbands. Therefore, the men have more privilege to select joint friendships, and the man's work friends are likely to be more important to improving the couple's social status. Second, marriage increases the amount of time women spend doing housework and subsequently decreases the amount of time available for socializing with friends. Third, women usually have primary responsibility for childrearing, which limits friendship interactions and, for full-time homemakers, eliminates the workplace as a context for making friends.

If marriage has a negative impact on women's friendships, does divorce have a positive one? There is some evidence that women's friend networks eventually expand after divorce, although there may be a temporary decrease if the couple's friends originated with the husband and their loyalty is to him, as is often the case. The major reason given for the increase in friendships by both white and Mexican American divorced women in a study by Wagner (1987) was that the ex-husband could no longer prevent them from having a more active social life.

In old age, friendships provide increased social support. The elderly population is largely comprised of women, many of whom do not have a spouse. Consequently, older women often expand their network of women friends and also are likely to begin to include more younger women and relatives as friends (Armstrong & Goldsteen, 1990). Having close friends is particularly important to widows' life satisfaction (Reinhardt & Fisher, 1989).

Throughout life, women's friendships appear to fulfill three major functions, according to Candy, Troll, and Levy (1981), who asked 172 women between the ages of fourteen and eighty to describe up to five best friendships. First, the most valued function for all age groups was intimacy-assistance. The women disclosed their most private or personal feelings to one another and gave or received help, including money, emotional support, and comfort. Second, they supplied status by conveying esteem for the friend or offering prestige. Friends viewed each other as important and encouraged other people to do so too. Power was the third friendship function. Being a friend gave the women the authority to give advice or influence their friends.

Psychological well-being is associated with certain aspects of friendship for women. Affirmation from a same-sex friend was reported by Goodenow (1985) to be the most important function in determining well-being among a large group of white, college-educated women, ages twenty-five to sixty-seven. Women whose friends were emotionally encouraging, treated them as worthwhile, supported their individuality, and enabled them to "be themselves" had higher self-esteem and more integrated identities, were more satisfied with life, and were less depressed than women whose friends were less affirming or who had no friends. Equality in friendship also was related to mental health. Women with friendships in which both women talked about the same amount, made about equal numbers of decisions, and received equal benefits reported more well-being. Lastly, having friendships that were easy to maintain was associated with positive mental health, whereas having friends who were hard to get along with, troublesome, or who "put down" their friends was related to psychological distress. Research on poor and working-class women indicates that the positive benefits of friendship cut across social class lines (e.g., Ferraro, Mutran, & Barresi, 1984).

VARIATION IN WOMEN'S FRIENDSHIP

The pattern of women's friendship described above is by no means universal. What accounts for differences in friendship among women? A comprehensive answer to this question is not available, but some examples will serve to demonstrate the effect various influences such as social class, race, sexual orientation, physical ability, and gender role have on friendship.

The role of social class illustrates how economic resources and class values affect friendship. According to Allan (1977), white working-class friendships tended to be situation-specific, with friends formed in one setting, such as a darts team, being confined to that setting, and rarely planned for outside it. Friends seldom were entertained at home, which was regarded as the exclusive preserve of the family. In contrast, white middle-class friendships were not limited to one sphere of activity. The relationships tended to "flower out" to other activities, including entertaining friends at home, and were often planned for the express purpose of seeing the friend, not for the activity itself. Also, in terms of intimacy, Hacker (1981) reported that women of working-class origins disclosed significantly more to their women friends than did upper-class women. These patterns might reflect class differences in resources and values: middle-class women have larger, more comfortable homes, have more funds for socializing, and are perhaps more likely to socialize as a couple, thus reducing opportunities for intimacy.

Race also influences friendship. A pattern of regarding friends as part of an extended family network appears to distinguish African Americans from white Americans, at least among the poor, working, and middle class. African American women on welfare were described by Stack (1974) as having set up a unique extended family network that included kin and a number of friends classified as kin. The networks shared resources, childrearing, and households, and enabled the women to survive on an inadequate income. Poor middle-aged and elderly African Americans also were found to seek help from a broad base, including friends and multiple family members, in contrast to whites, who relied on one family member (usually the spouse) almost exclusively (Gibson, 1982). Similarly, McAdoo (1980) reported that middle-class African American women, especially those who were single mothers, counted heavily on friends for financial assistance, emotional support, and child care.

Among young Mexican American women (Chicanas), the reliance on friends versus family followed a different pattern. Chicanas depended more on their families for support at the beginning of their first year of single parenthood, whereas white women focused more on their friends. However, both Chicanas and white women were using their friends more than family for support a year later (Wagner, 1987). These findings point to the need for race and culture to be taken into account more fully when describing friendship.

The case of professional black women demonstrates another way race and class interact to affect friendship. Professional black women operate almost entirely in a white male culture and continually must negotiate the stress of being bicultural, that is, of balancing the conflicting demands of the majority culture and the black community (Bell, 1990). Bonds with other black women help in identifying sources of racism and coping techniques. For instance, in an investigation of seventy-one professional black women, Denton (1990) found that friendships with other black women fulfilled many of the same functions reported earlier, providing social companionship, support, and instrumental bonding, including help and problem solving. However, in response to the question, "What are you able to do in life because of this friendship?" many women specifically told how the friendship helped them manage bicultural stress. "She helps me manage my feelings better with respect to negative situations at work. With her I can show my anger about whites on my job," replied one (p. 454). Bicultural support is also likely to be a characteristic of friendship for other women of color.

Sexual orientation is another variable affecting friendship about which there is little knowledge. Lesbians, particularly feminists, appear to place a very high value on women's friendship (Raymond, 1986). Friendship may be even more highly valued than romantic relationships, and often the friendship with a lover is regarded as more important than sexual aspects of the relationship (Rose, Zand, & Cini, 1994). This is not surprising, given that lesbians have been socialized similarly to other women. In a study comparing lesbians and heterosexual women, Rosenbluth (1990) found that both groups viewed friendships with women as being facilitated by similar interests, understanding, support, and the ability to deal with feelings. However, lesbians placed more emphasis than heterosexual women on equality and trust as being important to intimacy. Other differences no doubt exist, particularly in terms of how being in a relationship with a woman instead of a man affects women's friendships. Numerous questions remain to be explored.

Physical disability affects women's friendships with nondisabled women in at least three major ways (Fisher & Galler, 1988). First, opportunities to establish friendships often are limited for women with disabilities. Because nondisabled people tend to avoid interactions with the disabled, the disabled woman often must take the initiative when starting a friendship. Second, how reciprocity is to be achieved in the friendship must be negotiated so that both parties think that what they contribute and what they receive are fairly balanced. Typically, the nondisabled friend provides physical help or special accommodations to the disabled friend, who reciprocates by being especially attentive and supportive in the emotional sphere. Third, both the disabled friend and nondisabled friend must be willing to assume responsibility for the relationship. This often means the disabled woman will have to educate her friend about the disability. In turn, the nondisabled woman has the responsibility to use her knowledge to educate others and act as a liaison between her disabled friend and the rest of the world (Fisher & Galler, 1988).

Lastly, not all women's friendships fit the close, intimate prototype. One aspect of personality that has been shown to have an effect is gender role. Girls and women who have more "feminine" and androgynous personality traits tend to have more intimate friendships, possess more support from other people, and are less lonely than more "masculine" women or women who have few strong feminine or masculine traits (Williams, 1985). Thus, "feminine" expressive traits are more facilitative of friendship than are "masculine" instrumental ones.

These examples demonstrate that variations among women are actually so extensive that they may be more important to understanding any one woman's friendships than the more general pattern described for women earlier. They also suggest that women's friendship patterns overlap with men's considerably, a fact that often is overlooked when gender differences alone are the focus of discussion (Lott, 1990).

FRIENDSHIPS WITH MEN

Developing close cross-sex friendships poses a challenge for most women. Although the rules for establishing same-sex friendships are fairly consistent, even across cultures, the norms for cross-sex friendship are unclear (Argyle & Henderson, 1984). Many adults have no strategy for making friends with the other sex; they either "just happen" or occur "by default" when a romantic relationship fails or a sexual attraction is unreciprocated (Bell, 1981; Rose, 1985). The default pattern may account for the greater occurrence of cross-sex friendships among young single women, most of whom Rose (1985) found were able to identify a man other than a romantic partner as a close friend. Among middle-aged and married women fewer, about 25 percent to 66 percent, reported having a close cross-sex friend (e.g., Rose, 1985). Even fewer elderly women, about 4 percent to 20 percent, have close men friends (Adams, 1985; Babchuk & Anderson, 1989).

Because close cross-sex friendships are much less common than same-sex ones, they are often viewed as deviant, taboo, or suspect (O'Meara, 1989). No role models for platonic female-male relationships exist. Friendships between women and men depicted in movies and on television invariably end up as romances, as in the movie *When Harry Met Sally*. The cultural expectation that cross-sex interactions are sexually based places constraints on such interactions, especially for married women. A married woman who may not think twice about spending all day Saturday with a woman friend is likely to not even consider doing so with a man friend. To lessen the threat to the marital partner, cross-sex friendships usually are nested in relationships with other couples. This permits married women to have a larger number of "safe" men friends, but reduces the intimacy and frequency of interactions compared to those of single women (Booth & Hess, 1974).

Women and men appear to view the role of sexual attraction in cross-sex friendship differently. For instance, none of the women interviewed by Rose (1985) mentioned sexual attraction as motivating them to be friends with men, but most believed it was what primarily motivated men. The men proved the women correct. Single and married men alike gave sexual attraction as the most common reason for pursuing a cross-sex friendship. Once a friendship was established, however, sexual attraction was not necessary to maintain it.

Explanations for why women and men differ in their view about sexual attraction are varied. One is that heterosexual men are less able than heterosexual women to differentiate friendly from romantic cues in cross-sex interaction, as Shotland and Craig (1988) found, and so misinterpret friendship overtures from women as indicating sexual interest. Another is that women may tend to separate intimacy from sexuality more than men do. For example, Sapadin (1988) found that women were less likely than men to think that sex deepened friendship. Alternatively, Lipman-Blumen (1976) has proposed that because men have more power, resources, and status than women, women may be perceived as having little to offer in friendship other than sexuality. Lastly, both sexual orientation and gender role have an impact on the role of sexual attraction in friendship. When the other-sex friend is gay or lesbian, "the ubiquitous pressure for sex is absent . . . allowing the friends to relate more freely as individuals divorced of sexual availability" (Phillis & Stein, 1983, p. 222).

Similarly, nonconventional men were found to be more at ease in cross-sex friendships and view them as more appropriate than did traditionally sex-typed men (Bell, 1981).

If established, cross-sex friendships are highly valued for the help, companionship, and insight into the other sex that they provide (Rose, 1985; Sapadin, 1988). The course of such friendships is not always easy, however, particularly for women. Women and men bring different expectations to cross-sex friendships based on their prior experience in same-sex relationships. For instance, as noted earlier, women's friendships tend to focus on intimacy and expressiveness and to be "all purpose." Men's friendships tend to be "side-by-side." Shared activities, tasks, and sports are emphasized, and communication is less personal and generally more superficial (O'Meara, 1989). One likely consequence of these differing expectations is that women's desire for intimacy may go unmet in cross-sex friendships, or at least fall short of what can be attained in same-sex ones.

Indeed, evidence indicates that women experience what Bernard (1976) has called "social deprivation" in friendships with men. Rose (1985) found that women reported receiving less acceptance and intimacy in friendships with men than with women, whereas men received as much from both women and men. Men also often describe cross-sex friendships as being closer than women do and report deriving more therapeutic value from them (Aukett, Ritchie, & Mill, 1988; Buhrke & Fuqua, 1987). Furthermore, women report feeling happy more often in same-sex friendships than cross-sex ones, whereas men are happy more often in friendships with women (Helgeson, Shaver, & Dyer, 1987). Lastly, women describe friendships with men as being more superficial, patronizing, and sexist than men do (Sapadin, 1988).

Self-disclosure patterns are one reason women fare less well in cross-sex friendships. Women are more likely to reveal their weaknesses, and men their strengths (Hacker, 1981). Women talk more to men about feminine aspects of the self, such as how understanding of others they are or how often they express liking for others, than masculine aspects, such as how assertive they are or how strongly they usually defend their own opinions (Snell et al., 1988). The reverse is true for men. These patterns reinforce typical gender-role inequalities between women and men.

Friendship in marriage appears to be more satisfying for women than other cross-sex friendships, but less so than same-sex ones (O'Connor, 1992; Rawlins, 1992). Middle-class couples aspire to "an ideal of best friendship between the spouses" (Oliker, 1989, p. 33), and many couples do view each other as best friends. At their best, marital friendships "build the attachment and affective bond that make couples willing to go through the difficult processes of relationship repair" (Gottman, 1982, p. 119). However, other aspects of marriage contradict the conditions necessary for friendship to flourish (Rawlins, 1992). For example, friendships are voluntary attachments, whereas marriages are legally and often religiously sanctioned bonds. They also are not always relationships of equality. As in other cross-sex friendships, husbands tend to be happier with the friendship than wives and to consider their wives as their best friend and sole confidante (Gerstel, 1988; Oliker, 1989). On the other hand, wives value their friendships with husbands, but also typically have a female friend to whom they feel closer (Gouldner & Strong, 1987).

Despite the problems and inequalities in friendships with men, four benefits have been associated with them (Basow, 1992). Many women report particularly enjoying getting to see how men think and learning their perspectives about women. Second, women sometimes feel more comfortable revealing certain feelings (e.g., love) to men than to women friends. Third, women often like the companionship, activity orientation, and easier, less intense style of interaction of men friends. Fourth, women gain access to men's greater resources and status through friendship. Buhrke and Fuqua (1987) also found that women wanted more contact with men friends, wanted to be closer to them, and wanted more balance in those relationships, perhaps, as the authors concluded, in the hope of making those friendships more satisfying.

Although it appears from the preceding discussion that women and men are vastly different in their approaches to friendship, it is important to point out that they share more similarities than differences (Wright, 1988). This is good news, because as more women enter the workforce, opportunities for friendships will increase. Working women are more likely than homemakers to have men friends other than their spouses; married professional women who belong to professional and recreational associations and whose husbands also have professional jobs are almost certain to have men friends (Booth & Hess, 1974).

Women's greater professional roles have not yet changed the gender pattern described above, however. Cross-sex friendships among professionals studied by Sapadin (1988) were reportedly less enjoyable, intimate, and nurturing for women than men. In addition, even though men are more satisfied in cross-sex friendships than women, they are not welcoming to women as friends in the workplace. Lack of access to men's social networks has been identified as a major barrier to women's achievement (Epstein, 1971). Women scientists, professors, and medical students have difficulty finding male colleagues with whom to talk, study, or have lunch (e.g., Long, 1990). Men often exclude women from friendships and informal contexts such as athletic clubs, bars, and poker games where important contacts or decisions are made. Research on professional networks has shown that women's lack of contact with men, particularly higher-ranking ones, is detrimental to their careers (e.g., Rose, 1989). Women also experience social isolation and hostility from men in blue-collar jobs (Palmer & Lee, 1990; Schroedel, 1990). The resistance of this pattern to change points to the need to view friendship in a broader context.

THE WIDER CONTEXT OF FRIENDSHIP

Friendships are so much viewed as private, personal relationships in Western culture that how they are shaped by a wider social context is frequently ignored (O'Connor, 1992). People's general tendency is to focus on variables that lie within the individual, such as personality, in explaining women's and men's friendships. The almost exclusive attention to such person-centered variables overlooks situationally relevant factors external to the individual that also may determine behavior (Riger & Galligan, 1980).

Person-centered explanations of women's friendships suggest that female socialization encourages personality development that predisposes women to be more emotionally expressive, nurturing, and "relational." According to Chodorow's (1974) object-relations theory, identity development in girls follows a different path from that in boys primarily because universally women are almost exclusively responsible for infant care. The gender similarity between mother and daughter results in the mother identifying more with a girl than with a boy based on body sameness and support from cultural norms. This identification causes the mother to be more empathic to the daughter and to encourage a stronger connection between them. The mother is less likely to view the son as "like her" and also is under social pressure to encourage him to be separate and independent. These early experiences supposedly lead females to desire closeness in relationships with women and males to feel comfortable with distance.

Gilligan's (1982) theory of women's moral development also posits that women are more relational than men. She argues that female morality develops around the themes of caring for and being responsible to others. When faced with a moral dilemma, girls and women lean toward assessing the impact of their actions on others first and on the self second. In contrast, males value individual rights and fairness and are more inclined, when faced with a moral dilemma, to consider first how they will be affected and only secondarily how others will be affected.

In the same vein, "self-in-relation" theory contends that girls' internal mental representation of the self is a more encompassing one than occurs in boys (Jordan et al., 1991). This means that girls and women feel enhanced, satisfied, motivated, and empowered by being close to others and that their self-esteem is based on taking care of relationships.

Peer socialization may play a role in personality as well. According to Maccoby (1990), distinctive interaction styles develop in all-girl and all-boy groups. Female groups develop an *enabling* style that encourages social bonding. Enabling styles are those that acknowledge another's comments, express agreement, support whatever the partner is doing, and keep the interaction going. Male groups develop a *restrictive* style that is used to establish and protect dominance. A restrictive style tends to derail the interaction, such as threatening a partner, contradicting or interrupting, boasting, or topping the partner's story. Children's preference for same-sex play guarantees they will learn and prefer the styles of their group.

Viewed through the person-centered lens, then, women's close intimate friendship pattern can be attributed to a feminine personality. The core features coincide with gender stereotypes of women as warm, expressive, and talkative. Women's identity develops in the context of a system of relationships of which friendships form a part. The preference for dyadic interaction is based on early childhood experiences with the mother. Because this style of relating has intrapsychic origins, women are unlikely to be able to change them; also, problems in cross-sex friendships will be difficult to surmount.

Although person-centered explanations provide insight into the psychological dynamics of friendship, they are unable to account for numerous situational variables. For instance, Reis, Senchak, and Solomon (1985) found that men were capable of acting as intimately as women in same-sex interactions when the situation made it desirable to do so. These results raise the question of whether the gender differences posited by person-centered approaches are indeed ingrained in identity or are the outcome of other forces. Similarly, class, race, and other variations in friendships are not explained easily by person-centered views.

Situation-centered explanations provide an alternative paradigm for understanding friendship by underscoring structural and cultural forces in the environment that shape behavior. One approach suggests that power and resources are determinants of women's intimate and men's nonintimate style. According to Miller (1987), any dominant group in a society relegates activities it finds undesirable to the subordinate group. Subordinates "must learn to be attuned to the vicissitudes of mood, pleasure, and displeasure of the dominant group" (p. 39). Relationships that fit this pattern include parent-child, white-black, and male-female relationships. The subordinates in all cases are expected to be submissive, obedient, grateful, and nurturing to the dominant group. In terms of women and men specifically, women are expected to cater to men's claims of superiority. They also are responsible for maintaining the emotional bonds of the society. The social importance of this role is largely unrecognized. Consequently, women often look to other women for the nurturance and recognition they are denied as subordinates.

Situational factors such as lack of concrete resources, including time, money, and transportation, also place major constraints on women's friendships (O'Connor, 1992). For instance, among the seven hundred women studied by Green, Hebron, and Woodward (1990), few had free time for their own leisure activities, especially uninterrupted time. Domestic and family activities were given a higher priority than the women's individual pursuits. Wives continue to shoulder about 70 percent of the housework and child care responsibilities (Berardo, Shehan, & Leslie, 1987), spending about 19.5 hours per week compared to 9.8 hours for men (Pleck, 1985). Single mothers and married women who work for pay have increased opportunities to meet potential friends, but may not be able to pursue them if lunch hours or breaks are used to attend to family or household matters.

Women on the average earn less than men or are financially dependent on them. This affects both how much money they have to socialize with friends and their freedom to make such expenditures a priority. Finally, women are less likely than men to have a driving license or access to a car, particularly if they are poor or working-class (Allan, 1989). Thus, women often do not have the resources to engage in the routine sociability necessary to establish and maintain friendships.

In addition, women have less access to and control of public space than men. Male social control over playgrounds, bars, social clubs, basketball or racquetball courts, and pinball or video arcades effectively prohibits women from mingling with other women. Women unaccompanied by men are subject to stares, silent disapproval, joking or ridicule, sexual harassment, or open hostility (Green, Hebron, & Woodward, 1990). Fear of sexual or physical assault also inhibits many women from utilizing public facilities. As two young women friends explained a decision to cancel their plans to dine at a posh urban restaurant one Saturday night, "We were scared to walk from the parking lot to the restaurant by ourselves."

Public places more welcoming to women also have limitations. Traditional settings such as laundries or churches lack appeal for many women. Shopping malls, often frequented by women, are not designed to facilitate meeting new people. Alternative venues depend on a woman's race or social class. Very few public places other than churches exist for women of color to meet. Working-class women may meet at bingo games; middle-class women have more choices, such as aerobics classes or gyms. However, few of the above are as widely available geographically, are "drop-in," or are as inexpensive as the public spaces utilized freely by men.

Access to public space is easily available to women only if they accompany men. The necessity of a male escort precludes single women from interacting publicly primarily with other single women. Married women are able to socialize with friends publicly if their husbands are willing to participate. A husband is likely to be motivated to do so the more he likes the friends. As a result, his friendships may dominate the couple's social time. However, separation, divorce, or widowhood may jeopardize these ties. For instance, at many elite country clubs, membership renewal is withheld from women if they divorce or are widowed. Loss of the social setting in which the friendships were formed often causes the relationships to deteriorate. Men who divorce or are widowed retain their memberships, allowing their friendship patterns to continue uninterrupted.

By shifting the focus away from women's personality as a causal factor in friendship, the situation-centered explanations cited above highlight ways in which current social inequities create gender difference. Women's tendency to form dyadic same-sex friendships that emphasize talking is not surprising when viewed from this context. Women look to women to compensate for the intimacy, status, and nurturance lacking in marriage and society. They also turn to women because they are excluded from men's friendship networks. They generally meet in a domestic situation because they have few other places to go. Cars, clubs, bars, and other activities require financial resources, freedom of movement, transportation, and personal safety.

Men's greater access to resources and public space define a different context for their friendships—one in which group social activities occur easily and on a regular basis. Collective friendships rather than dyadic ones develop focusing on specific activities, such as work or sports. The friendships promote a strong group identity that both reflects and maintains male attitudes (Morris, 1985). Ease and comfort with and respect for the friend are more highly valued than expressing feelings or being affectionate. Men's nonintimate friendship style is used to establish their dominance in both same- and cross-sex friendships.

From the standpoint of social change, it is particularly important that situation-centered perspectives be taken into account when explaining friendships. A bias toward person-centered explanations implies that the cause of gender inequality lies within women by suggesting, for example, that women could overcome barriers to cross-sex colleague friendships by learning to adopt men's restrictive style of interaction. Situation-centered ones infer that women are excluded by men, not because they lack the right style, but because they lack power and resources. Thus, remedial efforts should be focused on the environment, not on women.

FRIENDSHIP AND FEMINISM

The feminist ideology of "sisterhood" as having the power to transform the self and society emphasizes the idea of friendship itself as being a force for social change. Friendships between women are believed to result in greater support and intimacy, increased personal power, awareness that "the personal is political," and ultimately, political activism (Strommen, 1977). In turn, feminism was thought to deepen friendship (Seiden & Bart, 1975). To date, friendship between women has helped create a social movement, but not to the extent originally hoped. This is because, depending on the social context, friendship can either be a repressive or liberating force.

One way friendship can repress women is by reinforcing gender status. O'Connor (1992) has pointed out that women's friendships may shore up unsatisfactory marriages by fulfilling the women's unmet intimacy needs and by diffusing anger and disappointment with the marriage. Oliker (1989) found that married women's friendships promoted marital stability by generating empathy for a woman's husband, using humor to defuse situations, reminding the woman of her financial dependence on her husband, and reinforcing her sensitivity to her children's needs for family stability. Ratcliff and Bogdan (1988) found that many friends were unsupportive when married women lost their jobs because they were opposed to the women working in the first place.

Friendships can reinforce the primacy of marriage and male dominance in violent relationships as well. Although many battered women do not have friends or do not tell them about the abuse, those who do confide in friends often receive limited or no help (Dobash & Dobash, 1980). The friends' offers of assistance depend on their beliefs about the sanctity of marriage and their access to resources, such as a spare room or money.

The bridal shower has been used to illustrate how gender status is reinforced by female friendship and social rituals (Cheal, 1989). The focus on the bride in marriage reflects the societal belief that marriage is more important to women than to men, wives' social and financial status generally being determined by the husband. The redistribution of resources that occurs at a shower through gift-giving enables friends to help the bride achieve a certain standard of living, similar to how resources were shared among the African American community observed by Stack (1974). However, "the female solidarity that women achieve within these networks produces a female consciousness, rather than a feminist consciousness" (Cheal, 1989, p. 9). The domestic gifts received confirm the legitimacy of the traditional gender arrangement with the woman as food server, domestic servant, and caregiver.

Women's gender status also is reinforced by the overvaluation of intimacy as a defining feature of women's friendship, according to Cancian (1986). First, disclosure of weakness—fears and disappointments—usually is interpreted as a sign of intimacy, not disclosure of victories and achievements. Thus, in friendships women emphasize their vulnerabilities rather than their skills, their helplessness rather than their power. Second, high expectations for intimacy may create tensions in relationships. The demands for "getting as well as giving" are sometimes emotionally and materially draining and burdensome (Rawlins, 1992). Women's tendency to get "up close and personal" also makes their friendships more fragile. By confronting strains in the relationship instead of ignoring them as men do, women more often risk severing the friendship (Rawlins, 1992). Lastly, the expectation that women's friendships be entirely supportive creates tension when negative emotions, such as anger, envy, and competition, are experienced.

Class and status homophily also inhibits women's friendships (O'Connor, 1992). Upper- and middle-class women may "look down" on lower-class women. Their class solidarity can be maintained by rejecting friendships with lower-class women or viewing their friendship overtures as "social climbing." Lower-class women, in turn, may view women of higher social standing as being snobbish or lacking in sensitivity about the constraints imposed by a less affluent lifestyle. Thus, class tensions have an adverse impact on women's ability to bond across class lines. Surprisingly, class barriers to friendship have received little attention, perhaps because friendship has been idealized as being a self-sacrificing relationship, not a self-serving one.

Status homophily in friendship helps reproduce class divisions in the workplace. Higher-ranking women often are advised not to develop close personal ties with lower-ranking women and, if promoted from the lower ranks, to break off old friendships and confine their affiliations to those of a similar rank. This advice effectively denies women in male-dominated occupations a support network, given that high-status men are unlikely to generously open their ranks to women.

Race divisions similarly impede sisterhood. Tensions between black and white women have been documented by See (1989), who investigated black women's responses to the feminist movement. Black women perceived white women to be insensitive to the discrimination black women and men had experienced and viewed white feminists as advancing an agenda that primarily would benefit white middle-class women. In the business world, black women also saw white women who had been promoted as unwilling to examine how their race privilege had benefited them professionally over black women who were not promoted. See's research suggests that although black and white women share similar burdens, unresolved antagonisms concerning race make friendships between them unlikely.

Women are also divided by sexual orientation. Heterosexual women acquire a number of privileges due to their willingness to mate with men that lesbians do not have, including respectability, spousal benefits, and job security. Those privileges could be jeopardized by friendships with lesbians; hence, heterosexual women may prefer to avoid them. Conversely, lesbians may reject heterosexual women for failing to renounce their privilege.

Friendships constitute a liberating force in women's lives, then, only under certain conditions. Friendships create a "moral universe," or social climate, which may either impede or promote growth (Gullestad, 1984). In order for friendships to effect change, that climate must promote gender and other forms of equality.

At their best, this is what feminist friendships do. Heterosexual and lesbian feminists surveyed by Rose and Roades (1987) claimed that feminism resulted in closer friendships, greater valuation of and loyalty toward women friends, and increased self-respect. Feminist friendships provided a support group and substitute kinship system that sustained feminist values.

The extent to which a social movement can be based on friendship or sisterhood has just begun to be explored. Friendship has been institutionalized in women's political groups, business networks, and professional caucuses with some success. On the other hand, as has been demonstrated, friendships are not uniformly positive. They may, indeed, affirm or heal, but they also may be a source of conflict, anxiety, or emotional pain. Moreover, the shape this deeply personal and private relationship takes is profoundly affected by structural forces maintaining gender, race, class, or other social divisions.

Thus, friendship is a prime example of how "the personal is political." As O'Connor (1992) pointed out, "Friendship is a personal relationship, but its importance transcends the purely personal: something which has only begun to be appreciated" (p. 193). Understanding it reveals key issues in women's lives.

REFERENCES

Adams, R. G. (1985). People would talk: Normative barriers to cross-sex friendships for elderly women. *The Gerontologist, 25,* 605-611.

Allan, G. (1977). Class variation in friendship patterns. *British Journal of Sociology, 28,* 389-393.

Allan, G. A. (1989). *Friendship: Developing a sociological perspective.* London: Harvester/Wheatsheaf.

Argyle, M., & Henderson, M. (1984). The rules of friendship. *Journal of Social and Personal Relationships, 1,* 211-237.

Aristotle. (Trans. 1962). *The Nicomachean ethics.* Book VIII, 214-273. Trans. Martin Oswald. New York: Bobbs-Merrill.

Armstrong, M. J., & Goldsteen, K. S. (1990). Friendship support patterns of older American women. *Journal of Aging Studies, 4,* 391-404.

Aukett, R., Ritchie, J., & Mill, K. (1988). Gender differences in friendship patterns. *Sex Roles, 19,* 57-66.

Babchuk, N., & Anderson, T. B. (1989). Older widows and married women: Their intimates and confidants. *International Journal of Aging and Human Development, 28,* 21-35.

Bardwick, J. (1979). *In transition.* New York: Holt, Rinehart & Winston.

Barth, R. J., & Kinder, B. N. (1988). A theoretical analysis of sex differences in same-sex friendships. *Sex Roles, 19,* 349-363.

Basow, S. (1992). *Gender: Stereotypes and roles.* 3rd ed. Pacific Grove, Calif.: Brooks/Cole.

Bell, E. (1990). The bicultural life experience of career-oriented black women. *Journal of Organizational Behavior, 11,* 459-477.

Bell, R. (1981). *Worlds of friendship.* Beverly Hills, Calif.: Sage.

Berardo, D. H., Shehan, C. L., & Leslie, G. R. (1987). A residue of tradition: Jobs, careers, and spouses' time in housework. *Journal of Marriage and the Family, 49,* 381-390.

Bernard, J. (1976). Homosociality and female depression. *Journal of Social Issues, 32,* 213-238.

Booth, A., & Hess, E. (1974). Cross-sex friendship. *Journal of Marriage and Family, 36,* 38-74.

Brain, R. (1974). *Friends and lovers.* New York: Basic Books.

Buhrke, R. A., & Fuqua, D. R. (1987). Sex differences in same- and cross-sex supportive relationships. *Sex Roles, 17,* 339-352.

Cancian, F. M. (1986). The feminization of love. *Signs, 11,* 692-709.

Candy, S. G., Troll, L. E., & Levy, S. G. (1981). A developmental exploration of friendship functions in women. *Psychology of Women Quarterly, 5,* 456-472.

Cheal, D. J. (1989). Women together: Bridal showers and gender membership. In B. J. Risman & P. Schwartz (Eds.), *Gender in intimate relationships* (pp. 87-93). Belmont, Calif.: Wadsworth.

Chodorow, N. (1974). *The reproduction of mothering.* Berkeley: University of California Press.

Clark, M., & Mills, J. (1979). Interpersonal attraction in exchange and communal relationships. *Journal of Personality and Social Psychology, 37,* 12-24.

Denton, T. C. (1990). Bonding and supportive relationships among black professional women: Rituals of restoration. *Journal of Organizational Behavior, 11,* 447-457.

Dobash, R. E., & Dobash, R. (1980). *Violence against wives: A case against the patriarchy.* London: Open Books.

Epstein, C. F. (1971). *Women's place.* Berkeley: University of California Press.

Faderman, L. (1981). *Surpassing the love of men.* New York: William Morrow.

Ferraro, K. F., Mutran, E., & Barresi, C. M. (1984). Widowhood, health, and friendship support in later life. *Journal of Health and Social Behavior, 25,* 245-259.

Fisher, B., & Galler, R. (1988). Friendship and fairness: How disability affects friendship between women. In M. Fine & A. Asch (Eds.), *Women with disabilities* (pp. 172-194). Philadelphia: Temple University Press.

Fischer, C. S., & Oliker, S. J. (1983). A research note on friendship, gender and the life cycle. *Social Forces, 62*, 124-133.

Gerstel, N. (1988). Divorce and kin ties: The importance of gender. *Journal of Marriage and the Family, 50*, 209-219.

Gibson, R. C. (1982). Blacks at middle and late life: Resources and coping. *Annals of the American Academy, 464*, 79-90.

Gilligan, C. (1982). *In a different voice.* Cambridge, Mass.: Harvard University Press.

Goodenow, C. (1985, August). *Women's friendships and their association with psychological well-being.* Paper presented at the annual meeting of the American Psychological Association, Los Angeles, Calif.

Goodenow, C., & Gaier, E. L. (1990, August). *Best friends: The close reciprocal friendships of married and unmarried women.* Paper presented at the meeting of the American Psychological Association, Washington, D.C.

Gottman, J. M. (1982). Emotional responsivenes in marital conversations. *Journal of Communication, 32*, 108-120.

Gouldner, H., & Strong, M. S. (1987). *Speaking of friendship: Middle class women and their friends.* New York: Greenwood.

Green, E., Hebron, S., & Woodward, D. (1990). *Women's leisure, what leisure?* London: Macmillan.

Gullestad, M. (1984). *Kitchen table society.* Oslo, Norway: Universitets forlaget.

Hacker, H. M. (1981). Blabbermouths and clams: Sex differences in self-disclosure in same-sex and cross-sex friendship dyads. *Psychology of Women Quarterly, 5*, 385-401.

Helgeson, V. S., Shaver, P., & Dyer, M. (1987). Prototypes of intimacy and distance in same-sex and opposite-sex relationships. *Journal of Social and Personal Relationships, 4*, 195-233.

Johnson, F. L., & Aries, E. J. (1983). Conversational patterns among same-sex pairs of late-adolescent close friends. *Journal of Genetic Psychology, 142*, 225-238.

Jordan, J. V., Kaplan, A. G., Miller, J. B., Stiver, I. P., & Surrey, J. L. (1991). *Women's growth in connection: Writings from the Stone Center.* New York: Guilford.

Lipman-Blumen, J. (1976). Toward a homosocial theory of sex roles: An explanation of the sex segregation of social institutions. In M. M. Blaxall & B. Reagan (Eds.), *Women and the workplace* (pp. 15-32). Chicago: University of Chicago.

Lepp, I. (1966). *The ways of friendship.* Trans. Bernard Murchland. New York: Macmillan.

Long, J. S. (1990). The origins of sex differences in science. *Social Forces, 68,* 1297-1315.

Lott, B. (1990). Dual natures or learned behavior: The challenge to feminist psychology. In R. T. Hare-Mustin & J. Maracek (Eds.), *Making a difference: Psychology and the construction of gender* (pp. 65-101). New Haven, Conn.: Yale University Press.

McAdoo, H. P. (1980). Black mothers and the extended family support network. In L. Rodgers-Rose, (Ed.), *The black woman* (pp. 125-144). Beverly Hills, Calif.: Sage.

Maccoby, E. (1990). Gender and relationships. *American Psychologist, 45,* 513-520.

Miller, J. B. (1987). *Toward a new psychology of women* (2nd ed.). Boston: Beacon.

Morris, L. (1985). Local social networks and domestic organizations: A study of redundant steelworkers and their wives. *Sociological Review, 33,* 327-341.

O'Connor, P. (1992). *Friendships between women: A Review.* New York: Guildford.

Oliker, S. J. (1989). *Best friends and marriage: Exchange among women.* Berkeley: University of California.

O'Meara, J. D. (1989). Cross-sex friendship: Four basic challenges of an ignored relationship. *Sex Roles, 21,* 525-543.

Palmer, H. T., & Lee, J. A. (1990). Female workers' acceptance in traditionally male-dominated blue collar jobs. *Sex Roles, 22,* 607-625.

Phillis, D. E., & Stein, P. J. (1983). Sink or swing? The lifestyles of single adults. In E. R. Allgeier & N. B. McCormick (Eds.), *Changing Boundaries* (pp. 202-225). Palo Alto, Calif.: Mayfield.

Pleck, J. H. (1985). *Working wives, working husbands.* Beverly Hills, Calif.: Sage.

Rake, J. M., Sr. (1970). Friendship: A fundamental description of its subjective dimension. *Humanitas, 6,* 161-176.

Ratcliff, K. S., & Bogdan, J. (1988). Unemployed women: When social support is not supportive. *Social Problems, 35,* 54-63.

Rawlins, W. K. (1992). *Friendship matters: Communication, dialectics, and the life course.* New York: Aldine de Gruyter.

Raymond, J. (1986). *A passion for friends.* London: The Women's Press.

Reinhardt, J. P., & Fisher, C. B. (1989). Kinship versus friendship: Social adaptation in married and widowed elderly women. In *Women in the Later Years* (pp. 191-211). New York: Haworth.

Reis, H. T., Senchak, M., & Solomon, B. (1985). Sex differences in the intimacy of social interaction: Further examination of potential explanations. *Journal of Personality and Social Psychology, 5,* 1204-1217.

Reisman, J. M. (1990). Intimacy in same-sex friendships. *Sex Roles, 23,* 65-82.

Riger, S., & Galligan, P. (1980). Women in management: An exploration of competing paradigms. *American Psychologist, 35,* 902-910.

Rose, S. (1984). How friendships end: Patterns among young adults. *Journal of Social and Personal Relationships, 1,* 267-277.

Rose, S. (1985). Same- and cross-sex friendships and the psychology of homosociality. *Sex Roles, 12,* 63-74.

Rose, S. (1989). Women biologists and the "old boy" network. *Women's Studies International Forum, 3,* 349-354.

Rose, S., & Roades, L. (1987). Feminism and women's friendships. *Psychology of Women Quarterly, 11,* 243-254.

Rose, S., & Serafica, F. C. (1986). Keeping and ending casual, close and best friendships. *Journal of Social and Personal Relationships, 3,* 275-288.

Rose, S., Zand, D., & Cini, M. (1994). Lesbian courtship rituals. In E. D. Rothblum & K. A. Brehony (Eds.), *The Boston marriage today: Romantic but asexual relationships between contemporary lesbians* (pp. 70-85). Amherst, Mass.: University of Massachusetts Press.

Rosenbluth, S. (1990, August). *Intimacy: Women's experiences of same-sex and cross-sex couples.* Paper presented at the meeting of the American Psychological Association, Boston, Mass.

Sadler, W. A. (1970). The experience of friendship. *Humanitas, 6,* 117-210.

Sapadin, L. A. (1988). Friendship and gender: Perspectives of professional men and women. *Journal of Social and Personal Relationships, 5,* 387-403.

Schroedel, J. R. (1990). Blue collar women: Paying the price at home and on the job. In H. Y. Grossman & N. L. Chester (Eds.), *The experience and meaning of work in women's lives* (pp. 142-165). Hillsdale, N.J.: Erlbaum.

See, L. A. L. (1989). Tensions between black women and white women: A study. *Affilia, 2,* 31-45.

Seiden, A. M., & Bart, P. (1975). Woman to woman: Is sisterhood powerful? In N. Glazer-Malbin (Ed.), *Old family/New family* (pp. 189-228). New York: D. Van Nostrand.

Sharabany, R., Gershoni, R., & Hofman, J. E. (1981). Girl friend, boy friend: Age and sex differences in development of intimate friendships. *Developmental Psychology, 17,* 800-808.

Shotland, R. L., & Craig, J. M. (1988). Can men and women differentiate between friendly and sexually interested behavior? *Social Psychology Quarterly, 51,* 66-73.

Shulman, N. (1975). Life cycle variations in patterns of friendship. *Journal of Marriage and the Family, 37,* 813-821.

Smith-Rosenberg, C. (1975). The female world of love and ritual: Relations between women in nineteenth-century America. *Signs, 1,* 1-29.

Snell, W. E., Jr., Belk, S. S., Flowers, A., & Warren, J. (1988). Women's and men's willingness to self-disclose to therapists and friends: The moderating influence of instrumental, expressive, masculine, and feminine topics. *Sex Roles, 18,* 769-776.

Stack, C. (1974). *All our kin: Strategies for survival in a black community.* New York: Harper & Row.

Strommen, E. A. (1977). Friendship. In E. Donelson & J. E. Gullahorn (Eds.), *Women: A psychological perspective* (pp. 154-167). New York: John Wiley & Sons.

Taylor, W. R., & Lasch, C. (1963). Kindred spirits: Sorority and family in New England, 1839-1846. *New England Quarterly, 36,* 23-41.

Wagner, R. (1987). Changes in the friend network during the first year of single parenthood for Mexican American and Anglo women. *Journal of Divorce, 11*(2), 89-109.

Williams, D. G. (1985). Gender, masculinity-femininity, and emotional intimacy in same-sex friendship. *Sex Roles, 12,* 587-600.

Wiseman, J. P. (1986). Friendship: Bonds and binds in a voluntary relationship. *Journal of Social and Personal Relationships, 3,* 191-211.

Wollstonecraft, M. (1967). *A vindication of the rights of woman.* New York: W.W. Norton.

Wright, P. (1974). The delineation and measurement of some key variables in the study of friendship. *Representative Research in Social Psychology, 5,* 196-207.

Wright, P. (1988). Interpreting research on gender differences in friendship: A case for moderation and a plea for caution. *Journal of Social and Personal Relationships, 5,* 367-373.

The Impact of Three Patriarchal Religions on Women

Rachel Josefowitz Siegel
Sudha Choldin
Jean H. Orost

INTRODUCTION

This chapter focuses on how Hinduism, Judaism, and Christianity influence the lives of women today. Established centuries ago, these three belief systems constitute a pervasively male-centered and male-serving force in our society that continues to legitimize and reinforce the patriarchy. Although it is not within the scope of this chapter to analyze or compare these religions, we can identify some common factors that impact specifically on women.

Historical Background

Religious beliefs, mythology, ritual, and symbols have been at the heart of all cultures throughout, and possibly before, recorded history (Eisler, 1987). They form the basis for the apparently universal longing to understand such profound mysteries as birth and death, unusual or frightening phenomena, the origins of peoples and their cultures, and one's sense of place and destiny in the cosmology of the universe. A sense of transcendence, or of a presence, force, or principle beyond external reality, led many early peoples to seek deities hidden within nature.

In cultures characterized by hunting and gathering, goddess worship grew out of reverence for nature and recognition of the awesomeness of the life-producing power of women (Goodman,

1988). Eisler's (1987) research into archeological data suggests a shift from goddess worship to patriarchal religions. This change seems to have coincided with the realization of the male role in reproduction and the development of tools that could be used to kill people or destroy nature. Males began to subjugate rather than to cooperate with nature and to assert dominance over women. Men may then have determined that their power over women, nature, and reproduction must be divinely ordained. They developed religious beliefs that were consistent with and supportive of this intent. The patriarchal religions addressed in this chapter—Judaism, Hinduism, and Christianity—express some of these ideologies and may have developed at the time of this shift from goddess worship to male deities, male-centered-ness, and male domination over women.

In India, Hinduism is a major ideological force that has shaped Indian culture and thinking. It has evolved, as it is prac-ticed today, out of a synthesis of many religions and cultures. The most influential of these is the religion of the Vedas, brought into India by the Aryans in 1500 B.C. This religion, together with the religions of the indigenous peoples of India and later the influences of Christianity and Islam, evolved into the complex beliefs, traditions, and customs of Hinduism. Because practices of Hinduism vary regionally, and even within a given region vary by class, it is difficult to come up with an exact definition of Hin-duism. In a broad sense all the sects and schisms that are derived from the Vedas can be defined as Hinduism.

Judaism, dating back over five thousand years, is both a reli-gion and the history of a varied and dispersed people. Although Christianity adopted the Hebrew Scriptures (Old Testament) from Judaism, Jews have consistently rejected the Christian Bible (New Testament). These two religions have developed into sepa-rate and unequal cultures and communities in which Christians invariably hold the majority and the power.

Christian beliefs and traditions have become dominant in European-American civilization. In North America, these beliefs permeate much of the generally accepted culture and legal struc-ture of society and have had a tremendous impact on the psy-chological development of males and females alike. Because many of the American colonies were established by conserva-tive Christian groups, the socialization of women in the United

States is still based on a belief that women are not only the source of sin and temptation, but are weaker, more susceptible to evil, and in need of the protection and control of men. Moreover, the prevalence of conservative Christian traditions in Europe and North America has led to discrimination against Native American, African American, Jewish, Hindu, Muslim, and other religious traditions.

The Impact of Patriarchal Religion on Women

Patriarchal religion today, through its institutions, leaders, literature, rituals, rules, and regulations, establishes systems and definitions of morality that affect the general population, including those individuals or groups who are neither religiously observant nor identified. Although particular practices differ among religions and even among different factions of a given religion, all patriarchal religions profess a morality that controls the intimate and everyday lives of women in the following manner:

1. by defining gender roles, including the limits of permissible sexual behavior, gender-specific dress codes, food restrictions and preparations, and gender-specific religious rituals and observances
2. by defining the family unit, including heterosexual imperatives, limitations of sexual partners, and ownership of women and children by male heads of household
3. by establishing rules and regulations that control reproduction
4. by establishing male hierarchies that perpetuate male dominance and female submissiveness within the family and within the religion, including institutionalized male leadership, scholarship, and power within each religion and the absence of women as deities, historical figures, role models, or priestly officiants.

Religious beliefs and religiously sanctioned customs further affect women:

1. by limiting women's participation in the formulation of ideology and in the enforcement of religiously based rules of conduct, thus teaching women to be silent

2. by determining and enforcing inheritance laws that keep women in economic dependency

3. by the use of masculine and at times hierarchical and military language in referring to the deity, thus suppressing any identification with the feminine, and/or cooperative, peace-loving aspects of the divinity

4. by insisting on adherence to a specific ideology and loyalty to its leaders and followers, separating and establishing hierarchies between ethnoreligious groups, between believers and nonbelievers, between observing or practicing members and those who don't, thus preventing alliances between women of different religions, different classes, and different geographic origins

5. by teaching and encouraging the externalization and projection of negative traits onto those who do not conform or belong to that religion, thus creating negative stereotypes and scapegoats

6. by justifying the societal control of women's bodies by predominantly male politicians, doctors, lawyers, and ministers, in the name of religiously sanctioned morality, thus limiting women's reproductive choices and sexual behaviors.

The Subliminal Nature of Religious Influences

Religious attitudes and beliefs permeate our culture so thoroughly that we are generally unaware of their impact on our lives, especially if we or our family of origin are not particularly observant or religiously identified. When we begin to trace childhood religious influences on our lives, or to attribute certain attitudes to our religious or nonreligious upbringing, we may find that these are inextricably mixed with factors of class, place of origin, color, and ethnicity. We also find it difficult to identify the fine nuances on a continuum of religious identification, belief system, or practice. Thus, we tend to assume that a woman is either religious or not, when in fact her religious identification is complex and at times conflicted.

In stereotyping or making generalizations about women of a religion other than our own or other than the predominant religion, we frequently fail to take these diverse factors into account, or to find out what kind of Indian or what kind of Christian or what kind of Jew we are meeting. Such stereotyping is often based on cultural and religious illiteracy and is especially oppressive in predominantly Christian countries where the prevalence of other religious groups and their non-Christian practices or preferences is consistently ignored or minimized.

JEWISH WOMEN

The Jewish woman exists in an environment in which she is directly affected by Jewish values, Jewish culture, Jewish religious and secular tradition, and Jewish gender roles. She also exists in an environment in which it is often dangerous to be a Jew, and especially uncomfortable to be a Jewish woman. She experiences the double oppression of being exposed to sexist and patriarchal customs within her own religion as well as sexist and anti-Jewish behavior from non-Jews. She has a complicated task in asserting her rights as a woman among Jews and as a Jew among non-Jews. If she is a feminist, she finds herself defending women and a feminist position in the Jewish community and defending Jews and a Jewish position in the feminist community. She may also find herself isolated and suspected of disloyalty in both communities when she criticizes Jews for indulging in racism or sexism, and when she criticizes feminists for indulging in anti-Semitism (Siegel, in press). When she traces the impact of her Jewish heritage on her own development, that inquiry must include the impact of living in a non-Jewish and overtly or covertly anti-Jewish environment.

Diversity among Jewish Women

The focus here is on Jewish women in North America. In this non-Jewish host culture, the diversity among Jewish women tends to be overlooked, resulting in frequent generalizations and stereotyping. Jews have been a wandering people since biblical times, and have been persecuted or barely tolerated in most of the countries in which they have lived. The impact of recent persecutions, and of the Holocaust in particular, is felt keenly by all Jewish women and their allies. For Jewish women who survived the Holocaust, whose parents or immediate relatives were survivors, and even those who fled Europe during those years, it is a trauma of unthinkable proportions that can never be completely healed.

Our families of origin have lived in a variety of host countries, sometimes for several generations, absorbing some of the language and customs of that country while retaining a core of Jewish customs and a religious and historical attachment to Jerusalem and the Holy Land. Our presence has been that of outsiders. We all observe the same holidays, use the same Hebrew prayers with different tunes and pronunciation, and relate to similar religiously based definitions of gender roles; yet Jews coming from different countries may differ in many particular customs.

Further diversity among Jewish women is present along religious lines. Being Jewish is not only a religious identity; it is also an ethnic and cultural identity. We range from being secular, areligious, or antireligious Jews, to being casually or occasionally observant of religious customs, to being religiously affiliated and actively observant within a Reform, Reconstructionist, Conservative, or Orthodox congregation (Grossman & Haut, 1992). In some localities, even more choices have become available with the emergence of progressive and innovative congregations. Among these are nonsexist or egalitarian congregations, gay/lesbian congregations, feminist prayer groups, and nonhierarchical Chavuroth, which are peer groups that meet for study, prayer, and community without an assigned spiritual leader.

Jewish women have a complex sense of Jewish identity that may change during different stages of life, being deeply affected by political and historical developments as well as personal life events and relationships. Whether we consider ourselves secular Jews or religious Jews, whether our parents spoke Yiddish, Ladino, or Judeo-Arabic, whether we are politically left or right, pro- or anti-Israeli occupation of occupied territories, wealthy or working-class, immigrant or third-generation, we are still responding on some level to Jewish messages, customs, and attitudes about women.

Jewish Attitudes and Practices Affecting Jewish Women

Traditional Jewish attitudes toward women are based on rigid gender roles. The differences between traditional Jewish gender roles and the gender roles that are commonly accepted by the

dominant population in North America have caused a devaluation of Jewish women that is not usually acknowledged. Jewish
women were often the breadwinners, shopkeepers, and traders in
the old country. They were highly respected for their skills as
mothers, homemakers, and providers of food and comfort for
the family. Soon after their migration to the North American con-
tinent, they were teased, ridiculed, and negatively stereotyped
for these same behaviors, living now in a culture that devalues
the nurturing and homemaking that is assigned to women
(Baum, Hyman & Michel, 1976; Siegel, 1986). Immigrant women
did not find the same opportunities in America. While working-
class Jewish women toiled in sweatshops, families who were able
to aspire to middle-class status relegated Jewish women back
into the home; their husbands now measured their own success
by how much they could provide for their families.

The resulting loss of dignity within the home and loss of role
outside the home are at the root of the negative "Jewish mother"
and "Jewish American princess" stereotypes (Beck, 1990;
Siegel,1986). Jewish assimilation into the American host culture
has also produced an artificial standard of female attractiveness
that causes Jewish women to feel inferior and less attractive than
their supposedly tall, blond, thin, straight-haired, and straight-
nosed non-Jewish counterparts.

Tensions have developed between generations and between
genders in the drama of wanting to become like other Americans while also wanting to retain a Jewish identity. Jewish women
have often become the scapegoats as Jewish men and sometimes
Jewish women have rejected them as intimate partners because
they looked or acted "too Jewish."

A Jewish girl learns very early on that she is not nearly as
important as her brothers. She learns that women are hardly ever
mentioned in the Bible, and have, until recent years, not been
counted as Jews when ten Jews are needed for a minyan (the
number of Jews needed for certain important prayers). She learns
that the ritual circumcision of Jewish boys, eight days after birth,
is the occasion for major celebration, whereas the naming of a
Jewish girl child had, until the current Jewish feminist movement, merited only minimal recognition in the synagogue. Furthermore, it is only in the past seventy years that Jewish girls of
twelve or thirteen have begun to celebrate their Jewish communal

coming of age with a bat mitzvah, similar to the bar mitzvah of their brothers. A Jewish girl also learns that in an Orthodox synagogue, she will be required to sit behind a curtain or barrier, in order that her sexuality not distract any man from prayer. She learns that the biblical injunctions are often addressed to men (as in "you and your wives and your sons and daughters, and your servants and the stranger that resides in your midst"). If she attends religious services in any but an egalitarian, Reconstructionist, or Reform synagogue, she finds that the language of prayer consistently refers to a male deity, the God of our fathers, God of Abraham, Isaac, and Jacob.

Over and over again she learns that men are the real Jews and she is the "other," that men deserve to be heard and listened to, and that what men do is important and is reserved for them. She even learns explicitly that the voice of woman is lascivious and must be silenced. The observant Orthodox Jewish woman is most consistently exposed to these exclusions and absences of female voices in Jewish religious history and practice. She may experience these exclusions as confirmations of her own place in a belief system that also values her in her primary role of mothering and caregiving (Kaufman, 1991).

Further devaluation of Jewish women within the Jewish community evolves from the high value placed on communal and religious activities that have excluded women. Men have been highly respected for their lifelong study of holy texts and commentaries and their leadership in religious and communal activities, whereas women have until very recently been excluded from Jewish institutions of higher learning, the rabbinate, and leadership positions. It is only in the past fifteen to twenty years that women have begun to have access to Jewish learning, the activity that is most highly prized among Jews.

Lessons about being a woman are embedded in Jewish history, Jewish Law, Jewish religious practice, and Jewish custom. The lessons repeatedly portray woman as "other," woman as absent or uncounted, woman defined by her function or relationship to man (Heschel, 1990), and woman whose sexuality must be curbed or covered to protect man from temptation. Woman is not central in Jewish history; she is only present as mother, daughter, sister, or wife. In these roles she is portrayed with some measure of respect and sometimes as a clever manipulator. "Judaism as a religion and historical experience has been shaped almost exclusively by men, as attested by the standard Jewish history textbooks which almost never mention women" (Heschel, 1990, p. 32). Although these lessons about the marginality of Jewish women are easily found in Jewish texts, and have been documented by Jewish feminist scholars, they are consistently denied or minimized by the Jewish establishment.

Jewish women react to these messages with a variety of responses that range from rejecting everything religious or everything Jewish, to fully accepting their assigned position, embracing it and feeling virtuous and valued within these parameters (Kaufman, 1991). Most Jewish women fall somewhere between these extremes, living with ambivalence and compromise, expressing or swallowing their anger, often afraid to rock the boat for fear of exposing themselves or their community to external anti-Semitism. Furthermore, Jewish women are often unaware that these demeaning messages have undermined their self-esteem. They frequently attribute their ensuing discomfort to individual pathology, rather than recognizing that the individual pain is caused by a system and communal structure that deny them full participation.

Idealization and Denial

The idealizing image of the Jewish wife and mother, combined with the pejorative images of the Jewish mother and the Jewish American princess, are used to deny the powerlessness of women in the Jewish community and to convey an image of the Jewish woman as holding all the power in the family. This denial is so prevalent that Jewish women themselves have internalized it and tend to fear the use of their own power (Kaye/Kantrowitz, 1990).

Ideals of Jewish family life portray Jewish men as gentle scholars and Jewish women as self-less mothers. Both Jewish women and Jewish men have difficulty living up to these ideals and reconciling these values with the more "American" ideals of independence and male dominance. The Jewish ideal of *shalom bayit*, peace in the home, or its illusion, is held onto, even when it does not exist. Although Jews resist and deny the fact that marital violence exists among Jews, it is as common in Jewish families as in non-Jewish families. The Jewish woman who is battered has the additional hurdle of exposing her family as deviant in the Jewish community. She is often subjected to disbelief and to powerful pressure from Jewish community representatives, and is asked to minimize or cover up the violence so that the illusion of shalom bayit can be maintained. Her shame becomes a communal shame and she may feel even more trapped, powerless, and guilty than her non-Jewish sisters (Giller, 1990).

Sexuality and Reproduction

Religion is one of the strongest forces defining a woman's sexuality, even when she herself does not believe or practice religiously, or has not been brought up in a religious home, because some attitudes and behaviors may be conveyed long after the belief system has changed. Jewish messages about sexuality are somewhat ambivalent, although on the whole positive. Sex is not considered a sin when practiced within acceptable confines. It is an important and pleasurable activity, to be enjoyed by both man and woman within marriage. Married heterosexual activity is encouraged, and a man is expected to respect and satisfy his wife's sexual needs. These messages are positive as well as consistently heterosexual and marriage-oriented. There is no specific biblical injunction against lesbianism, but the very absence of any mention of a lesbian option carries a powerful message of disapproval. Blessings said on the occasion of the naming of a girl or at her bat mitzvah invariably include the phrase, "and may she be brought to the wedding canopy."

Since Adam and Eve, woman has been portrayed as the ultimate sexual temptress whose body must be hidden from man's eyes, for his sexuality is considered both innocent and uncontrollable. In Orthodox communities, a woman is expected to keep her arms and legs covered, and to cover her hair, or even shave her head when she gets married. Orthodox custom forbids a man from touching or even looking at any woman other than his wife.

Woman is also considered unclean during menstruation as well as after childbirth, and is to cleanse her body in a ritual bath before resuming sexual relations, lest she defile her male partner's body with her uncleanness. Many Jewish women, far removed from these customs, still carry the sense of bodily shame and uncleanness that these practices taught their mothers and foremothers, and many Jewish men still carry this attitude of avoidance toward the bodily secretions of women.

The Jewish woman also learns that she is supposed to find meaning and satisfaction within the confines of her female role; she is told that the survival of the Jewish people depends on her getting married and having Jewish children. Since the Holocaust, the burden of Jewish survival is felt deeply by many Jews. "Be fruitful and multiply" assumes new meaning when an ethnic group has lost over 6 million members. The responsibility for Jewish survival, being placed on women's reproductive function, directly increases and perpetuates Jewish biases against single women, childless women, and lesbians. The concomitant fear of Jewish annihilation or disappearance also reinforces Jewish attitudes against intermarriage. Some Jewish leaders, educators, and rabbis are beginning to realize that Jewish survival can better be served by welcoming and reaching out to intermarried couples and their children and by making all Jewish women feel more included and visible, instead of driving them away from Judaism by strict adherence to sexist practices.

The pressure to reproduce does not, in Jewish law or custom, translate into rigid measures or attitudes against abortion or contraception. In Jewish religion, the saving of a life overrides all other religious injunctions, and this concept is applied to the life of the mother rather than the life of the fetus. Although abortion is generally not viewed as the method of choice, the necessity for keeping that option available has been defended by all but the most orthodox fringe. Even among the ultraorthodox, abortion is viewed as an option, but it is reserved for extreme circumstances and to be regulated by male rabbis and physicians.

Food and Food Preparation

The Jewish dietary laws are called laws of kashruth, or keeping kosher. Forbidden foods include pork and pork products as well as all kinds of shellfish. Keeping kosher further requires a separation between meat and milk that involves separate sets of dishes, cookware, and utensils. The observance of these dietary laws comes easily to women who were brought up in a kosher home, but it is complicated, confusing, and intimidating to anyone who comes to it without this background. Like other customs, keeping kosher is practiced on a continuum; individual families make accommodations that may shift over a lifetime and that may seem strange, illogical, or irrational to others. The degree of keeping kosher is often an emotionally loaded issue that can become a bone of contention between partners or between generations.

Traditionally, the Jewish woman carries most if not all the responsibility for keeping a kosher kitchen. Her role in the kitchen thus assumes the additional importance of maintaining Jewish tradition; she is in some sense responsible not only for her family's nutritional well-being, but also for keeping their bodies ritually kosher. Food preparation thus becomes a religious act and a link in the chain that maintains the survival of Jewish customs and the Jewish people.

The laws of kashruth also serve to isolate and divide those who observe from those who do not. The sharing of food becomes an area of complex explanations and negotiations that can easily test good will on both sides and often leads to divisiveness among Jews as well as between Jews and non-Jewish friends and neighbors.

Value Conflicts and Divergences

Klal Israel, the concept of worldwide Jewish community, is imbedded in Jewish consciousness and has been nurtured and maintained throughout the dispersion and exile from the Promised Land. The Jewish family is viewed as central to the survival of Klal Israel in a non-Jewish and usually anti-Jewish world. The development of the individual takes place in the context of family and community. Concepts of separation and individuation, though espoused by many if not most Jewish therapists, are essentially alien and in conflict with Jewish community-centered and family-centered values. Because Jewish mothers bear most of the burden of transmitting Jewish values within the home, and because these values, or their divergence from "American" values, are not talked about, Jewish mothers often get blamed for the ensuing value conflict or confusion. In therapy terms they are often labeled as overprotective, enmeshed, or clinging .

The divergence of values that many therapists fail to notice when working with Jewish clients also reflects and takes place in the context of a much broader lack of information and acknowledgment of Jewish customs and Jewish values in a non-Jewish environment. Non-Jews and some Jews are frequently unaware of the pervasively non-Jewish nature of their customs and assumptions, and the general absence of attention to Jewishness in their midst, even within the most progressive or liberal American communities, in which Jews have never been overtly oppressed or persecuted. The term "Judeo-Christian," so loosely and frequently applied to Western culture, is but one example of commonly used phrases or assumptions that imply a false sense of unity between Jewish and Christian traditions. Such language erases the differences and denies the differential power structure between the dominantly Christian majority culture and the Jewish minority culture. Jewish women often find themselves in situations where their Jewishness is overlooked. When that happens, we feel the way many women feel when men make generalizations and assumptions based on male experience or the way many gays and lesbians feel when heterosexuals make assumptions that exclude homosexuals.

Jews who seem to fit into the host culture or to pass, are often falsely assumed not to be very Jewish anymore. Another false assumption is that being Jewish should not make any difference, just as being a woman should not make any difference in male environments. Yet it does make a difference. A Jewish woman who does not observe any Jewish holidays, may still be uncomfortable when you wish her a Merry Christmas, for Christmas is not her holiday. And a Jewish mother raising a child in this environment has a difficult task figuring out what to teach her child about coping and surviving in an environment that does not positively recognize the Jewishness of her child.

Jew Hating and Jew Baiting

Expressions of anti-Jewish sentiments abound in non-Jewish environments, as does cultural illiteracy about Jewish culture and beliefs. Anti-Semitism ranges from overt persecution and annihilation to the much more subtle and covertly insidious forms that are more commonly found in North America. Casual references that assume inclusivity are commonly made about Christmas, Easter, New Year, Jesus, your church, church-going, and the like. Christian symbols are used in public places and ham is served at public gatherings; meetings and conferences are scheduled on the Jewish Sabbath or Jewish Holy Days; and public schools or colleges make insufficient or no preparations to assure that Jewish students will not be disadvantaged by school being open on Jewish Holy Days. When generalized statements are made that assume everyone to be Christian, the exclusion of Jews is similar to the exclusion of homosexuals when statements are made assuming everyone to be heterosexual.

Therapists and feminists are not immune to prejudice and need to become more aware of their participation in anti-Jewish behaviors and attitudes. Some anti-Semitism is directed specifically against Jewish women who end up being undefended within the Jewish community as well as among their feminist sisters.

Jewish women are exposed to a combined form of misogyny and anti-Semitism, indulged in by both Jews and non-Jews, through the supposedly harmless jokes about the Jewish American princess, the JAP, and earlier jokes about the Jewish mother (Beck, 1990; Siegel, 1986). *Lilith* magazine drew attention to *"JAP" Bating on Campus* with their lead articles (Chayat, 1987; Rubenstein, 1987; Schnur, 1987). JAP baiting on college campuses had by then reached alarming proportions and turned into overt harassment of female Jewish students before any action was taken by college authorities or the Jewish community.

This level of anti-Semitism would not have been tolerated by Jews had it been directed at Jewish men, and this level of violence against women would probably not have been tolerated by feminists, had it been directed at non-Jewish women. At feminist gatherings, Jewish women are often subsumed under white women, perceived as being equally privileged, only perhaps more loud and pushy. When diversities are explored, Jewish women often have difficulty being perceived as oppressed as well as privileged. Although often present in large numbers, Jewish women have trouble raising their own issues and concerns; they have too often been met with rejection and denial when they have tried, and have learned to keep silent (Siegel & Cole, 1990). One could say that Jewish women collude in their own oppression with their silence, but one could also say that their non-Jewish feminist sisters have a responsibility to examine each incident or behavior that falls short of recognizing the needs of Jewish women, and to create an environment in which it is safe for Jewish women to speak.

Unfortunately Jewish women have learned that they cannot automatically rely on such safety within women's gatherings. Pogrebin (1991) reported on the Jew-hating, directed at Jewish women, which erupted at the United Nations International Women's Decade Conferences in Mexico City in 1975 and in Copenhagen in 1980. Jewish women were called paranoid when they came home and tried to tell their stories. Pogrebin (1991) writes: "I cannot think of any feminist context in which a woman's testimony—whether about sexism or racism—would be disregarded or labeled 'female paranoia.' Why the gap when women speak bitterness about anti-Semitism?" (p. 206).

Hope for the Future

Jewish women have made great strides in the past two decades in claiming the right to participate in all religious functions and to take positions of authority and leadership in the Jewish community. Jewish women have become rabbis, cantors, and scholars, and have collaborated with non-Jewish religious feminists in transforming traditional texts, rewriting traditional prayer language, and creating new prayers and new rituals. Jewish women are creating their own prayer groups, study groups, and Rosh Hodesh (new moon) groups. They are exploring new rituals (Adelman, 1986; Levine, 1991), expanding Jewish scholarship (Heschel, 1983; Plaskow, 1990), and searching ancient sources for traces of female rituals and goddess worship. Jewish women are also in the process of making their Jewish issues more visible among feminists. They are integrating Jewish and feminist values, each in her own way, and applying these synthesized values to the personal and political work that is meaningful to each.

Counseling Issues

In counseling Jewish women, the therapist, Jewish or non-Jewish, needs first of all to examine her own biases toward Jews in general and toward Jewish women or certain kinds of Jewish women. The therapist also has a responsibility to inform herself about this particular client's specific Jewish background and to pay attention to the Jewish aspects of her client's life. Furthermore, the therapist would do well to remember that a particular personal trait or family pattern could be based on a history of Jewish oppression or on a Jewish value system that may be in discord with dominant "American" values or even with what current psychological theory considers normal or healthy. In the process of healing, the therapist needs to assist the Jewish client in sorting out and naming those aspects of her Jewish heritage that are valuable to her, as well as naming the oppressive aspects. The Jewish client can then focus on how she can best use that information. The therapist who is well informed about the issues of Jewish women can be a valuable resource in the client's search for a positive and informed Jewish identity.

CHRISTIANITY AND THE PSYCHOLOGY OF WOMEN

According to much Christian theology, humankind is made in the image of God, the divine creator, who is all-powerful and usually conceived of as male or Father. Some interpreters insist that woman was derivative and therefore created to be inferior to man. Original perfection is believed to have been marred by woman having introduced sin into the world. Although Jesus treated and regarded women as equal in all respects, later church leaders returned to earlier patriarchal treatment of women as inferior and needing guidance and protection. Although official doctrine declares that all people can be reconciled to God through acceptance of Jesus as the son of God and personal commitment to a life of obedience to the Bible, in effect, in most Christian religious groups, women must still struggle to be recognized as eligible to exercise the same spiritual gifts and offices as men.

Women's Position in Catholic Churches

In Roman Catholicism women are not permitted to hold priestly offices, because they are believed not to appropriately represent the maleness of Jesus Christ. Throughout the centuries of Catholicism, the worship of Mary developed, in which all the feminine attributes of God plus the attribution of asexuality came to be associated with the earthly mother of Jesus. Thus there developed for women a choice between emulating Mary, through a total lifelong commitment to avoiding sexuality and separating oneself from the world, or following in the steps of sinful Eve, and earning salvation from the sin of sexuality by producing babies as new members for the Church. The emphasis for most women is on suffering, self-sacrifice, and guilt coupled with fear that enough is never quite enough when it comes to laying down one's life as Christ did. The only way of escape for many women who did not want to repeat the life pattern of motherhood was to be "called of God" to serve as a nun. Many women religious throughout church history have had opportunities, even within the patriarchal superstructure, to develop their talents and abilities, and even to exercise considerable power and influence over both men and women.

Early in church history, the Eastern Orthodox Church split with Roman Catholicism; many countries today have their own version of Orthodox churches, which have differing rituals, traditions, and teachings that reflect the country or culture. Despite being limited to some extremely patriarchal, restrictive, and proscriptive roles, women have nevertheless been a very powerful force within these churches in maintaining a cultural heritage, especially among groups that have been transplanted to other countries.

Women in "Mainline" Protestant Churches

Protestant churches stress each individual's relationship to God, but the writings of early Protestant leaders made it clear that women were subject to men. In the twentieth-century United States, however, especially in "mainline" Protestant churches, such as Episcopalian, Presbyterian, and Methodist, there has been considerable emphasis on various social justice issues and an increasing awareness of the importance of the role of women. Most of these churches now grant full participation to women, and most have reluctantly begun to ordain women to the clergy. Still remaining to be fully included however are lesbians and gays, the differently abled, and, in many church communities, those whose cultural or socioeconomic background is not white or middle-class. These "socially acceptable" churches, often at the heart of political as well as religious respectability in many communities, have been continuously losing membership over the past two decades.

Women in Fundamentalist and Pentecostal Churches

Also within the Protestant sector of Christendom are those churches generally referred to as fundamentalist, which claim to be based on a literal interpretation of a divinely inspired, inerrant Bible. Central to their theology is a personal and individual salvation experience, in which one admits one's utter sinfulness and inability to live a good life and accepts the offer of reconciliation with a wrathful God through the substitutionary death of Jesus, God's son. Thus, one is allowed to enter into "fellowship" with other members of the church; continued acceptance by this group is predicated on behaviors consistent with their particular version of Christian living.

In his book, *The Dangers of Growing Up in a Christian Home* (1986), Donald Sloat described the typical home of Christians who have made the commitment to this lifestyle paramount in their lives. The man is seen as the ruler in home and church life; wives and children not properly submissive come under censure or punishment. Sloat states that "Parents use scripture and God to control their children, avoid personal responsibility for their behavior, and justify negative child rearing practices" such as beating their children (p. 85). He also notes that certain personality types who desire power gravitate to churches that assign and socially sanction the almost limitless power of husbands over wives and children, as well as pastors over their whole congregation. This is especially true in small, independent churches.

Pentecostalism, another Protestant variation, best known by the largest denomination within that group, the Assemblies of God, emphasizes personal salvation followed by the receiving of the power of the Holy Spirit, through which people demonstrate various gifts and sometimes unusual behaviors. These churches emphasize emotional experiences more than cognition, in contrast to the fundamentalists, and vary a great deal in their attitudes toward women, although most teach a female submission to male leadership both in the home and in the church. Women are generally allowed to "exercise their gifts" more readily in these churches than in the fundamental ones, some of which still require women to wear dresses, keep their heads covered, and never speak in the church.

Positive Aspects of Religion in the Lives of Christian Women

This chapter paints a rather bleak picture of women in the Christian church. Why, then, is it that women appear to be the mainstay of most churches? To understand one aspect of this phenomenon, we need to look at nineteenth-century U.S. history. Historians have referred to "the cult of true womanhood" as an almost sacred ideal to which most became dedicated (MacHaffie, 1986):

> Reversing the traditional view of women as prone to sin, they were idealized as paragons of virtue and piety while men were cast in the role of sensuous beasts. Because of her moral purity, the true woman was given formidable tasks in safeguarding the social order of the new American republic. . . . Religion became an integral part of the domestic sphere over which women were to reign. Women were viewed as imitators of Christ. . . . Some men pursued wealth and prestige, often in very non-Christian ways, yet they continued to profess belief in the importance of traditional moral and religious values. They may have quieted their consciences by assigning to women those areas of life they held dear but treated lightly. (pp. 94-95)

In some ways, the feminine mystique of the 1950s represented a return to this philosophy.

Religious rituals and cultural traditions help people maintain a sense of place and security in the face of stress and societal upheaval. Many women are quite aware of and comfortable with their roles in helping maintain stability during such times. Moreover, the immersion in religious acts, words, and images in early childhood has proven to be permanent and very impervious to later, more cognitively derived religious beliefs (Pratt, 1950). Thus, depending on whether one is exposed to affirming God images, religious traditions can be very positive and sustaining.

There are other strengths of various religious traditions. Most recognize the importance of a community of people with shared beliefs who can support and encourage one another, the importance of a higher power to giving meaning and purpose to life, and models of heroic historic characters who miraculously or with great courage were able to overcome tremendous obstacles in life. Many women report significant and empowering spiritual experiences that provide individual life sustenance in spite of the institutionalized patriarchy.

Throughout church history, and certainly within the recent history of the United States, women who have been very strong in their Christian faith have been at the forefront of various peace and justice campaigns. In the last century, for example, Elizabeth Cady Stanton (1895-98), who compiled *The Women's Bible*, and Sojourner Truth, both women of strong faith, led many women and men in the abolition and women's suffrage movements. Other outstanding women of that time, including Lucretia Mott, Phoebe Palmer, Aimee McPherson, Mary Baker Eddy, Alma White, and Frances Willard, the director of the Women's Christian Temperance Union, led various religious groups. Today, Mother Theresa is a model of Christian faith in action, as are many women who work in soup kitchens, welcome battered children and pregnant teens into their homes, lobby, write, and stand as witnesses against injustice wherever it is found, even within the church itself.

Some Negative Aspects

Many negative influences on the psychological development of women have been experienced in Christian churches. Although many of the following traits can be seen in all women who are victims of oppression and abuse, they commonly appear among Christian women.

Fear.   At the core of the faith is the fear of death. The belief in an eternal life of reward and joy helps dispel some of this fear, but it is replaced by an anxiety lest one lose one's "salvation." The prospect of being judged at the end of life by a male God, with a male Jesus at his side telling him who is and who is not deserving, based on their obedience (sometimes interpreted as suffering and self-sacrifice to the males they are to serve), keeps many women in continuous fear. This may take the form of fearful people-serving and a lack of development of the self. Many fundamentalists have been taught to fear psychology as the word of the devil, talking to or believing anyone outside their church, their own thoughts and imaginations, and virtually everything and everyone "in the world," which belongs to Satan.

Caregiving and guilt.   Marshall (1985), writing in the *Journal of Psychology and Christianity*, described the tremendous obstacle to growth that occurs because of what she describes as the primary Christian virtue for women: the role of caregiver. This role places on women the responsibility for everyone's happiness and assigns tremendous guilt to women who are not able to make everything and everyone turn out okay. The risk of self-definition and the fear of potential conflict if a woman takes herself out of the role of universal caregiver serve to keep many women, and consequently their families, enmeshed and unable to grow as individuals. Some groups rely very heavily on instilling feelings of guilt for minor infractions or even wayward thoughts. Those burdened with heavy loads of guilt become easy prey for various cults that emphasize earning acceptance through self-denial.

Powerlessness.   In patriarchal institutions women have been relegated to powerlessness, and within churches women may be taught that this is God-ordained. Many Christian women have learned that they were designed as weak creatures. Such helplessness not only leads to their victimization but also precludes their learning how to exercise judgment and to take responsibility for decision making. It is impossible to "war against God" without encountering a great deal of anxiety and external resistance, which has often been the case with feminist theologians who have dared to challenge these institutions.

Isolation.   Although many women feel isolated from one another, many religious women belong to sects that keep them physically isolated from the general culture in a way in which other women are not. In some groups, for example, all media, reading material, and social contact are restricted to those that are approved by the male leadership. Women may not be allowed to work outside the home or have friends outside the church. There is also a growing trend to keep these women busy "home-schooling" their children, so that the children do not learn about the wider culture. Church meetings sometimes take up several nights each week, providing some contact with others, but the content of conversation and thought is very carefully prescribed. Although these extremes are practiced by only a small minority of Christians, the isolating practices of even the more traditional religions are seen by outsiders to be anachronistic and irrelevant to life in today's culture.

Dualistic thinking.   Christian philosophical thought grew out of Neo-Platonism, with its emphasis on the dualism of "reality," emphasizing mind over body, man over nature, and woman as the embodiment of all that is inferior. Christianity is dominated by dualistic thinking, making it difficult to pursue any issues of cognitive complexity or problematic morality. Consequently, the church usually chooses one side of every complex issue and declares that it occupies the moral high ground, making it then mandatory and sometimes a test of salvation for all "true believers."

This tendency to dichotomize pervades most major political issues in the United States. Complex problems such as abortion, AIDS, heterosexism, pornography, welfare, child care, family life, sexual abuse, wife battering, workplace discrimination, racism, nationalism, and classism tend to be reduced in Christian rhetoric to God's way versus "man's way" or right versus wrong. All of these issues have a deep impact on women, who must live out the complexity of real-life situations in everyday relationships where doctrines and theologizing seem very remote and intangible. While women may be silenced and revictimized by this system, they are simultaneously used by male policy makers in waging their lobbying, petitions, sit-ins, and politically expedient campaigns to retain their own political and economic power.

The Impact of Feminism on Biblical Theology

Throughout the history of organized religious institutions, patriarchy has used God-talk and male-dominated interpretations of the Bible to justify the ravaging of women and the earth. Such theology has been used to justify the murder and persecution of multiple groups of people whose religions, lifestyles, landholdings, or possessions were believed to interfere with the male leadership's view of entitlement. As women and some other persecuted peoples have found voice, new theologies have been constructed. These are based on a reclamation of the concept of liberation and justice for all people, so movingly described but so often overlooked in the Bible. Catholic theologian Rosemary Radford Reuther (1983) describes the God of the Bible, who, when stripped of patriarchal interpretation and language, has always been identified with liberation from bondage and the unification of diverse groups in an egalitarian society. Women, those from various cultures, the abused, AIDS victims, lesbians, gay men, children, and other groups oppressed by Christianity are beginning to reclaim this lost heritage. Beginning with new translations of the Bible that reclaim the original languages from the patriarchal assumptions of a male God, to the creation of *An Inclusive Language Lectionary* (1987), women are beginning to establish their place in Christian theology and practice.

What happens, then, when women begin to construct or reconstruct their own theology? A significant collaboration between Christian and Jewish feminists occurred when Carol Christ and Judith Plaskow coedited *Womanspirit Rising: A Feminist Reader in Religion* (1979). They describe two strands of feminist theology. One school usually referred to as reformist theologians, speak of an egalitarian or sex-transcendent God. Much of their research is devoted to redeeming from sacred writings, history, and religious traditions, that which they believe to be the truth of an egalitarian god who has been wrongly interpreted through patriarchal theology. Examples of such Christian theologians would be Elisabeth Schussler Fiorenza (1984), Rosemary Radford Reuther (1983), Letty Russell (1985), David Scholer (1986), and Phyllis Trible (1978). Jewish feminist thologians within the reformist tradition include Aviva Cantor (1987), Susannah Heschel (1983), and Judith Plaskow (1990). Some call themselves biblical feminists, referring to their affirmation of the authority of the Bible, though recognizing the effects of patriarchal distortions and mistranslations. Among African American Christian women, Luisah Teish (1989), a Yuroba priestess, and Deborah Williams (1989) are reclaiming a sense of spiritual connection with ancestors and proclaiming womanist theology based on concepts of survival as well as community building and maintenance.

On the other hand, another important strand of feminist theology looks for models of a female ascendent deity or spirituality. Such theologians as Mary Daly (1973) have rejected the traditions and biblical texts as hopelessly patriarchal and are constructing new theological formulations. Others, such as Zsuzsanna Budapest (1979), Starhawk (1979, 1989), and Merlin Stone (1976), have gone back to prebiblical, pre-Hebraic mythology to the early goddesses to rekindle new patterns of spirituality for women. Dhyani Ywahoo (1989) describes the value of Native American ritual and tradition for reclaiming a unity with the land and the universe as a prerequisite to ecological social action.

Feminist theologian Elisabeth Schuessler Fiorenza, in *Weaving the Visions: New Patterns in Feminist Spirituality* (Plaskow & Christ, 1989), writes about feminist pressures to reject all biblical religion as hopelessly sexist to the core, and hence irrelevant to the spiritual development of contemporary women. Such, a position in her eyes,

> too quickly concedes that women have no authentic history within biblical religion and too easily relinquishes women's feminist biblical heritage. Nor can such a stance do justice to the positive experiences of contemporary women within biblical religion. . . . Insofar as biblical religion is still influential today, a cultural and social feminist transformation of Western society must take into account the Biblical story and the historical impact of the biblical tradition. Western women are not able to discard completely and forget our own personal, cultural, or religious Christian history. We will either transform it into a new liberating future or continue to be subject to its tyranny whether we recognize its power or not. (p. 34)

Clinical Issues

When a therapist works with women coming from a strong Christian faith tradition, it is important to determine the underlying fears and anxieties that support various strongly held religious views. Those accustomed to talking in religious language may have difficulty articulating their thoughts or feelings in any other way. Therefore, before introducing new interpretations or challenging assumptions, care should be taken to discover and address the underlying issues. However, those with a strong tradition of dependence on the scriptures as the only source of "truth" will need a counselor who is well versed in the texts that have generally been used to keep women in subjection. Promotion of contact with other women, listening and telling stories, reading feminist theology for themselves, and rereading the Bible with a liberation perspective can be utilized in therapy to provide hope, affirmations of persons as wholes, processes of growth and change, survival strategies, and powerful female role models. As women begin to trust their own experiences and thoughts as truth, Jesus' words, "The truth shall set you free," can give courage.

HINDU IDEOLOGY, CUSTOMS, AND OPPRESSION

Like most religions Hinduism provides answers to questions about the nature of divinity and life after death. It also offers detailed guidance as to how its followers should conduct their ethical and social lives. Hinduism is more than a religion; it is a way of life. Many of the traditions and customs that are essentially oppressive can be traced to Hindu religious and social laws. For almost three thousand years Hinduism has believed in a divinely ordained, stratified system of social classes called varnas, which are further divided into castes. Each caste has its own norms of conduct. Hinduism believes that the four class/varna system is essential to the preservation of the social order. As well, for centuries there has existed a group of people—the untouchable—who are ranked below the lowest caste. Despite the 1950 Indian constitution that outlawed untouchability and guaranteed civil liberties to all groups, there exist many groups of people in India who are denied their fundamental civil rights.

The most oppressed members of these groups are women. They are twice oppressed: by virtue of their membership in an oppressed group and by virtue of their being women. This oppression is expressed by restricting women's movement and decision making, by controlling both their access to economic resources and their choice and conditions of labor, and by regulating sexuality. This denial of civil rights and oppression is legitimized through ideology and custom. Besides addressing itself to social order as a whole, Hinduism also addresses itself to the preservation of the family. The traditional family is a joint family, with the male head of the household having absolute authority over all members and family property. This concentration of power has the potential for extreme oppression within the family. Within Hinduism marriage is indissoluble, even before consummation, and there is no widow remarriage. Divorce and widow remarriage are rare, despite legislative attempts to modify what are essentially religious dictates.

Ideology and Custom

As Maritza Montero (1990) asserts, ideology is both a system of cognitive processes and a system of social meanings that evolve when unequal groups interact. She goes on to explain that within a particular ideological construct are subsumed a variety of behaviors which "considered separately, describe individual reactions to . . . stressful situations, oppression, discrimination, and other aversive environments. When people think about such environments within the constraints of ideological frameworks, they are prone to accept unfairness, discrimination . . . as due to the natural and proper functioning of society" (p. 46).

Ideology serves as the overarching construct that legitimizes a people's behavior. It mediates the understanding of both the victim and the victimizer, so they see their world, laws, and customs as fair and equitable.

To understand the impact of ideology and tradition on the Indian woman, it is important to understand the concept of womanhood as proposed by Hindu ideology and popularized by the mass media. This ideological concept of the ideal woman, embodied by the women in the epics Ramayan and Mahabharat, is broadly accepted and is in turn translated into various customs and traditions. According to Hindu ideology, a woman's means to salvation and fulfillment lies with her husband (Dhruvrajan, 1990). This ideology translates as subordination of women by men, for only by serving her husband diligently and putting him above all else will a woman find meaning in life. According to Dhruvrajan (1990) the underlying premise of this ideology is that women are considered ritually pollutable and lacking in physical strength and will power, whereas men are believed to be ritually pure and physically and emotionally strong. Therefore, in keeping with this premise, for life to proceed in an orderly fashion a man, who is by nature pure and rational, should be in control of a woman, who is by nature pollutable and irrational.

This ideology serves to camouflage injustice and inequality and transform oppressive social structures into acceptable social norms. The conceptual framework of a given ideology helps explain this oppression. In the case of the Indian woman it helps explain how she is able to accept what to others appears to be an untenable situation. It is not that she is incapable of understanding her situation, but rather that her reality is mediated by ideological constraints.

Restricting Freedom of Movement

A crucial aspect of Indian women's oppression is their restriction of movement. A woman's movement is determined by the men in the family; women, through force of tradition and religious ideology, have come to regard these restrictions as acceptable and even desirable (Horowitz & Kishwar, 1984). This orientation is strengthened by the fact that disregarding these restrictions could lead to a loss of respectability, not only for the woman who disregards them, but for her entire family (Kishwar, 1984a; Marker cited in Dankelman & Davidson, 1988). The idealized women of the epics were chaste not just in deeds, but in thoughts as well; one way to ensure that Indian women emulate this idealized chastity is to limit their access to the public world.

Restriction of movement and segregation of women is also considered a mark of higher social status and respectability. This restriction and seclusion operates in different ways and at various levels. It may be expressed as physical segregation. This could mean restricting the woman to certain parts of the house or to the family compound, or it could be instituted through establishing segregated wards in hospitals, segregated schools and colleges, and segregated compartments on public transportation. Restriction and seclusion may be expressed as social segregation (i.e., limited social contacts and interactions). A woman may be allowed to interact only with specified family members or only with female colleagues at school or work.

Finally, restriction and seclusion may be expressed in terms of how the female body is covered and clothed. A woman may be expected to be in complete purdah (i.e., covered from head to toe with netting over the eye area to allow her to see), or she may be required to cover herself with a dupatta, a large scarf draped over her shoulders and breasts and sometimes covering her head and part of her face (Kishwar, 1984a; Marker cited in Dankelman & Davidson, 1988).

Restriction of movement and freedom are differently experienced by women of different social classes. For the poor rural woman there is less distinction between the public and private spheres. This blurring between work and home leads to less restriction of movement but at the same time leads to inhumanly long working hours. She works both in the fields and at home and this can mean fifteen to seventeen hours a day of hard physical labor (Brahme, 1984). For the middle-class woman, the distinction between private and public spheres is much clearer, and her restriction of movement is defined by this distinction and expressed in terms of separation of home from schools, colleges, and work. These public institutions mirror the restrictions placed on women by families. Colleges and schools place strict curfews and restrictions on female students. Kishwar (1984a) describes how female students are restricted from stepping outside the college or school compounds; when they are permitted to leave on outings, restrictions are placed in terms of time and activities and chaperoning is required.

With such stringent restriction of movement comes not only loss of control, but also loss of access to information and ability to function in the public domain. With such restriction of movement women are dependent on men. Men have access to information; they also have knowledge and ability to function in the public domain; this allows them to control women. Restricting women's movement is a very powerful mechanism for engendering a sense of powerlessness and helplessness in women.

Restricted Access to Economic Resources and Labor

Because India is a secular state, it ensures the existence of different religious ways of life. This, as Dhruvrajan (1990) noted, places private, family life under the purview of religion,whereas public life ostensibly comes under secular law. In India the family structure is patriarchal. This structure is supported by religious ideology that contends that men are by nature rational and should therefore have control of women, who are not. This ideology supports males as heads of households. As the head of the household, the male is the owner of family income, family land, and other economic assets; women have no control over economic assets, their labor, or their income. Whether a woman will be allowed to work outside of the home is determined by the male head of the household. As Kishwar (t984a) explains, "This makes women's situations in many ways similar to that of a bonded laborer because, like others in bondage, women perform crucial services for society, but they do not have the freedom to decide the conditions of their own labor" (p. 234).

Despite the Hindu Succession Act of 1955, which gave women the right to inherit parental property, women have in reality limited access to property. Loopholes in the act enable both the private and the public spheres to ignore the act and deny women their right to own property. As Kishwar (1984a) noted, when the government confers land to a disadvantaged group, it does so to the male heads of the household. In a predominantly agriculture-based society, where land is a major economic resource, the social structures that deny a woman ownership of the land contribute to her economic bondage.

This tradition that disallows women's ownership of land is further protected by the custom of dowry. Dowries provide a family with economic and moral justification for denying a woman the right to own land. The giving of dowry preempts the daughter's rights to her share of the land, thereby preventing her husband from making a claim on her behalf. In addition, dowry causes a family to view a female child as an economic liability and a male child as an economic asset. This is because the dowry, though provided in the name of the daughter, is given to her husband and his family. The woman is therefore economically dependent on the male and at the bottom of economic hierarchy both before and after her marriage.

This economic dependence, legitimized by ideology and tradition, is reinforced by legal and governmental institutions. Kishwar (1984b) notes that a married woman requires her husband's signature to apply for a passport. Ration cards are issued in the husband's name. Custody as well as adoption procedures are biased in favor of the male. Thus the patriarchal family structure, which requires a hierarchial relationship of male dominance and female subordination, is supported by ideology and custom and contributes to women's economic dependence and helplessness.

Restrictions on Sexuality

The economic, political, religious, and cultural systems that view a husband as a woman's only means of salvation, place a great deal of pressure on a family to get its daughters married early. This, together with the ideology of *kanyadaan*—a view that holds that a girl is a gift to be presented by the father to the husband—tends to promote marriage as the ultimate goal of a girl's existence. A girl is considered *parayadhan*, someone else's belonging. Therefore, the sooner she is handed over to her rightful owner in an undamaged state, the better. "There is a deep-rooted cultural fear of having a grown-up, unmarried daughter capable of bearing children on one's hands, and a great urge to get her married at any cost and as soon as possible" (Kishwar, 1984a, p. 9). A great emphasis is placed on an unmarried woman's virginity. This leads to marriage at an early age and serves as an effective control for women's sexuality. A woman who has been raped or sexually molested is often disowned by her father or husband. This restricts women's mobility. These factors, when combined with the patrilocal tradition (i.e., a tradition that dictates that a girl has to marry outside her own village and move to her husband's home), ensure that a girl will feel completely dependent on her husband's family. The patrilocal tradition that serves to loosen a girl's ties with her parental family also denies her access to emotional and day-to-day support. This lack of support makes the transition from adolescence to adulthood more difficult for the girl. At the same time it ensures her husband's control over her behavior and, should the marriage break down, it leaves her vulnerable to maltreatment.

Transformed Images of Women

Though feminist thinkers analyzing Indian ideology recognize that traditional Hindu religion plays a major role in the oppression of women (Dhruvrajan, 1990), they have not as yet revised the scriptures, reinterpreting the traditional texts with the goal of restoring a sense of power to women. In part this could be due to the urgency of other issues such as the physical safety of women. Women's deprivation in terms of food allocation and health care makes them vulnerable to illness and death. This concern together with dowry murders and bride burning have been the focus of the feminist movement in India (Kishwar, 1984b, 1987). Therefore, although the scriptures have been examined for their impact on cultural traditions and for their role in normalizing practices that are oppressive to women, there has not been to date a feminist revision of the *Ramayan* or the *Mahabharat*.

The Sita of the Ramayan is a powerful role model for women. She is traditionally portrayed as self-effacing and subservient, but as Kishwar (1984b) has noted, Gandhi was able to transform this age-old symbol of a subservient Sita into a woman of power who was able to maintain her self-respect and integrity both in her relationship with her husband and during her captivity. Gandhi also transformed Mirabai, a religious poetess, into a woman who was able to face down her persecutors while rejecting the traditional roles of wife and mother. Gandhi was able to use these transformed symbols of womanhood to inspire women to join the freedom movement that eventually led to India's independence in 1947. The transformations effected by Gandhi were not sustained, and the old ideology took root again. However, Gandhi's efforts point to the fact that the traditional scriptures and texts have within them tremendous potential to combat practices oppressive to women. As feminists begin to reconstruct these symbols of womanhood, Indian women will be able to overcome the destructive traditions while retaining their cultural and spiritual heritage.

Understanding the cultural traditions and the ideologies that support these traditions serves two purposes: it expands our understanding of the Indian woman's condition, and it sensitizes us to the issues an Indian woman struggles with when she moves into a Western culture.

Issues Regarding Intervention with Immigrant Indian Women

When working with immigrant Indian women in North America it is important to address a number of factors such as gender, ethnicity/race, and whether the women are recent, first-, or second-generation immigrants. The immigrant Indian woman has to struggle with conflict between her own norms and majority group norms. If she has children, she is confronted with the issue of raising children whose beliefs may be in conflict with her own. Subsequent generations may shift in focus to intergenerational and intrafamilial conflict. The immigrant woman may find herself trying to preserve her ethnic identity and culture—a culture that is also a source of oppression and restriction. At the same time she may find herself trying to incorporate Western traditions which, though they offer greater personal freedom, are also subtly or overtly racist and rejecting. In this sense the Indian woman is caught between two worlds, neither of which is totally accepting and supportive.

Although there is considerable literature that addresses the concerns of cross-cultural counseling, there is little that addresses the specific issues of working with immigrant Indian women. It is important for the Indian woman to understand the traditions and ideologies that influence her worldview, as well as the problems these traditions may pose. To deny the former would be to reject her cultural identity, and to deny the latter would be to accept cultural oppression. Once she has some understanding of the cultural assumptions that shape and influence her identity, she can begin to integrate and reject aspects of her ethnic culture as well as those of the Western culture. Then she can share this understanding with other women. This will enable non-Indian women to understand her better and help other Indian women deal with issues of racism and sexism.

FEMINIST SPIRITUALITY TODAY

Although Hindu women have been primarily concerned with how religious ideology is interpreted and its effect on the safety and survival of Indian women, they have as yet paid little attention to the language of prayer or to feminist interpretations of religious texts. Christian and Jewish women, however, are experiencing a creative wave of feminist thinking, writing, and practice in areas of women's religion and spirituality. They are engaged in the process of applying feminist analysis to their religious traditions, feminizing existing prayers and rituals, reimagining religious texts to include women, finding evidence of early woman-centered and goddess worshiping religions, reclaiming goddess rituals, and creating new rituals. Women of different faiths and different religious traditions are also beginning to speak together and to write and create together (Goldenberg, 1979; Mollenkott, 1987; Christ & Plaskow, 1979), as we are in this chapter.

Imagine a religion based on truly egalitarian principles and practices and stripped of those aspects that are oppressive to women. Women could find in such a religion a possible and potential source of moral teaching, spiritual enrichment, life-affirming rituals, communal and cooperative action, communal caring, and relationship-centered life-span development. Some of us are working toward such goals within our own religions or are creating new forms of worship and community based on egalitarian and cooperative principles.

The spiritual energy of feminist women and the networking and sharing of ideas through discussions and publications are beginning to have a revolutionary impact on established religions. Women's voices are counteracting the alienation of women from each other, as well as the heterosexual agendas, limitations of gender roles, and hierarchical structures of male-dominated and male-defined religions. As in other aspects of women's liberation, women are beginning to be heard in religious institutions. Yet real change is much too slow and sporadic.

CONCLUSION

In the psychology of religion field, gender issues have been largely ignored. However, Jonte-Pace (1985) states that androcentric theologians have succumbed to a primitive or infantile stage of development when they split objects into good and bad. The splitting of the Goddess from male images of God and the delineation of idealized and evil images of woman have been the result. She suggests that our very survival in a world increasingly bent toward destruction might depend on a reintegration of opposites. Maturity in religion, Jonte-Pace proposes, requires an integration of diversity, a tolerance for ambivalence, and compassion for all creation. This can come only when images of God include the "divine feminine" (Mollenkott, 1983), and when the virgin/whore dichotomization of women can be eliminated.

Generally speaking, life crises often challenge existing behaviors and attitudes as well as beliefs and allegiances. Such events can become opportunities to examine one's faith, belief system, or religious practice. Therapists who are well versed in the religious traditions of their clients and who have or are exploring the impact of religion on their own lives as women can be very helpful. They can explore new possibilities with their clients without threatening the faithful or religiously observant woman.

The specific problems experienced by Hindu, Christian and Jewish women differ to the extent that they are culture bound, but the underlying structures that create these problems have much in common. Once we can understand the religiously reinforced patriarchal social and political systems that support the specific oppressions of women, we will be able to stop thinking of women's problems in a specific culture as "other" and extraordinary.

Maltreatment of women is legitimized and accepted in most societies. For the most part, national governments and international political bodies do not recognize and do not offer protection to women who have been maltreated. Some nations are occasionally willing to offer sanctuary to those who are fleeing persecution for reasons of race, religion, or membership in a particular group. The same nations, however, are unwilling to offer sanctuary to women who are persecuted by virtue of being female (Dubois & Ruiz, 1990; Karl, 1983).

To separate and restrict our understanding of women's oppression by culture, country, and religion, is to overlook the socioeconomic, political, and religiously based structure that supports the oppression. These structures are the common theme that bind women across culture and geography. Screened by ideology and custom, these structures restrict and oppress women. Religion, ideology, and custom not only make invisible victims out of women; they also serve to divide women by class and culture, thus making it difficult to perceive the links between gender subordination and oppression based on class and culture. To be able to make those links, we need to involve women from different classes, religions, and ethnic backgrounds.

If feminist critique is to be a critique of women's conditions, there will need to be a diversity within the critique to address the needs of all women. In this chapter, although the three of us have communicated across our diversities and been challenged by it, we have also been very aware that each of us could only speak out of her own experience and knowledge base. We know that a much richer diversity is needed. We hope that our effort might serve as a springboard for broader explorations of the topic.

REFERENCES

Adelman, P. V. (1986). *Miriam's well: Rituals for Jewish women around the year*. Fresh Meadows, N.Y.: Biblio Press.

Baum, C., Hyman, P., & Michel, S. (Eds.) (1976). *The Jewish woman in America*. New York: Dial.

Beck, E. T. (1990). Therapy's double dilemma: Anti-Semitism and mysogyny. In R. J. Siegel & E. Cole (Eds.), *Jewish women in therapy: Seen but not heard* (pp.19-30). New York: Harrington Park Press.

Brahme, S. (1984). The growing burdens of women. In M. Kishwar & R. Vanita (Eds.), *In search of answers: Indian women's voices from Manushi* (pp. 49-62). London: Zed Books.

Budapest, Z. (1979). Self blessing-ritual In C. C. Christ & J. Plaskow (Eds.), *Womanspirit rising* (pp. 269-272). New York: Harper & Row.

Cantor, A. (1987). *The Jewish woman.* New York: Biblio Press.

Chayat, S. (1987, Fall). "JAP" baiting on the college scene. *Lilith. The Jewish Women's Magazine,* pp. 6-7.

Christ, C. C., & Plaskow, J. (Eds.). (1979). *Womanspirit rising: A feminist reader in religion.* New York: Harper & Row.

Daly, M. (1973). *Beyond God the father: Toward a philosophy of women's liberation.* Boston: Beacon Press.

Dankelman, I., & Davidson, J. (1988). *Women and environment in the third world: Alliance for the future.* London: Earthscan Publications.

Dhruvrajan, V. (1990). Religious ideology, Hindu women, and development in India. *Journal of Social Issues, 46*(3), 57-69.

Dubois, E. C., & Ruiz, V. L. (1990). *Unequal sisters.* New York: Routledge.

Eisler, R. (1987). *The chalice and the blade: Our history, our future.* San Francisco: HarperCollins.

Fiorenza, E. S. (1984). Emerging issues in feminist biblical interpretation. In J. L. Weidman (Ed.), *Christian feminism: Visions of a new humanity* (p. 34). New York: Harper & Row.

Giller, B. (1990). All in the family: Violence in the Jewish home. In R. J. Siegel & E. Cole (Eds.), *Jewish women in therapy: Seen but not heard* (pp. 101-109). New York: Harrington Park Press.

Goldenberg, N. (1979). *Changing of the gods: Feminism and the end of traditional religions.* Boston: Beacon Press.

Goodman, F. (1988). *Ecstasy, ritual, and alternate reality.* Bloomington, Ind.: Indiana University Press.

Grossman, S., & Haut, R. (Eds.). (1992). *Daughters of the king: Women in the synagogue: A survey of history, halachah and contemporary reality.* Philadelphia: Jewish Publication Society of America.

Heschel, S. (1983). *On being a Jewish feminist.* New York: Schocken.

Heschel, S. (1990). Jewish feminism and women's identity. In R. J. Siegel & E. Cole, (Eds.), *Jewish women in therapy: Seen but not heard* (pp. 31-39). New York: Harrington Park Press.

Horowitz, B., & Kishwar, M. (1984). Family life—the unequal deal. In M. Kishwar & R. Vanita (Eds.), *In search of answers: Indian women's voices from Manushi* (pp. 69-103). London: Zed Books.

Jonte-Pace, D. (1985). *Goddess, Gods, and object relations theory: Toward a feminist psychology of religion.* Paper presented at the meeting of the American Academy of Religion, Anaheim, Calif.

Karl, M. (1983). Women and rural development: An overview. *Women in development: A resource guide for organization and development*. Geneva: ISIS Women's International Information and Communication Services.

Kaufman, D. R. (1991). *Rachel's daughters: Newly orthodox Jewish women.* New Brunswick, N.J.: Rutgers University Press.

Kaye/Kantrowitz. (1990). The issue is power: Some notes on Jewish women and therapy. In R. J. Siegel & E. Cole, (Eds.), *Jewish women in therapy: Seen but not heard* (pp. 7-18). New York: Harrington Park Press.

Kishwar, M. (1984a). Introduction. In M. Kishwar & R. Vanita (Eds.), *In search of answers: Indian women's voices from Manushi* (pp. 1-41). London: Zed Books.

Kishwar, M. (1984b). Some aspects of bondage. In M. Kishwar & R. Vanita (Eds.), *In search of answers: Indian women's voices from Manushi* (pp. 104-124). London: Zed Books.

Kishwar, M. (1987). The burning Roop Kanwar. *Manushi*, 42-43, 10-13.

Levine, E. R. (Ed.). (1991). *A ceremonies sampler: New rites, celebrations, and observances of Jewish women.* San Diego, Calif.: Woman's Institute for Continuing Jewish Education.

MacHaffie, B. J. (1986). *Her story: Women in Christian tradition.* Philadelphia: Fortress Press.

Marshall, D. (1985). Current issues of women and therapy. *Journal of Psychology and Christianity, 6*(1), 62-72.

Mollenkott, V. (1983). *The divine feminine: Biblical imagery of God as female.* New York: Crossroads.

Mollenkott, V. R. (Ed.). (1987). *Women of faith in dialogue.* New York: Crossroad.

Montero, M. (1990). Ideology and psychosocial research in third world contexts. *Journal of Social Issues, 46*(3), 46-59.

Plaskow, J. (1990). *Standing again at Sinai: Judaism from a feminist perspective.* San Francisco: Harper & Row.

Plaskow, J., & Christ, C. C. (Eds.). (1989). *Weaving the vision: New patterns in feminist spirituality.* New York: Harper & Row.

Pogrebin, L. C. (1991). *Deborah, Golda, and me: Being female and Jewish in America.* New York: Crown.

Pratt, J. B. (1950). *Eternal values in religion.* New York: Macmillan.

Reuther, R. R. (1983). *Sexism and God talk: Toward a feminist theology.* Boston: Beacon Press.

Rubenstein, J. A. (1987, Fall). Confronting the perpetrators—Antisemitism at Syracuse University. *Lilith. The Jewish Women's Magazine*, pp. 8-9.

Russell, L. (1985). *Feminist interpretation of the Bible.* Philadelphia: Westminster Press.

Schnur, S. (1987, Fall). Blazes of truth: When is a JAP not a yuppie? *Lilith. The Jewish Women's Magazine,* pp. 10-11.

Scholer, D. M. (1986). The place of women in the church's ministry. In A. Mickelson, (Ed.), *Women, authority, and the Bible* (pp. 193-224). Downers Grove, Ill.: InterVarsity Press.

Siegel, R. J. (1986). Antisemitism and sexism in stereotypes of Jewish women. *Women & Therapy, 5*(2/3), 249-257.

Siegel, R. J. (in press). Overcoming bias through awareness, mutual encouragement and commitment. In J. Adelman & G. Enguidanos-Clark (Eds.), *Racism in the lives of women: Testimony, theory, and guides to antiracist practice.* New York: Haworth Press.

Siegel, R. J., & Cole, E., (Eds.). (1990). *Jewish women in therapy: Seen but not heard.* New York: Harrington Park Press.

Sloat, D. (1986). *The dangers of growing up in a Christian home.* Nashville: Thomas Nelson.

Starhawk (1979). Witchcraft and women's culture. In C. C. Christ & J. Plaskow (Eds.), *Womanspirit rising* (pp. 259-268). New York: Harper & Row.

Starhawk (1989). Ritual of bonding. In J. Plaskow & C. C. Christ (Eds.), *Weaving the vision* (pp. 326-335). New York: Harper & Row.

Stone, M. (1976). *When God was a woman.* London: Quarter Books.

Teish, L. (1989). Ancestor reverence. In J. Plaskow & C. C. Christ (Eds.), *Weaving the vision* (pp. 87-92). New York: Harper & Row.

Trible, P. (1978). *God and the rhetoric of sexuality.* Philadelphia: Fortress Press.

Williams, D. (1989). Womanist theology. In J. Plaskow & C. C. Christ (Eds.), *Weaving the vision* (pp. 179-186). New York: Harper & Row.

Ywahoo, D. (1989). Renewing the sacred hoop. In J. Plaskow & C. C. Christ (Eds.), *Weaving the vision* (pp. 274-280). New York: Harper & Row.

AUTHORS' NOTE

The three authors collaborated in writing the introductory and concluding sections of this chapter. The section on Jewish women was written by Rachel Josefowitz Siegel, who wishes to thank Rabbi Deborah Brin for her critical reading and constructive comments. "Christianity and the Psychology of Women" was written by Jean H. Orost. The section on Hindu ideology, customs, and oppression was written by Sudha Choldin. Versions of this section were presented at the Canadian Research Institute for the Advancement of Women, 15th Annual Conference, Edmonton, Canada, November 9, 1991, and at the International Council of Psychologists regional meeting in Padua, Italy, July 10, 1992. A panel discussion based on this chapter was presented at the Association for Women in Psychology Annual Conference, Oakland, California, March 1994.

Women and Achievement

Darlene C. DeFour
Michele A. Paludi

In 1986 Paludi and Fankell-Hauser interviewed eighty women, ten each from the following age groups: late teens, twenties, thirties, forties, fifties, sixties, seventies, and eighties. This sample included women who were beginning their careers, who were in the middle of their achievement paths, and who had retired. Also included in this sample were women who were or had not been employed outside the home. Paludi and Fankell-Hauser used the following standardized interview items with each woman:

What, specifically, do you want to accomplish in the next few years?

What specific steps do you plan to take to achieve these goals?

What blocks in yourself will you have to overcome to achieve these goals?

What blocks in the world will you have to overcome to achieve these goals?

How do you feel about the possibility of achieving these goals? Of failing to achieve them?

How do your parent(s) feel about the possibility of your achieving these goals? Of failing to achieve them?

How does your mate feel about your achieving these goals?

How do your children feel about your achieving these goals?

How do your women acquaintances feel about your achieving these goals?

How do your men acquaintances feel about your achieving these goals?

Who, if anyone, are the people (or person) you would like to be like? That is, who are the people you try to model yourself after? Describe the different role models you've had over the course of your life.

Have you ever been in a situation where you were about to succeed at something and wondered if it was worth it or got afraid of the success or something it might produce?[1]

A theme that emerged from the women's responses concerned developmental discontinuities in women's achievement striving. Compared to older women, younger women were more concerned with competitive achievement. Older women (in the fifty to eighty age groups) reported that their achievement striving increased when they were in the "child launching" phase of their relationships. They reported feeling accepted at that stage by both male and female peers and relatives.

Achievement striving was also likely to be characteristic of women whose parents reinforced and encouraged achievement efforts and who were reared in dual-earner families. These women viewed their relationship with their parent(s) as warmer, closer, more sharing, and more supportive than did other women.

The achievement goals identified by women included "having a successful relationship with my mate," "graduating from college," "getting a driver's license," "being a good parent," "being independent," and "becoming self-actualized." In order of most to least concern, the following personal blocks were reported by women as preventing them from reaching their goals: procrastination, lack of self-confidence, fear of meeting/interacting with people, fear of failing, worrying too much, and being a perfectionist. Women also reported blocks in the world that would prevent them from succeeding: lack of

---

[1] Reprinted by permission of Cambridge University Press.

jobs/opportunities, lack of financial aid/social security, sex, age, and other people's opinions (especially their spouse and children).

In women's own voices:

A lot has to do with the environment in which I grew up. My parents were never one to say well you have got to get this grade or we have got to keep up with the Jones or they never—that was not their frame of reference. I brought home all As one time and they said you aren't doing any work and it's true, I wasn't. Success or failure was never measured in the terms that traditionally people think about—like how much money you make or do you have a car or something. My whole upbringing during this time these things were not measures of success or failure. It was more are you an honest person, do you have respect for others, do you care about others, do you care enough about yourself to educate yourself and to learn things and make a contribution and just be a decent person. That is success and failure not any of the more traditional measurements. (p. 95)

I've never been afraid of my successes, although I have succeeded at something and wondered if it was worth it. I can work toward a goal and achieve it and then it's done and I'm proud, but something is always missing. I guess I expect fireworks to go off. I like to succeed at something, but then, on the other hand, it seems like after it's done, it was no big deal after all. (p. 94)

I have to admit I have worried about my family's reaction to my success in an outside situation, necessitated by being out of town for extended periods of time. I decided I cannot do both, so opted for my family's needs/desires to be fulfilled first by me. They have first call upon me now. One most vocal about the situation was my oldest daughter, who consciously seems to feel she'd have to take my place, and she did not want to. I felt it was selfish of me not to finish the job of raising children in the best way I knew how. (p. 94)

In this chapter we will discuss women's achievement and career development. Specifically, we will discuss achievement-related motives and their implications for real-life behaviors. We'll review the personality factors as well as societal factors contributing to individuals' career decisions and work patterns, noting age, gender, and ethnic comparisons. We'll use the interview items presented above to guide our discussion.

WHAT, SPECIFICALLY, DO YOU WANT TO ACCOMPLISH IN THE NEXT FEW YEARS?

Trends over the past twenty-five years and recent statistics suggest the importance of occupational pursuits in the plans and lives of women. The career and life choices women make are stereotypically female occupational fields; the result is occupational sex segregation. For example, among first- and second-graders there has been considerable evidence of gender bias in the kinds of jobs children think about in terms of their future employment (Archer, 1984; Fine, 1987; Franken, 1983). Third- and fifth-grade girls most often select as occupations nurse, teacher, and stewardess, and do not select police officer, truck driver, pilot, and architect (McKay & Miller, 1982). Betz (in press) reported that highly feminine stereotyped activities among third- through seventh-graders included knitting, sewing, selling perfume, and being a secretary. Once set, girls' range of occupations is difficult to change. When they reach high school, many adolescent girls restrict their occupational aspirations. They tend to focus on jobs that bring less status and less money than the jobs that boys think about.

The sex of the actual job holders appears to be one basis of occupational stereotypes (Paludi & Fankell-Hauser, 1986). In fact, high school girls express more interest in traditionally male occupations when they are told that sex ratios will be balanced in the future. The lack of other women in an occupation deters women from aspiring to that occupation (Betz, in press; Betz & Fitzgerald, 1987).

The educational system communicates "appropriate" occupational behaviors for girls and women. Many school systems literally direct girls into different courses by a differential "tracking system," whereby girls are taught to think only in terms of becoming teachers, nurses, and secretaries (Alexander & Cook, 1982). Programs taken in the junior high years funnel girls into traditionally feminine courses (e.g., home economics and typing).

In spite of the fact that sexism is found in many schools and that girls are covertly, if not overtly, treated differently than boys by the educational system, women have many of the same academic goals as men have (Klein, 1992). Women want to learn academic skills that will better prepare them to be self-sufficient and skilled in abilities that could lead to high-paying positions in the labor market, although the fact remains that fewer women than men pursue advanced programs that will lead them into the higher-status and better-paying occupations such as medicine and law (Betz, in press).

According to Betz (in press), by age twenty-nine, the brightest men are beginning to manifest their intellectual potential; the brightest women fall further short of their potential for educational and occupational achievement. Arnold's (as reported in Betz, in press) research also supports this finding. In 1981 forty-six women and thirty-four men who graduated as valedictorians and salutatorians of their Illinois high school classes were interviewed about their career goals and plans. Additional interviews took place in 1984, 1985, and 1988. Results suggested that all but four students (two women; two men) finished college and performed well (mean grade point averages of 3.6 and 3.5 for the women and men, respectively). Arnold reported that gender differences started to emerge immediately after high school. For example, there was a decline in the intellectual self-confidence of women, a persistent concern among women about combining career and family, and differences in the extent and level of planned labor force participation. In fact, six women abandoned the career goal of becoming a physician. Two-thirds of the women valedictorians but none of the men planned to reduce or interrupt their labor force participation for childrearing.

Arnold also reported that women and men valedictorians were pursuing careers in traditionally male areas of science, business, law, medicine, and academia. A substantial proportion of women (but no men) were pursuing traditionally female caregiving or helping professions. Arnold noted that differences in educational and career achievements among the men can be predicted by individual differences in ability, motivation, job experience, and college prestige. The only useful predictor among women is career versus family priorities.

Thus, the workforce will continue to be sex-segregated as most occupations remain dominated by one sex or the other (Betz & Fitzgerald, 1987). In the United States, employed women earn less than 70 percent of men's wages. Black women earn less money than women or men of any ethnic group, and they earn substantially less than do black men (Betz, in press; Smith, 1983). Similar to white women, black women are concentrated in low-paying, stereotypic "feminine" jobs, such as domestic and service jobs. The average employed woman must work nearly eight and a half days to earn as much as the average employed man earns in five. Disparity between women's and men's incomes still exists when job category, education, and experience are taken into account. This salary disparity is in large part due to the cultural belief that men should earn more than women because men are the primary "breadwinners" of the family.

WHAT SPECIFIC STEPS DO YOU PLAN TO TAKE TO ACHIEVE THESE GOALS?

Super (1957) divided individuals' career pathways into five distinct stages:

Growth Stage (birth-14 years)

Exploration Stage (15-24)

Establishment Stage (25-44)

Maintenance Stage (45-64)

Decline Stage (age 65 and older).

Super's major concern was with the manner in which individuals searched for an appropriate occupation: playing at various roles and activities in childhood; assessing needs, abilities, and interests in adolescence; establishing and focusing on the selected vocation in adulthood. He believed that children move from no interest in vocations (0-3 years), to extensive fantasies about careers (4-10 years), to career interests based on likes and dislikes (10-12), to beginning to take ability into account in their career choices (13-14 years). More realistic career choices are made from about fifteen to twenty-four years; the individual often makes an initial vocational commitment and may begin a first trial job in the latter part of the stage.

There is a danger of overinterpretation when considering Super's theory. For example, it does not take into account women's unique career patterns. It is unreasonable to accept Super's assumption that all individuals (especially women) go through a single set of stages in one vocational pathway. Women may participate in several jobs before making a major vocational commitment to one of them. Women are more likely than men to change careers at midlife (Mednick & Thomas, in press), and many first begin to prepare for a career in midlife.

This theory does not address the fact that most women have children for whom they are primarily responsible and thus may need to or want to take some time out from full-time careers for childrearing or to work or go to school part-time. By having only one career pattern in mind (i.e., full-time, uninterrupted work), institutions may essentially eliminate women from many career opportunities.

Ethnic minority women have been more likely to be in the labor force than white women. From 1978 to the present the rate of labor force participation of white women increased much more rapidly than that of ethnic minority women (Mednick & Thomas, in press). The fact that ethnic minority women have participated in the labor force because of financial necessity (rather than or in addition to self-development) is an important contributor to how ethnic minority women view integrating a lifestyle and work roles. In addition, black women are more likely than white women to be unemployed, work in low-paying jobs, and live in poverty (Betz, in press). There is a growing segment of black women who are pursuing careers. In 1981, for example, black women received 60 percent of all college/university degrees awarded to black individuals. However, this advantage for black women drops considerably at the doctoral degree level (Mednick & Thomas, in press).

WHAT BLOCKS IN YOURSELF WILL YOU HAVE TO OVERCOME TO ACHIEVE THESE GOALS?

In this section, some major barriers to individuals' career choices will be reviewed. Barriers are variables leading or related to the tendency to make gender-role stereotypical choices (Betz, in press).

Causal Attributions for Success and Failure

Weiner (1972) proposed a cognitive attribution theory of achievement motivation to explain the differences between high- and low-achievement individuals. This theory regards the differential persistence of high- and low-achieving persons as due to the different attributions they make regarding the causes of their success and failure. According to Weiner, high-achievement individuals take charge of their own achievements; they believe themselves to be the cause of their successes (because of ability and hard work). Low-achievement persons, on the other hand, attribute their successes to external causes (to teachers' mistakes or an easy test) and their failures to internal ones (lack of ability).

Several researchers have studied the self-attributions for the causes of success and failure. Betz (in press), for example, concluded that women were more likely than men to attribute their successes to luck and their failures to low ability. Meta-analyses of the research in this area (e.g., Frieze et al., 1982) suggest that for success men make only slightly more attributions to ability than do women, and women make only slightly more attributions to luck. Explanations for the small effect size in this research concern the manner in which the information was elicited, either causally worded (e.g., "To what extent do you think your performance on this task was caused by luck?") or informationally worded (e.g., "How much ability to perform this task do you think you have?"). Women make more luck attributions to causal questions, but not to information ones.

WHAT BLOCKS IN THE WORLD WILL YOU HAVE TO OVERCOME TO ACHIEVE THESE GOALS?

Performance Evaluation

Deaux and Emswiller (1974) observed that equivalent performances by women and men are not explained by the same attributions. Performance by a man on a masculine task is typically attributed to skill, whereas an equivalent performance by a woman on the same task is seen to be more influenced by luck. Feldman-Summers and Kiesler's (1974) study indicated that men attributed more ability to a male physician than to a female physician. Men also attributed the female physician's success to ease of course and a large amount of effort.

Although the devaluation of women is considered to be well established, it has not always been replicated. The male bias observed in the Goldberg (1968) study has not been replicated with older women who are not college students. In addition, women are as likely to be evaluated as competent as men when their performance is (1) acknowledged by an authoritative individual (Taynor & Deaux, 1975); (2) judged on explicit criteria (Issacs, 1981; Jacobson & Effertz, 1974); (3) judged by unqualified experts in the particular field (Ward, 1981); or (4) successful in male-populated occupations or activities (Taynor & Deaux, 1973).

Perhaps one explanation for the inconsistencies in results concerns individuals' implicit assumptions about femininity and masculinity that are brought with them to research settings. For example, Paludi and Strayer (1985) focused on the interaction of the sex-typing of the task with the sex of the participants in the research. Results of this study suggested that an article written by a man was valued more positively than if the author was not identified as a man. In addition, women and men made assumptions about the sex of an author whose name was ambiguous. Eighty-seven percent of the participants attributed an article on politics to a man and 96 percent attributed an article on the psychology of women to a woman. Explanations given by participants for their decisions about the author's sex centered around stereotypes about femininity and masculinity:

Men are associated with economics, business, and politics.

The author seemed to have insight to the woman's feeling and could relate. I don't think a man would have that kind of insight (p. 358).

Individuals' assumptions about women and femininity are not easily modified in research settings; thus, they probably account for the inconsistency in the results of the research on performance evaluation. Starer and Denmark (1974) found that women made less promale evaluations when they made judgments alone than when in the presence of men. Thus, the sex composition of the group in which the evaluations are made is an important variable. Women in all-women groups endorsed more profeminist ideas after reading articles by women than did women in mixed-sex groups. This research suggests, therefore, that men in groups trigger negative biases against women.

In work settings, men are rated higher than equivalent women in performing certain tasks and job qualifications. Similarly, women receive lower recognition and economic rewards for their work than men, and lower prestige, knowledge, and expertise are attributed to them as well. Widely accepted stereotypes depict men, but not women, as having the requisite skills and characteristics for managerial and leadership positions. Business professionals indicated a strong preference for male applicants for a stereotypically masculine job even when similar information on the résumés of female and male applicants had led to perceptions of similar personality traits (Glick, Zion, & Nelson, 1988). These stereotypes persist even though gender differences were not found in leadership ability or job performance (Doyle & Paludi, 1991).

As a result of male teachers and employers attributing women's successes to luck rather than skill, women's level of aspiration remains low. Therefore, many women never establish any occupational life plan or prepare themselves for a career.

Lack of Child Care Provisions

The majority of women with children work outside the home. The most recent rate of maternal employment for two-parent families with school age children is 71 percent (Hoffman, 1989). In 1987 53 percent of women with children age one and under were in the labor force. This rate is more than double the rate of 24 percent in 1970 (Hoffman, 1989). Black women with school age children are more likely to be employed than white or Hispanic women with children (Reid & Paludi, in press).

The reasons for women working outside the home are related primarily to financial needs and personal self-actualization (Scarr, Phillips, & McCartney, 1989). As a result of the decline in family income from 1973 to 1988, families must have two incomes to support themselves at a level previously achieved by one wage earner. Single, widowed, and divorced women with children must work to try to avoid poverty.

Employed women with children have also reported wanting to work for the social support, adult companionship, and social networks offered by workplaces (Repetti, Matthews, & Waldron, 1989). Hoffman (1989) described employment for mothers as a morale boost and a buffer against the stress of family roles. Research on the impact of maternal employment on children has generally found no negative effects on the children (Hoffman, 1989). Maternal employment appears to have a positive influence on adolescents, particularly daughters. They are more likely to be self-confident, to achieve better grades in school, and to pursue careers themselves (Hoffman, 1984).

Overall, child care researchers have found that when children are in high quality care, there is no negative impact on their emotional adjustment or relationship with their mother (Etaugh, 1984; Hoffman, 1989). Child care has been found to have no negative effects on the intellectual development of children, and may have a positive impact on children from economically disadvantaged homes. The social behavior of children attending day care has been found to show increases in both positive and negative peer-oriented behaviors.

The Department of Labor has estimated that by 1995 women will comprise two-thirds of all new employees (Johnson, 1987). Eighty percent of women are expected to have children during their career path. Despite these statistics, as well as the research that indicates the positive effects of maternal employment and quality day care on children, the United States is still ambivalent about employed mothers and day care. As Scarr, Phillips, and McCartney (1989) stated, "we have a shameful national dilemma: More than 50% of American mothers of infants and preschool children are now in the labor force and require child care services, but there is no coherent national policy on parental leaves or on child care services for working parents" (p. 1404).

This "national dilemma" is unique to the United States. Women in France have a job-protected leave of six weeks before childbirth. Women in Italy have a six-month job-protected leave paid at a flat rate that is equal to the average income for women. They also have available to them an unpaid job-protected leave for one year following this six-month period. In Sweden, parents have the right to a leave following the birth of their children that is paid at 90 percent of one parent's salary for nine months. This is followed by a fixed minimum benefit for an additional three months. Parents also have the option of taking an unpaid, but job-protected leave until their child is eighteen months old. They may also work a six-hour day until their child is eight years old.

In the United States, policies on child care and maternal leave reflect myths about all women's "personality" and career goals, as well as what is involved in caring for infants (Paludi, 1992). In reality, there is wide variation in women's responses to the birth process. Some women (especially midlife women) need an extended rest period following delivery if the pregnancy and/or birth was difficult (Etaugh, 1990). Some women and their babies require three or more months to adjust to a breastfeeding routine. Other women may return to work more quickly.

Traditional occupational policies reflect the separation of family and work life and the societal expectation that mothers remain at home to care for their children. There is thus a general incompatibility between the workplace and family demands, as well as the relative lack of provisions to ease women's integration of these roles. These conditions may be expected to produce greater potential stress and conflict among employed mothers who hold the primary responsibility for childrearing and child care. Many businesses have adopted family-oriented policies such as job sharing, flexible work hours, or employer-sponsored day care as an employee benefit. These organizations have found positive ramifications for the businesses as well as for parents, including lower absenteeism, higher morale, positive publicity, lower rate of turnover, child care hours that conform to work hours, and access to quality infant and child care (Anderson-Kulman & Paludi, 1986).

Sexual Harassment

Women experience sexual harassment in many forms—from sexist remarks and covert physical contact (patting, brushing against their bodies) to blatant propositions and sexual assaults (Paludi, 1990; Paludi & Barickman, 1991). Sexual harassment is clearly prohibited as a form of sex discrimination, under both Title IX of the 1972 Education Amendments and, for employees, Title VII of the 1964 Civil Rights Act.

In addition, guidelines first issued by the Equal Employment Opportunity Commission (interpreting Title VII) and adopted in 1981 by the Office for Civil Rights further specify the range of sexual harassment covered by these statutes. According to these guidelines, behavior constitutes sexual harassment when:

- The person engaging in such behavior explicitly or implicitly makes your submission to it a term or condition of your employment or academic standing.

- The person engaging is such behavior makes decisions affecting your employment or academic life according to whether you accept or reject that behavior.

- The person's behavior is an attempt to interfere, or has the effect of interfering, with your work or academic performance, or creates an intimidating, hostile, or offensive working or learning environment.

The last condition—the creation of "an intimidating, hostile, or offensive working or learning environment"—is particularly significant because it covers the most pervasive form of sexual harassment. Sexual harassment claims are not limited simply to those for which a tangible job benefit is withheld ("quid pro quo" sexual harassment), but includes those in which the individual is subjected to an offensive, discriminatory work environment ("hostile environment" sexual harassment).

Although generalizations are difficult given the differing methodologies and samples used, the best estimate is that one out of every two women will be sexually harassed at some point during her academic or working life, indicating that harassment is the most widespread of all forms of sexual victimization studied (Paludi & Barickman, 1991).

Two of the largest studies of workplace sexual harassment will be summarized below. The first was conducted by the United States Merit Systems Protection Board (Merit Systems, 1981). This study addressed sexual harassment in the federal workplace and suggested that 42 percent of all women employees reported being sexually harassed. Merit Systems reported that many incidents occurred repeatedly, were of long duration, and had a sizable practical impact, costing the government an estimated minimum of $189 million over the two-year period covered by the research project.

Results also indicated that 33 percent of the women reported receiving unwanted sexual remarks, 28 percent reported suggestive looks, and 26 percent reported being deliberately touched. These behaviors were classified as "less severe" types of sexual harassment. When "more severe" forms of sexual harassment were addressed, 15 percent of the women reported experiencing pressure for dates, 9 percent reported being directly pressured for sexual favors, and 9 percent had received unwanted letters and telephone calls. One percent of the sample had experienced actual or attempted rape or assault. Merit Systems repeated their study of workplace sexual harassment in 1987 and reported identical results to their 1981 findings.

Research by Gutek (1985) with women in the civilian workplace reports similar findings as well: approximately half the female workforce experiences sexual harassment. Based on telephone interviews generated through random digit dialing procedures, Gutek's results suggested that 53 percent of women had reported one incident they believed was sexual harassment during their working lives, including degrading, insulting comments (15%), sexual touching (24%), socializing expected as part of the job requirement (11%), and expected sexual activity (8%).

There have been some studies reported in the literature that suggest that group differences in sexual harassment are common. For example, Gold (1987) reported that her sample of blue-collar tradeswomen experienced significantly higher levels of all forms of sexual harassment than did either white-collar professional women or pink-collar clerical women. Baker (1989) studied a sample of one hundred women employed in either traditional or nontraditional occupations, where traditionality was defined by the gender distribution in the work group. Baker also divided the traditional group into pink- and blue-collar workers. The pink-collar group included women who were secretaries and clerical workers. The blue-collar group included women who were industrial workers. Baker reported that high levels of sexual harassment are associated with having low numbers of women in the work group. For example, machinists reported significantly high frequencies of all levels of sexual harassment, whereas the traditional blue-collar workers reported very low levels. Clerical women reported experiences that were more similar to those of the traditional blue-collar workers than the nontraditional blue-collar workers. Baker also reported that women in the pink-collar and traditional blue-collar groups encountered just as many men as the machinists during the workday, but were treated differently. Thus, these results suggest that as women approach numerical parity in various segments of the workforce, sexual harassment may decline.

Research does suggest that although some forms of sexual harassment are more frequent than others, none of them are rare, suggesting that the experience of sexual harassment approaches a normative event in women's job lifespan (Fitzgerald, in press). Similarly, sexual harassment is experienced by women students at an alarming rate. For example, Dzeich and Weiner (1984) reported that 30 percent of undergraduate women experience one or more levels of sexual harassment from at least one of their professors during their four years of college. When definitions of sexual harassment include sexist remarks and other forms of "gender harassment," the incidence rate in undergraduate populations nears 90 percent.

Bailey and Richards (1985) reported that of 246 women graduate students in their sample, 13 percent indicated they had been sexually harassed, 21 percent had not enrolled in a course to avoid such behavior, and 16 percent indicated they had been directly assaulted. Bond (1988) reported that 75 percent of the 229 women members of APA Division 27 who responded to her survey experienced jokes with sexual themes during their graduate training, 69 percent were subjected to sexist comments demeaning to women, and 58 percent of the women reported experiencing sexist remarks about their clothing, body, or sexual activities. All of these findings indicate that when definitions of sexual victimization include sexual and gender harassment, it becomes clear that the sexual victimization of women is pervasive: literally millions of women each year experience victimization in the college/university setting.

Fitzgerald and Omerod (in press) noted that the outcomes of the harassment/victimization process can be examined from three main perspectives: work-related, psychological or emotional, and physiological or health-related.

Work-related outcomes. In the original Merit Systems study, 10 percent of the women who reported they were sexually harassed reported changing jobs as a result. In their more recent study, Merit Systems (1987) noted that over 36,000 federal employees left their jobs due to sexual harassment in the two-year period covered by their study. This incidence rate included individuals who quit, were fired, were transferred, or were reassigned because of unwanted sexual attention. Additional research has documented decreased morale and absenteeism, decreased job satisfaction, performance decrements, and damage to interpersonal relationships at work (Baker, 1989).

Similar findings have been reported with women undergraduate and graduate students. For example, students who have been sexually harassed typically change their major or educational program as an outcome of the harassment. Students also may drop courses, avoid courses, or avoid certain professors as a way of coping with unwanted sexual attention.

Psychological outcomes. The consequences to women students and employees of being harassed have been devastating to their emotional health, including depression, helplessness, strong fear reactions, loss of control, disruption of their lives, and decreased motivation (Quina, 1990; Rabinowitz, 1990). Research has indicated that, depending on the severity of the harassment, between 21 percent and 82 percent of women report that their emotional condition deteriorated as a result of the sexual harassment. Furthermore, like victims of rape who go to court, sexual harassment victims experience a second victimization when they attempt to deal with the situation through legal and/or institutional means. Stereotypes about sexual harassment and women's victimization blame women for the harassment. These stereotypes center around the myths that sexual harassment is a form of seduction, that women secretly want to be sexually harassed, and that women do not tell the truth.

Physiological outcomes. The following physical symptoms have been reported in the literature concerning academic and workplace sexual harassment: headaches, sleep disturbances, disordered eating, gastrointestinal disorders, nausea, weight loss or gain, and crying spells (Rabinowitz, 1990). Recently, researchers and clinicians have argued that victims of sexual harassment can exhibit a "postabuse" syndrome characterized by shock, emotional numbing, constriction of affect, flashbacks, and other signs of anxiety and depression. As Fitzgerald (1993) recently noted, "the available data are sufficient to support the conclusion that harassment constitutes a serious risk to women's health and well-being. Given the tens of thousands of women who are victimized in this manner, the enormity of this problem becomes increasingly and alarmingly clear" (p. 22).

Sandler (1988) and DeFour (1990) have indicated that on many campuses ethnic minority women are victims of sexual harassment because of the stereotypes and myths that portray minority women as sexually active, exotic, and erotic. There is thus an interface of racism and sexism in some elements of sexual harassment.

In addition, physically challenged women experience a considerable amount of psychological victimization when reporting sexual harassment due to stereotypes about their sexuality and attractiveness. Lesbian women have been the victims of gender harassment and other forms of sexual harassment because of homophobic attitudes. Feminist women are often specifically targeted for sexual harassment (Paludi & Barickman, 1991; Sandler & Paludi, in press).

Sex Discrimination

As the research on sexual harassment suggests, the progress of women in higher education and the workforce has long been impeded by sex discrimination. It was not until 1833 that the first woman was even allowed admission to a college, Oberlin College in Ohio. But even at Oberlin, a highly progressive institution for its day, women primarily learned the arts and home economics, which were "intended to prepare them for homemaking or teaching" (Deckard, 1983, p. 245). Oberlin's women students were discouraged from pursuing academic programs considered "too strenuous" for women such as science and commerce, which were areas of study considered suitable "for men only" (Flexner, 1971). Women were required to engage in nonacademic duties: "Washing the men's clothes, caring for their rooms, serving them at table, listening to their orations, but themselves remaining respectfully silent in public assemblages, the Oberlin 'coeds' were being prepared for intelligent motherhood and a properly subservient wifehood" (Flexner, 1971, p. 30).

There may be higher admission requirements for women than men applicants, sex quotas for admission, discrimination in the award of financial aid, and age restrictions on enrollment that constitute age and sex discrimination against women (Betz, in press). Men have traditionally received most of the financial aid and awards, including the G.I. Bill, ROTC, athletic scholarships, and prestigious awards reserved for men, such as the Rhodes Scholarship program (recently also awarded to women).

Bernard (1988) has characterized the effects of such discriminatory behavior as the "inferiority curriculum" that contributes to women students feeling depressed and frustrated, doubting their competency and self-worth. Freeman (1975) described education for women as the "null environment." A null environment is an environment that neither encourages nor discourages women—it simply ignores them. The impact of the null environment is to leave women at the mercy of whatever personal and/or environmental resources to which they have access.

FACILITATORS AND GATEKEEPERS
OF WOMEN'S ACHIEVEMENT

In this section, some major facilitators related to individuals' career choices will be reviewed. Facilitators are factors related to broadened career options and higher educational and career achievements.

Maternal Employment

One powerful facilitator of women's and men's career development is maternal employment (Betz, in press). Daughters of employed mothers are more career-oriented (versus home-oriented) than are daughters of homemakers (Hoffman, 1989). Sons and daughters of employed mothers are less stereotyped in their gender-role preferences, and daughters of employed mothers are more willing to pursue nontraditional careers than daughters of homemakers. Employed mothers place considerable emphasis on independence training.

Research with ethnic minority individuals consistently has suggested that maternal employment is positively associated with academic achievement. In addition to maternal employment per se are the effects of the mothers' feelings about work. Women's primary role decisions of career, noncareer work, or homemaking did not parallel those of their mothers but were related to their mothers' messages to them. In addition to mothers' encouragement of their daughters' success is their concomitant lack of pressure toward culturally defined expectations of femininity. Mothers who exert less pressure on their daughters to date, marry, and mother have more career-oriented daughters (Betz, in press). Research has suggested a greater flexibility and permissiveness in middle-class homes regardless of ethnicity. This flexibility leads to the availability of masculine activity choices for girls (Betz, in press). In working-class homes, parents are more concerned that their children adhere strictly to sex-appropriate behavior, as it is stereotypically defined (Nadelman, 1974). Hill (1988) noted that lesbian mothers perceived their daughters and sons to be more similar in characteristics than did heterosexual mothers. Lesbian mothers held masculine role expectations of their daughters.

WHO, IF ANYONE, ARE THE PEOPLE (OR PERSON) YOU WOULD LIKE TO BE LIKE? THAT IS, WHO ARE THE PEOPLE YOU TRY TO MODEL YOURSELF AFTER? DESCRIBE THE DIFFERENT ROLE MODELS YOU'VE HAD OVER THE COURSE OF YOUR LIFE

Researchers, teachers, and employers have often suggested that role models and mentors are important—in fact, necessary—for individuals' career development. Schockett and Haring-Hidore (1985) identified two major functions of mentoring: psychosocial and vocational. Vocational functions include educating, consulting/teaching, sponsoring, and protecting. Psychosocial functions include role modeling, encouraging, counseling, and being a transitional figure. Each of these components can be defined as follows:

Educating: teaching, challenging, and evaluating

Consulting/Coaching: acquainting a protégé with the political structures in the academy; implementing the protégé's goals

Sponsoring: promoting a protégé's work to colleagues

Protecting: shielding a protégé from negative publicity or from damaging contacts with individuals in power

Role Modeling: providing opportunities for a protégé to observe the mentor interact with colleagues, deal with conflicts, and/or integrate lifestyle and career

Encouraging: building a protégé's confidence

Counseling: discussing the protégé's fears career and/or personal concerns

Being a Transitional Figure: becoming a colleague with the protégé; reciprocal sharing of ideas and assistance.

Not all individuals who are "mentors" will fulfill all of these vocational and psychosocial functions; not all "protégés" want all of these behaviors from one person. In addition, there are styles of mentoring in which any of the psychosocial and vocational functions can be expressed. Two styles recently receiving attention are "grooming mentoring" and "networking mentoring." Grooming mentoring involves a more experienced person who uses power and/or position to educate, open doors, and sponsor a less mature professional who is seeking to ascend the career ladder. An egalitarian alternative to this type of mentoring is called "networking mentoring" (Swoboda & Millar, 1986).

In networking mentoring, two or more people play the roles of mentor and protégé to each other at different times. This is an egalitarian rather than hierarchical approach and is based on the notion of mutual enhancement. Its advantages include that it is open to all individuals, not just a select few who find someone to groom them. Furthermore, there are fewer relational problems resulting from intensity of the relationship, greater self-reliance, less resentment by colleagues concerning favoritism, an opportunity to learn how to mentor, and no setbacks related to a mentor's career and/or personal problems (Paludi & DeFour, 1992).

Recently, Paludi and DeFour (1992) reported incidence data with their new instrument, the Mentoring Experiences Questionnaire. In a national sample of 120 graduate students and faculty members (from the City University of New York schools and from the Association of Black Psychologists, Modern Language Association, American Sociological Association, American Association of University Professors, and the National Association of Women Deans, Administrators, and Counselors), they found the following results: (1) mentoring is more common among graduate students than among undergraduate students; (2) more women than men endorse psychosocial functions of mentoring relationships, such as receiving advice (mostly from women) on personal problems, receiving information on dealing with role strain involved in combining a career and family life, and being assisted with personal development; (3) more men than women endorse the vocational functions of mentoring relationships, such as being guided from one stage of their career to subsequent stages, being coached on submitting a paper for publication, having a faculty member share their knowledge and expertise (mostly from men); (4) women report not being given instruction to complete their projects, e.g., that a "null environment" has been set up for them in which no information is shared; and (5) more women than men report problems in mentoring relationships (especially with men mentors), including unwanted attempts to be drawn into a discussion of personal or sexual issues and not being included in a mentor's professional network.

Schockett et al. (1983) identified the following stages of mentoring relationships:

- Initiation (begins as the mentor provides educating and role modeling for the protégé)
- Cultivation (includes consulting and coaching, encouraging, sponsoring, protecting—the relationship grows stronger)
- Separation (ambivalence is experienced as mentor and protégé begin a process of psychological disengagement)
- Redefinition (the primary function of the mentor is one of moving from a transitional figure to friend).

The results of research by DeFour (1990) and Moses (1988) provide compelling evidence of the importance of black faculty in the retention of black graduate and undergraduate students. Contact with black faculty is associated with better academic performance and psychological well-being. Black faculty may serve as role models for black students.

As black women faculty have noted:

Because of the paucity of black professors at my university, I am placed in the dilemma of being all things to all black students. Note that there are only two other females (in a university of 16,000 students), one in the school of medicine and the other in agriculture—and both . . . have little contact with black students.

White professors contribute to this problem of overwork for me because they refer black students who are experiencing difficulties to me.

When I first arrived at the university (my first professional appointment) I enjoyed the attention I received. After a short while, however, I realized that the responsibility associated with being the only black female in my college, and only one of a handful in the university, was overwhelming. I have suffered several instances of burnout and exhaustion. As a consequence I have learned to maintain a less visible profile as a coping and survival strategy. (Moses, 1988, pp. 15-16)

HAVE YOU EVER BEEN IN A SITUATION WHERE YOU WERE ABOUT TO SUCCEED AT SOMETHING AND WONDERED IF IT WAS WORTH IT OR GOT AFRAID OF THE SUCCESS OR SOMETHING IT MIGHT PRODUCE?

Motive to Avoid Success

Horner (1968) introduced the construct "motive to avoid success" to the achievement motivation literature. She believed that in competitive achievement situations, especially those in which important men are present (e.g., prospective dates, boyfriends), women have a tendency to become anxious about being successful. Horner considered this avoidance motive to be present because of the expectation of negative consequences as a result of succeeding (e.g., loss of femininity, social rejection, and disapproval).

She thus suggested that fear of success acted as a motive and accounted for the major part of the withdrawal of women from higher education and work. However, Horner's findings are not as robust as originally assumed (Paludi, 1984). For example, Monahan and her colleagues (Monahan, Kuhn, & Shaver, 1974) and Solomon (1975) demonstrated that a cultural interpretation of fear of success is preferable to an intrapsychic one.

Based on a review of studies subsequent to Horner's original experiment, the following conclusions may be made:

Inconsistent data exist to support the hypothesis that fear of success is less likely among black women and more likely among white women.

Fear of success has shown no consistent relationship to ability—IQ, career goals—in women.

Inconsistent data exist to support a relationship between fear of success and gender-role identity.

No reliable age or gender differences in fear of success have been observed.

Whether fear of success taps a motive or cultural stereotype is not clear.

Career Counseling

In order to be effective, career counselors need to be aware that the choices women and men have made concerning their careers may have been constrained by gender-role stereotypes, discriminatory behavior, home versus career conflicts, and math anxiety. Counselors can facilitate women's career development by restoring to them options societal pressures have taken away from them (Betz, in press).

This process can involve several techniques, including encouraging women to make decisions that leave their options open until *they* are ready to reject them for appropriate reasons, asking women how their beliefs about women and women's roles influence their choices about their careers, and then sharing with women the research on women's vocational development. Counselors need to introduce adolescent girls to women role models, work with girls to manage anxiety about a career, and provide active support and encouragement of girls' efforts to develop skills and competencies.

Counselors also need to give support and encouragement to women as they confront barriers to meeting their career goals. Betz (in press) recommends the following counseling interventions with women:

Plan ahead to deal with potentially difficult situations (e.g., "But I'll be one of the only women in that profession—how will I survive? and "But I know it's very difficult for women to obtain apprenticeships in that field").

Obtain quality education and/or training and gain needed skills in job hunting, résumé writing, interviewing, assertion, and information seeking.

Locate support systems, role models, and mentors.

Deal with discrimination, sexual harassment, and the like when necessary.

Doubly strong support for women of color is needed because they face the dual barriers of gender and ethnic/minority status.

SUGGESTIONS FOR FUTURE RESEARCH: SEX EQUITY IN EDUCATION

There is considerable literature to support the contention that education and training are important elements in improving women's place in the labor force (Paludi & Barickman, 1991). The Project on the Status and Education of Women (1982) and Klein (1992) have focused attention on sex equity in education, which includes retraining faculty, student affairs personnel, and administrators to empower women and eliminate the "chilly climate."

Other psychologists have focused their work on intervention in adolescent girls' lives so that the girls will not have negative self-identities. For example, Gilligan, Lyons, and Hanmer (1990) worked with adolescent girls at the Emma Willard School in Troy, New York. Gilligan and her colleagues reported that until girls are eleven years old, they typically assert themselves, speak openly about what they are feeling, and accept conflict as a healthy part of relationships. Gilligan reported, however, that at adolescence, many girls begin to use statements such as "I don't know." They fear that speaking their opinions and voicing their feelings will anger people; consequently they keep silent. They settle for idealized relationships in which all people are "nice." Belenky et al. (1986) also reported that women whom they interviewed believed themselves to be "voiceless" and "mindless," incapable of learning from authority. Gilligan suggests that adolescent girls encounter a "wall of prohibition." Gilligan and her colleagues (1990) developed programs for helping women teachers assess their relationships with girls and their own gender-role stereotypes and the ways in which they had been silenced themselves during adolescence. The goal of the intervention in the lives of adolescent girls is to make these girls feel central, not marginal, to education and work. This goal suggests new agendas for the vocational psychology of women.

Occupations that are considered successful usually have a masculine bias. Success may be represented by achievement at a prestigious occupation, academic excellence, and other accomplishments that are associated with masculine values. Consequently, accomplishments that are associated with traditionally feminine values receive little or no attention. Women may manage a household and children and yet this kind of accomplishment has traditionally not been studied in the topic of achievement motivation and work (Paludi, 1992). The field of career psychology needs to redefine achievement and achievement-related issues in a way that does not keep women's realities and choices invisible. This will be accomplished by affirming values that women bring to education, work, and relationships.

REFERENCES

Alexander, K., & Cook, M. (1982). Curricula and coursework: A surprise ending to a familiar story. *American Sociological Review, 47,* 626-640.

Anderson-Kulman, R., & Paludi, M. A. (1986). Working mothers and the family context: Predicting positive coping. *Journal of Vocational Behavior, 28,* 241-253.

Archer, C. (1984). Children's attitudes toward sex-role division in adult occupational roles. *Sex Roles, 10,* 1-10.

Bailey, N., & Richards, M. (1985, August). *Tarnishing the ivory tower: Sexual harassment in graduate training programs in psychology.* Paper presented at the annual meeting of the American Psychological Association, Los Angeles, Calif.

Baker, N. (1989). *Sexual harassment and job satisfaction in traditional and nontraditional industrial occupations.* Unpublished doctoral dissertation, California School of Professional Psychology, Los Angeles, Calif.

Belenky, M. F., Clinchy, B. M., Goldberger, N. R., & Tarule, J. M. (1986). *Women's ways of knowing: The development of self, voice, and mind.* New York: Basic.

Bernard, J. (1988). The inferiority curriculum. *Psychology of Women Quarterly, 12,* 261-268.

Betz, N. (in press). Career development. In F. L. Denmark & M. A. Paludi (Eds.), *Handbook on the psychology of women.* Westport, Conn.: Greenwood.

Betz, N., & Fitzgerald, L. F. (1987). *The career psychology of women.* New York: Academic Press.

Bond, M. (1988). Division 27 sexual harassment survey: Definition, impact, and environmental context. *Community Psychologist, 21,* 7-10.

Deaux, K., & Emswiller, T. (1974). Explanations of successful performance on sex-linked tasks: What's skill for the male is luck for the female. *Journal of Personality and Social Psychology, 29,* 80-85.

Deckard, B. (1983). *The women's movement.* New York: Harper & Row.

DeFour, D. C. (1990). The interface of racism and sexism in sexual harassment. In M. A. Paludi (Ed.), *Ivory power: Sexual harassment on campus* (pp. 45-52). Albany: State University of New York Press.

Doyle, J., & Paludi, M. A. (1991). *Sex and gender: The human experience.* Dubuque, Iowa: Wm. C. Brown.

Dzeich, B., & Weiner, L. (1984). *The lecherous professor.* Boston, Mass.: Beacon.

Etaugh, C. (1984). Effects of maternal employment on children: Implications for the family therapist. In S. H. Cramer (Ed.), *Family therapy collections: Vol. 10, Perspectives on work and the family* (pp. 16-39). Rockville, Md.: Aspen Systems.

Etaugh, C. (1990). Images of women: Myths and realities. In M. A. Paludi & G. A. Steuernagel (Eds.), *Foundations for the feminist restructuring of the academic disciplines* (pp. 39-68). New York: Haworth Press.

Feldman-Summers, S. A., & Kiesler, S. (1974). Those who are number two try harder: The effect of sex on attributions of causality. *Journal of Personality and Social Psychology, 30,* 846-855.

Fine, M. (1987). Silencing in public schools. *Language Arts, 64,* 157-174.

Fitzgerald, L. F. (in press). *Sexual harassment in higher education: Concepts and issues.* Washington, D.C.: National Education Association.

Fitzgerald, L. F., & Omerod, A. (in press). Breaking silence: The sexual harassment of women in academia and the workplace. In F. Denmark & M. Paludi (Eds.), *Handbook on the psychology of women.* New York: Greenwood.

Flexner, E. (1971). *Century of struggle.* New York: Atheneum.

Franken, M. (1983). Sex role expectations in children's vocational aspirations and perceptions of occupations. *Psychology of Women Quarterly, 8,* 59-68.

Freeman, J. (1975). How to discriminate against women without really trying. In J. Freeman (Ed.), *Women* (pp. 194-208). Palo Alto, Calif.: Mayfield.

Frieze, I., Whitley, B., Hanusa, B., & McHugh, M. (1982). Assessing the theoretical models for sex differences in causal attributions for success and failure. *Sex Roles, 8,* 333-343.

Gilligan, C., Lyons, N. P., & Hanmer, T. J. (Eds.). (1990). *Making connections: The relational worlds of adolescent girls at Emma Willard School.* Cambridge, Mass.: Harvard University Press.

Glick, P., Zion, C., & Nelson, C. (1988). What mediates sex discrimination in hiring decisions? *Journal of Personality and Social Psychology, 55,* 178-186.

Gold, Y. (1987, August). *The sexualization of the workplace: Sexual harassment of pink, white and blue collar workers.* Paper presented at the annual conference of the American Psychological Association, New York.

Goldberg, P. (1968). Are women prejudiced against women? *Transaction, 5,* 28-30.

Gutek, B. (1985). *Sex and the workplace.* San Francisco, Calif.: Jossey-Bass.

Hill, M. (1988). Child-rearing attitudes of black lesbian mothers. In Boston Lesbian Psychologies Collective (Eds.), *Lesbian psychologies: Explorations and challenges* (pp. 215-226). Urbana, Ill.: University of Illinois Press.

Hoffman, L. W. (1984). Work, family, and the socialization of the child. In R. D. Parke (Ed.), *Review of child development research* (vol. 7, pp. 223-281). Chicago: University of Chicago Press.

Hoffman, L. W. (1989). Effects of maternal employment in the two-parent family. *American Psychologist, 44,* 283-292.

Horner, M. (1968). *Sex differences in achievement motivation and performance in competitive and noncompetitive situations.* Unpublished doctoral dissertation, University of Michigan.

Issacs, M. B. (1981). Sex-role stereotyping and the evaluation of the performance of women: Changing trends. *Psychology of Women Quarterly, 6,* 187-195.

Jacobson, M. B., & Effertz, J. (1974). Sex-roles and leadership: Perceptions of the leaders and the led. *Organizational Behavior and Human Performance, 12,* 383-396.

Johnson, W. B. (1987). *Workforce 2000: Work and workers for the 21st century.* Indianapolis: Hudson Institute.

Klein, S. S. (Ed.). (1992). *Sex equity and sexuality in education.* Albany: State University of New York Press.

MacKay, W. R., & Miller, C. A. (1982). Relations of socioeconomic status and sex variables to the complexity of worker functions on the occupational choices of elementary school children. *Journal of Vocational Behavior, 20,* 31-37.

Mednick, M., & Thomas, V. (in press). Women and achievement. In F. L. Denmark & M. A. Paludi (Eds.), *Handbook on the psychology of women.* Westport, Conn.: Greenwood.

Monahan, L., Kuhn, D., & Shaver, P. (1974). Intrapsychic vs. cultural explanations of the fear of success motive. *Journal of Personality and Social Psychology, 29*, 60-64.

Moses, Y. (1988). *Black women in the academy.* Washington, D.C.: Project on the Status and Education of Women.

Nadelman, L. (1974). Sex identity in American children: Memory, knowledge and preference tests. *Developmental Psychology, 10*, 413-417.

Paludi, M. A. (1984). Psychometric properties and underlying assumptions of four objective measures of fear of success. *Sex Roles, 10*, 765-781.

Paludi, M. A. (1992). *Psychology of women.* Dubuque, Iowa: Wm. C. Brown.

Paludi, M. A. (Ed.). (1990). *Ivory power: Sexual harassment on campus.* Albany: State University of New York Press.

Paludi, M. A., & Barickman, R. B. (1991). *Academic and workplace sexual harassment: A resource manual.* Albany: State University of New York Press.

Paludi, M. A., & DeFour, D. C. (1992). The mentoring experiences questionnaire: Initial psychometric analyses. *Mentoring International, 6*, 19-23.

Paludi, M. A., & Fankell-Hauser, J. (1986). An idiographic approach to the study of women's achievement strivings. *Psychology of Women Quarterly, 10*, 89-100.

Paludi, M. A., & Strayer, L. (1985). What's in an author's name? Differential evaluations of performance as a function of author's name. *Sex Roles, 12*, 353-361.

Project on the Status and Education of Women (1982). *The classroom climate: A chilly one for girls.* Washington, D.C.: Association of American Colleges.

Quina, K. (1990). The victimizations of women. In M. Paludi (Ed.), *Ivory power: Sexual harassment on campus* (pp. 93-102). Albany: State University of New York Press.

Rabinowitz, V. C. (1990). Coping with sexual harassment. In M. Paludi (Ed.), *Ivory power: Sexual harassment on campus* (pp. 103-118). Albany: State University of New York Press.

Reid, P. T., & Paludi, M. A. (in press). Psychology of women: Conception to adolescence. In F. L. Denmark & M. A. Paludi (Eds.), *Handbook on the psychology of women.* Westport, Conn.: Greenwood.

Repetti, R., Matthews, K., & Waldron, I. (1989). Effects of paid employment on women's mental and physical health. *American Psychologist, 44*, 1394-1401.

Sandler, B. (1988, March). *Sexual harassment: A new issue for institutions or these are the times that try men's souls.* Paper presented at the Conference on Sexual Harassment on Campus, New York, N.Y.

Sandler, B., & Paludi, M. (in press). *Educator's guide to controlling sexual harassment.* Washington, D.C.: Thompson.

Scarr, S., Phillips, D., & McCarney, K. (1989). Working mothers and their families. *American Psychologist, 44,* 1402-1409.

Schockett, M., & Haring-Hidore, M. (1985). Factor analytic support for psychological and vocational mentoring functions. *Psychological Reports, 57,* 627-630.

Schockett, M., et al. (1983, April). *A proposed model of mentoring.* Paper presented at the meeting of the American Educational Research Association, Anaheim, Calif.

Smith, E. (1983). Issues in racial minorities' career behavior. In W. B. Walsh & S. Osipow (Eds.), *Handbook of vocational psychology* (pp. 161-222). Hillsdale, N.J.: Erlbaum.

Solomon, L. Z. (1975). Perception of a successful person of the same sex or the opposite sex. *Journal of Social Psychology, 85,* 133-134.

Starer, R., & Denmark, F. (1974). Discrimination against aspiring women. *International Journal of Group Tensions, 5,* 65-70.

Super, D. (1957). *The psychology of careers.* New York: Harper & Row.

Swobda, M. J., & Millar, S. B. (1986). Networking-mentoring: Career strategy of women in academic administration. *Journal of NAWDAC, 49,* 8-13.

Taynor, J., & Deaux, K. (1973). When women are more deserving than men: Equity, attribution, and perceived sex differences. *Journal of Personality and Social Psychology, 3,* 360-367.

Taynor, J., & Deaux, K. (1975). Equity and perceived sex differences: Role behavior as defined by the task, the mode, and the actor. *Journal of Personality and Social Psychology, 3,* 381-390.

United States Merit Systems Protection Board, Office of Merit Systems Review and Studies (1981). *Sexual harassment in the federal workplace: Is it a problem?* Washington, D.C.: USGPO.

Ward, C. (1981). Prejudice against women: Who, when, and why? *Sex Roles, 7,* 163-171.

Weiner, B. (1972). *Theories of motivation and attribution theory.* Morristown, N.J.: General Learning Press.

Coping with Challenges: College Experiences of Older Women and Women with Disabilities

Lillian P. Holcomb
Carol B. Giesen

The purpose of this chapter is to introduce concerns of both older women and women with disabilities as they experience their undergraduate college years. Although the viewpoints and needs of these two populations of women students differ to a degree, they share commonalities in terms of the "cumulative burdens" they bring to the college experience from earlier confrontation with and oppression from a variety of systems (e.g., medical, economic, educational, legal). This is significant, as current services on many campuses are inadequate to meet their needs at a time when traditional students' numbers on campus are decreasing and "special," "diverse," or "minority" students are increasing. The entry of observable numbers of older women and women with disabilities (in addition to the rise in the number of women students overall) creates a concern for college administrators, faculty, and staff, who must now learn new pedagogical and technological methods to work with them. The presence on campus of women in these "minority groups" illustrates their unwillingness to continue accepting sexist/ageist/disableist traditional professionals' stereotypes of them as helpless, passive, dependent "stay-at-homes."

For the purpose of this chapter, the term "older women" is defined as women over age forty who are entering college for the first time or reentering campus life after a lengthy break in their studies. "Women with/of disability" or "disabled women" refers to college women of any age who self-identify as living with ongoing physical conditions such as mobility impairment, blindness, deafness, or other such circumstances for which architectural and attitudinal social barriers have limited their inclusion and participation. "Older disabled women" identifies previously nondisabled students who have developed disability as a function of aging (such as osteoporosis) or students with a disability since birth who have added impairment due to the function of aging (arthritis added to congenital blindness, for example). "Commonality in diversity" indicates the shared issues of older and/or disabled women who come to the campus with considerable background diversity. A blind twenty-year-old white lesbian, a nondisabled sixty-five-year-old heterosexual African American woman, and a fifty-year-old Native American woman student using a wheelchair may all experience lack of access to campus because of sexist, ageist, and disableist attitudes.

Although it is true that all special/diverse populations including ethnic and sexual minority groups on campus share a certain amount of the social stigma of prejudice with nonminority women, it must be noted that the populations of women of disability and older women are unique in that they share a life situation that is inescapable to all human beings currently alive. That is, all (regardless of ethnic or sexual minority status) will grow older; all are vulnerable to accidents and illnesses resulting in their immediate membership in the minority group known as "persons of disability." For those few who avoid accidents or illness up to the moment of death, death results because by definition disability has already occurred. When a white lesbian awakens tomorrow, it is unlikely she will have become an Asian heterosexual, but she will have aged overnight and may have experienced a stroke in her sleep or mobility impairment resulting from an encounter with a rapist intruder.

It is important to clarify that although women students with disabilities share certain experiences of disability stigma with disabled men on campus and certain experiences of sexism with nondisabled women on campus, the interactive aspects of sexism and disableism impact their lives in a very different manner. The same is true of older women students who share experiences with older men or with younger women, but the interactive aspects of sexism and ageism impact their lives in a unique way as well. For an increasing number of women students who are simultaneously older and disabled, the interaction of sexism, ageism, and disableism functions in ways that distinguish their college experiences from those of young blind male students or older nondisabled African American men on campus. Traditional professionals' concepts of "older people" or "disabled people" tend not to address the needs of older women as distinct from older men or disabled women as distinct from disabled men. This clarification is necessary for student service programs to be rendered useful to older and/or disabled women students.

REVIEW OF THE LITERATURE

The body of literature that addresses the concerns of women of disability and older women is pathbreaking, albeit sparse; especially minimal are empirical studies of their college experiences. As the entry of significant numbers of women of disability and older women to undergraduate degree programs is a fairly recent phenomenon, there is insufficient documentation on the specific needs of college *women* who are both older and disabled. A review of the literature on the challenges within community systems (e.g., economic, medical, educational, legal) that both disabled and older women have confronted will follow.

Older Women

Until the late 1970s research findings on older women students tended to focus on older students taking special purpose recreational or job-training courses. Steadily increasing numbers of older women students returning to four-year colleges have begun to call attention to this group and their unique needs (Swift, Colvin, & Mills, 1987), achievements (Cleave-Hogg, 1990; Giesen, 1991), and problems (Leavitt, 1989). The small amount of research available suggests that the challenges they must overcome, like challenges presented to disabled women, are generated in part by social attitudes and institutional practices and in part by their own individual past experiences. The importance of the successes of these older women for other women is yet to be clearly defined.

Older women enter college with many of the same future goals as younger people, although, for many, their motivation may be based more on practical experience than on idealism. Some are among those forming a significant part of the total number of the older poor (Roff & Atherton, 1989) or have been employed at lower-paying jobs with little likelihood of promotion and less adequate benefits (Grambs, 1989). Some have experienced discrimination by government helping agencies (Palmore, 1990); others have been deserted by spouses, left financially disadvantaged by a husband's death, or lost their jobs to younger workers (Giesen, 1991; Giesen, in press).

Others with more positive life experiences have been employed at professional or paraprofessional levels (Beutell & O'Hara, 1987), have been full-time homemakers or single heads of households with minimal or no financial disadvantages, or have combined full- or part-time employment with full-time homemaking. For these women, as well as those who have experienced a harsher lifestyle, returning to college presents the opportunity to move beyond the present circumstances of their lives and to take advantage of the role that education plays in enhancing their sense of self-sufficiency and self-esteem (Giesen, 1991; Hiemstra, 1985).

The problems that older women encounter as they return to the higher educational system reflect a composite of broad and general social prejudices against older people as well as more specific negative attitudes on the part of educators (Merriam & Lumsden, 1985). Older people, in general, are often considered to be stubborn, dependent, cranky, forgetful, unable to learn new information, and likely to be senile or have other mental impairments (Palmore, 1990). Older women, in particular, are likely to be considered as even less capable, competent, and attractive than older men (Giesen, 1989).

Further, educators commonly employ an economic perspective in their attitudes toward their student populations. That is, the primary purpose of education is perceived to be serving economic interests. It is younger students rather than older students who will spend twenty, thirty, or more years contributing to the national economy (Merriam & Lumsden, 1985).

In addition, difficulties may be created for older women students as the result of overprotectiveness. The belief that they need and want to be sheltered from the rigors and stresses of the higher education system may only occasionally be expressed by social agencies and educators but is frequently stated by families and friends. Although this attitude appears, and no doubt is intended to be, nurturant, it also conveys the message that older women students are more likely to fail to successfully carry out their educational plans (Giesen, 1991).

Despite the implicit assumptions conveyed by social prejudices, older women students tend to be among the more highly motivated, conscientious, and serious students in the classroom (Cleave-Hogg, 1990; Giesen, 1990; Grambs, 1989). They generally bring to their college work many attributes related to academic achievement, such as autonomy, independence, goal directedness, and a mature sense of responsibility (Hiemstra, 1985). Moreover, their experiences in social relationships and with life events often benefit instructors and younger students alike by facilitating classroom discussions and highlighting lecture content.

The present increasing economic pressures are likely to continue to place even heavier burdens on women who must earn their own livelihoods or who are responsible for the livelihood of children or older parents. These economic pressures, in combination with the generally lower level of educational attainment of older people (Lumsden, 1985), create demands that can best be met by further education. Finally, many women wish to continue to learn about the world and themselves and enhance their sense of accomplishment.

Evidence of these goals is found in the rapidly increasing numbers of older women applying for admission to four-year or community colleges. Once admitted, their performance makes it clear that their place in the classroom can no longer be disputed. Although the challenges, problems, and barriers presented by social prejudices and institutional misconceptions must be overcome by each older woman who enters college, her ability to excel adds more evidence that the current discriminatory academic atmosphere confronted by older women in general must be altered.

Women with Disabilities

Public access laws (1973 Rehabilitation Act and 1990 Americans with Disabilities Act) have made possible the entry of women with long-term, early onset, and congenital disabilities into higher education for the first time in history. A few pioneer studies of the college concerns of these women have been conducted recently (Hopkins-Best, Wiinamaki, & Yurcisin, 1985; Kroeger & Pazandak, 1990; Marshall, 1990). Earlier, less empirical literature exists concerning educational access and its relationship to rehabilitation services for disabled women (Atkins, 1982; Holcomb, 1984; Lesh & Marshall, 1984; O'Toole & Weeks, 1978). Women and disability issues specific to careers and employment and concerned with educational access and the rehabilitation system have been addressed by Hollingsworth and Mastroberti (1983), Russo and Jansen (1988), and Vash (1982).

According to Bowe (1984), women of disability are only half as likely as nondisabled women to have any postsecondary education; compared to only one in twenty-eight nondisabled women with fewer than eight years of formal education, as many as one in six disabled women have such inadequate precollege preparation. Disabled women participate in higher education at different ages but often are late entry or require greater number of years to finish an undergraduate degree as compared to the general nondisabled population. The disabled women students in Marshall's (1990) study were on average twenty-five years old.

One reason women with disabilities enter college later or require more years to complete an undergraduate degree is the sexism within the vocational rehabilitation system, which has the power to approve educational and job-training referrals and opportunities for people with disabilities (Barker, 1982; Lesh & Marshall, 1984). Fewer traditional college-age women (under age 35) are referred for vocational rehabilitation services (Region V Division of Vocational Rehabilitation Services study cited in Kroeger & Pazandak, 1990; Mudrick, 1987); when they are accepted for services, their cases can be closed as "successfully rehabilitated homemakers" who increased housework performance rather than obtained salaried employment (Danek & Lawrence, 1985). Fewer women of disability receive vocational rehabilitation services to attend college because they are more likely to have chronic hidden disabilities that become visible later in life, as compared to men who have "important" obvious accidents and injuries—disabilities "earned" as youthful athletes, employees, or war veterans (Asch & Fine, 1988; Kutza, 1985).

Fewer career opportunities are open to women with disabilities than to disabled men (Hopkins-Best, Murphy, & Yurcisin, 1988), even when they obtain a college education (Asch & Fine, 1988). Disabled women's unemployment rate of up to 75 percent and their earning only about half the income of nondisabled women or men with disabilities (Imdieke, 1988; Saxton, 1988; Women and Disability Awareness Project, 1984) is a national disgrace.

Early-onset or congenitally disabled women are college-delayed due to childhood confrontations with the medical system. These confrontations at times consisted of disputes with physicians about errors written about the girls in their medical files—errors that follow them to college and throughout life (Hannaford, 1985; Holcomb, 1991). Disabled girls treated inadequately by the medical system often have been born into poverty to parents (especially mothers) already living in unhealthy, economically deprived conditions to which disability caregiving expenses are an added burden (Asch & Fine, 1988; Durham, 1986). A second generation of poverty is created; as they become young adults, these disabled daughters are further isolated and financially deprived as few job or marriage opportunities exist and they are forced onto public welfare and social security/Medicare (Altman, 1985; Kutza, 1985). They may experience early involvement with the legal system because violence and abuse occur frequently behind the closed doors of institutions and parental homes ("Care That Kills," 1986; Davis, 1989), and continue into adulthood because there are few crisis services designed especially for women with disabilities (Grothaus, 1985; O'Toole, 1990). These conditions create humiliation and low self-esteem (Connors, 1985; Saviola, 1981), which combine to delay college entry and interfere with the ability to concentrate on meeting the coursework deadlines so critical to completing a degree within the designated timespan.

The early education system delays college preparation by its inadequate choice for disabled children: residential schools where the girls are placed with "their own kind" (other disabled children) or public school mainstreaming, where "special attention" is given to disabled girls. Inadequacies of public school mainstreaming include deficits in funding and disability-specific technology, few role models, and exposure to mockery and teasing by nondisabled children (Peterson & Pelarski, 1974; Phillips, 1986;

Simons, 1991). Residential schools are advantageous because they provide a peer culture that offers friendships and relevant learning equipment, but the cultural lag of these schools isolates disabled girls from the nondisabled college preparation world, and perpetuates sexism through outdated gender-role portrayals in their textbooks and curriculum (Holcomb, 1984; Myers, 1991).

Commonalities in Diversity

Although no empirical study that addressed the interactive components of ageism, disableism, and sexism as experienced on the college campus by nondisabled older women, disabled younger women, or older women of disability could be located, there is pioneering professional work being done that unites the concerns of persons of disability and older persons without emphasis on women's perspectives (Gibson & Durano, 1989; Munson, 1987). Because caregiving is a primary mutual concern of both older and disabled persons and the majority of caregivers are female (Sommers & Shields, 1987), women's perspectives are beginning to be included (Kinderknecht, 1989). Women's perspectives in the literature on aging and disability illustrate two sides of a coin: "facing age with disability and facing disability with age" (Holcomb & Chai, 1988). The concept of facing aging with disability is emphasized in Trieschmann's (1987) textbook (including sections on aging disabled women), which focuses on persons already disabled since youth who now have to deal with growing older. The concept of facing disability with age is presented by Porcino (1983) and Doress, Siegal, The Midlife and Older Women's Book Project, and the Boston Women's Health Book Collective (1987) in terms of such disabilities as osteoporosis and impairments of vision and hearing that appear as a function of aging process.

The interaction of older women experiencing disability for the first time and women just entering midlife and older years with an experience of disability since birth or youth is discussed by Matthews (1983) in her work on institutionalization and by Simon (1988) in her study of integration based on the single lifestyles of previously nondisabled, never-married, old women and women with lifelong disability. Although Kriegsman and Bregman (1985) and Mudrick (1987) do not describe on-campus experiences of older women of disability, they do analyze the employment dilemma that results when, through a combination of sexism, ageism, and disableism, these women are unable to benefit from the vocational rehabilitation system and its referrals to educational opportunities.

From the older women's community-at-large, there is a growth of less formal literature on unity with regard to the commonality of interests of older women and women with disabilities across diverse sexual and ethnic minority communities. Although there is yet no significant documentation of shared college experiences, the Older Women's League (Lederer, 1991), the Seattle Women's Commission Project on Ageism and Disableism (Holcomb, 1990), and the Gray Panthers Disability Task Force (Owen, 1988) recognize mutual problems from several oppressive systems that hold in common their reinforcement of poverty for "seniors and disabled": inaccessible housing, transportation, and health services. Lederer (1991) and Holcomb (1990) concluded that disabled and older women's anxiety about each other intensifies because of their struggle to compete for diminishing economic resources at the same time that their unity could be used to strengthen their resources and support systems.

COMMONALITIES SHARED ACROSS THE DIVERSITY OF OLDER WOMEN AND WOMEN WITH DISABILITIES IN TODAY'S COLLEGE LIFE

Older college women and women of disability share two major problems of "cumulative burdens" brought to their campus life from earlier confrontations with a variety of systems (medical, economic, education, legal) plus discrimination and oppression while on campus. Both disabled and older women students must create unique responses to cope with attitudinal and architectural barriers that limit their access to and participation in coursework and campus activities. Few current services meet their needs in the same way concerns are already being addressed on campus for disabled or older men students and nondisabled or young women students.

"Cumulative Burdens"

Both older women and women of disability bring with them to the campus a variety of experiences termed "burdens": discrimination experienced in their younger years as a function of exposure to "helper" social systems, which have become barriers. "Helping agencies" (legal, educational, medical, economic) supposedly designed to assist "special populations" (women, persons of disability, older people) may reinforce stereotypes of their clients as needing protective benefactors, instead of spending money, time, and energy to remove social barriers that exclude these women.

Older women.   For older women in today's world, the "helping" systems of society may become barriers to the attainment of the very goals they were designed to facilitate. Displaced homemakers, widows, or women unemployed as the result of economic changes, for example, may find that age and gender (and sometimes lack of previous work experience) are perceived as liabilities by members of various helping agencies. Age, in particular, may become a liability for women who have been employed in low-wage occupations or who have been full-time homemakers.

The problems are illustrated by the questions that are asked in the helping process and by the outcomes that helping agencies perceive as appropriate for older women who are entering the job market or trying to improve their occupational status. Women who have been employed in a low-wage service occupation and who also received state or local assistance may be asked to give a rationale for wishing to have a higher-paying job or even asked why they think they deserve better jobs. Further, it is sometimes pointed out that the cost of earning a higher wage will be the termination of social services and, in some cases where housing aid is provided, the necessity of repaying the agency for the monies previously expended.

The future opportunities predicted for such women are also often limited in scope. Despite the advantages of beginning with small increments in occupational status, self-improvement, and goal attainment, older women may be perceived by helping agencies as being unable to move beyond these first small improvements. Consequently, suggestions, plans, and assistance leave out the possibility of long-term achievements and are often predicated on the agencies' view that only small life-improvements are possible for older women.

In the second author's experience, nearly a quarter of older women college students whose backgrounds included being displaced from their homes by divorce, employment at low-wage occupations, assistance by helping agencies, or lower socioeconomic homes encountered these problems. Their estimated capabilities were based on their age, past history, and the "age-istic" view that because they were older, previously not well off financially, or with an employment history of low-wage occupations, they could not be expected to move very far beyond their present status.

The number of women dissuaded from trying to help themselves by furthering their education cannot be estimated; large numbers of older women do not appear in classrooms, vocational training labs, or job-training seminars. Effects of these attitudes on women who do go on to college, however, can be described; older women bring with them into the college classroom the self-doubts and anxieties arising from their encounters with the social system. Their society has implied that they are not capable of moving very far beyond their present life and occupational statuses, and their perceptions of their life experiences have been distorted by their acceptance of these social biases.

After entering college and discovering their ability to succeed in academic work, such self-perceptions begin to change but, prior to that, the path to matriculation often presents traps and barriers that arise from both assistance programs and college regulations. The women's doubts and anxieties about the likelihood that they can succeed add to the difficulty of overcoming such bureaucratic obstacles (Giesen, 1991).

Women with disabilities.   Many disabled girls receive negative messages about themselves as lazy, stupid cripples (Marshall, 1990) with little hope of achieving adulthood competence. When they come in contact with "helping agencies," these messages are often reinforced as the legal, medical, economic, and educational systems perceive of them in interacting sexist and disableist terms, resulting in "double handicap"/"double jeopardy" (Deegan & Brooks, 1985) or "double burden" (Saviola, 1981).   Confrontation with interacting sexism and disableism creates a situation of "rolelessness" (Fine & Asch, 1985) because there are no roles or role models for disabled girls in terms of being an adult woman or a disabled adult. A disabled girl grows up with "double jeopardy" because she occupies two statuses society views negatively, unlike disabled boys who have male status or nondisabled girls who have at least traditional female roles open to them. Homemaker roles and traditional female jobs (e.g., secretary, receptionist, nurse) are not open to disabled women, because many men (including disabled men) view them as unmarriageable and unattractive. Nontraditional, male-dominated careers that might offer these women an opportunity to earn a wage to support themselves without husbands (survival with disabilities is expensive) usually have architectural barriers and require unattainable years of graduate-level university preparation. The early educational system of either mainstreaming or residential school placement does not equip disabled girls for an adult woman's role and rarely provides adequate transition to a college setting. Parents may continue to keep this unemployable, unmarriageable, disabled daughter at home for as many years as they can provide for her needs, knowing one day they will die or become too disabled themselves to assist her, and then leave her to survive alone.

Therefore, it is with only a great deal of survivalist effort that women with disabilities make it at all to the college campus. They may enter their college years with this "cumulative burden" of discrimination from early education mainstreaming or residential school, be living in poverty on social security/Medicare or public welfare, and possibly have been involved with the legal system due to having been sexually abused. In addition, congenital or early-onset disabled women have a growing file of physician diagnoses and prognoses following them from within the medical system. The male/nondisabled system of establishment power has never really believed these women could succeed, and disabled women often come to believe in failure themselves because they grew up hearing little else but how doubly devalued they are.

Commonalities in diversity.   Older women and women of disability experience dual devaluation by society. They are viewed as incompetent, and not much is expected of them because counselors in helping agencies may see them as poor investments: older women who have little time left to achieve and disabled women whose lives are nonproductive. This may be especially true if they spent earlier years at home being taken care of by a salaried husband or parents, or have been living in poverty because of the isolation of never having married, being divorced, widowed, or displaced homemakers. Older or disabled women must summon tremendous energy to believe in themselves when others do not.

The older disabled woman comes to the college experience with the burden of triple jeopardy/triple discrimination: sexism, ageism, disableism. As an older woman she experiences role-lessness because she no longer meets the pretty young woman standard; as a disabled woman she experiences rolelessness because she never has been considered marriageable. Both aging and disability are viewed by society's legal, economic, educational, and medical systems as phenomena to be avoided, cured, or disposed of (especially in women); older disabled women are thus not assisted in their attempt to attain a college degree. With this burden of negative messages of failure, such women enter the campus already doubtful. To this will be added the necessity of changing their own self-perceptions as they challenge attitudinal and architectural barriers on the campus, which virtually invite them to become academic failures and threaten to withdraw assistance from helping agencies if they do.

Systemic Discrimination and Oppression
in the Academic Environment

While in the academic environment, disabled and older women students must cope with attitudinal and architectural barriers that limit their access to and participation in coursework and campus activities. They must become very creative in their responses and find ways to survive, for there are few services and programs designed to meet their complex needs.

Older women's barriers in the academic environment. Programs specifically intended to assist women to enter college often present the most stressful of the barriers that must be overcome. Such programs may offer full tuition and fees or provide funds for transportation or child care. Typical of these programs are those that provide funds for college courses but require that the student begin with a full-time courseload in order to receive the assistance. No recognition is given to the extent of the demands placed on the prospective student, who is required to begin college-level work with no time for renewing learning skills and no allowance for remedial work unless it is done in addition to the full-time courseload.

The only additional requirement needed for such programs to assume the dimensions of a prescription for failure is to add the demand that students also continue to work part- or full-time to support themselves. For women who attempt to matriculate in these programs, the contrast between the attitudes of society and its agencies in regard to older women's abilities and the heavy and inflexible demands of some college assistance programs constitutes a double-bind condition that is both discriminatory and oppressive.

Overcoming these barriers to push themselves through the first college semester demands dogged determination and the inner strength to cope with academic requirements intended to challenge students who have been exercising their formal learning skills for the past twelve years. Older women students are also expected to be efficient at reading comprehension, test taking, note taking, rote memory, and essay composition. They must be able to cope with the initial confusion, doubt, and anxiety of this burden as they continue to work at improving learning skills. Women must also be able to cope with self-recrimination and fear of failure when their first test grades or semester course grades are lower than expected. Some must find strength to go on even when they have failed a course.

As older women students continue through the first semester and on to the next level of courses, they often discover that not only do they have the ability to succeed but they have several advantages over younger students. One of these advantages is the work-oriented attitude that most older students bring to their academic efforts. College coursework is now their "job" and they tend to be very good at fulfilling their job responsibilities. An additional advantage is that they generally do not participate in the undergraduate social search for emotional relationships or social status. They are, as many have said, "free" of these needs.

Other challenges are a part of the early adjustment to college period as well. Learning the procedures of course registration, changing courses, using library facilities, and managing time present difficulties for older women who do not have the same access to the dormitory, cafeteria, or between-class discussions that are available to the younger resident students. Access to information distributed through the campus mail or placed on dormitory bulletin boards remains limited for commuter students even though most colleges make efforts to see that it is disseminated widely.

Informal and spontaneous interactions with advisors and faculty are also limited for older returning women students. For many, the need to continue working either part- or full-time at some occupation reduces the time they have available to seek out assistance. They may, for example, be unable to avail themselves of tutoring services offered in the evenings or on weekends, and they may have to take time off from work in order to be on campus during faculty office hours. Other problems are posed by courses that require out-of-class work that must be done in the evenings. Fine arts courses, for example, may require extra time spent in the studio, attending concerts, or participating in the preparation and staging of plays. For many older women, particularly those who must remain employed, such course requirements cannot be met.

Disabled women's barriers in the academic environment. Personal communications with coordinators and directors of campus disability services offices and student commissions (S. A. Kroeger, June 1990; J. Lonergan, September 1991; C. Rozumalski, October 1991) indicate the following barriers for women of disability in the academic environment: architectural deficits of "historic old buildings" (constructed originally without barrier-free design because persons with disabilities were not expected to participate in college life); hilly, inaccessible campus grounds that lack curb cuts; unmonitored "handicapped-designated" parking stalls used by nondisabled people; inadequate funding for disability support services (e.g., sign language interpreters, lift-equipped vans and transportation across campus at all needed hours and days, readers, note-takers, computer access); insufficient numbers of personal care attendants and the lack of campus funds to hire them for disabled students; lack of escort/transportation services when disabled women use isolated, dark building entrances (e.g., someone nearby to assist opening a heavy door there may be the campus rapist). Judy Lonergan (personal communication, September 1991) has suggested that the recruitment of women with disabilities is particularly important in math, science, engineering, and architecture departments, which have been barriers of exclusion to women and which could do so much to remove architectural barriers.

Kroeger and Pazandak's (1990) study found that disabled college women felt excluded on campus to a greater degree than did men with disabilities. Disabled women students expressed less confidence in finding help on campus if they needed it. Women with disabilities are particularly at risk if help is needed suddenly because of imminent attack or rape due to their being stranded or isolated in a building without sufficient architectural access (e.g., inadequate lighting; no ramped exit; waiting alone for an attendant, reader, or note-taker who never appears at the appointed hour or who perpetrates an attack). The demands of full-time courseloads are also a burden for disabled women, who require extra time and energy to find ways around inaccessible campus architecture, study using braille, or hike to class on crutches. Some disabled women must be certain that attendants are available to assist in everyday living (e.g., eating, going to bed, transferring to wheelchair) while under pressure to compete for grades—no small task given their often inadequate college preparation.

Commonalities of barriers in the academic environment.   Two shared barriers for both older women and women of disability are safety concerns and problems of time and energy management in an inaccessible academic environment that was not originally designed to include them. Although older and disabled women students who commute to college escape violence from dormitory intruders, both are targets for assault in other situations. Disabled women students may be dependent on an abusive male attendant for assistance with coursework and daily living activities; older women may be attacked in isolated parking lots with poor lighting and few security guards.

Traditional college academic and social programs often exclude both disabled and older women students from participation in a full campus life because their time and energy demands are already consumed elsewhere. Spontaneous meetings with young, nondisabled students and faculty members become nearly impossible in a tight schedule. The full-time inflexible courseload requirement in tuition and funding programs is a burden for disabled and older women students who must cope with these added survival responsibilities. With little space in the schedule for campus socializing, disabled and older women, by default, may become more serious students— although, perhaps, for different reasons.

Commonalities of responses of older and disabled women. Feelings of self-doubt, anger, and frustration at barriers while access is so available to younger and nondisabled students create the need to develop bonds with peers or allies who understand the life circumstances of those who are older and disabled and who share the need to discover new ways to solve problems beyond initial negative responses of the bureaucracy. Despite injustices, survival techniques must be discovered if college degrees are to be completed. Uniting in support groups, learning to manage frustrations, developing "tough survivor" personality traits, and creating new services are among the common strategies. Strategies must include ways to control vulnerability to violence on campus and wise time and energy usage. Both older and disabled women often report that they become more organized, serious, and task-oriented in their academic work. This is an advantage they share over young, nondisabled students who may not respond with such high motivation levels because their survival does not depend on it to the same degree or for the same reasons.

IMPROVING SERVICES ON CAMPUS

The concept of an interactive needs model to address the complexities of multiple minority "special populations" (lesbians of color, older women with disabilities, etc.) is generally unknown on today's campus. Accustomed to schedules associated with traditional students (i.e., young, white, nondisabled males), campus personnel may feel relieved if some organization can "take care of the problem" when students of only one minority status (female *or* ethnic *or* older *or* disabled *or* gay/lesbian) arrive with unique needs. The existence of students with needs who are members of more than one minority group is an overwhelming complexity for traditional campuses.

Current Services

Among services that currently exist to assist older women students, the advising services of continuing education staff members often stand out as examples of the type of help that can be most useful. In some continuing education programs, staff members are not only experienced in course requirements and university procedures but are also able to advise students on seeking additional funding, finding part-time or full-time work, and obtaining good quality child care. Beyond the continuing education staff, however, services specific to the needs of older women students are often nonexistent.

With regard to women with disabilities, the on-campus experience of the first author plus communications with a variety of disability and women's programs (S. A. Kroeger, June 1990; J. Lonergan, September 1991; C. Rozumalski, October 1991) indicates information and referral, advocacy, and counseling or consultation services are used frequently. Disability centers offer such services as an accompaniment to accessing a barrier-filled campus by providing sign language interpreters, readers, notetakers, adaptive braille computer, and textbook tape-recording. Women's centers offer information and referral, advocacy, and counseling or consultation services to assist women in accessing programs that have traditionally excluded them. The problems of older disabled women students are rarely addressed because continuing education programs, women's centers, and disability resource services usually do not deal with the intersections of sexism, ageism, and disableism.

Future Services Needed

What older women in both academic and extracurricular programs require are expanded hours for facilities, more flexible scheduling for courses (particularly required courses in majors), and the addition or rearrangement of advising times for students who must work. In general, administrations are not positively disposed toward meeting these needs and current fiscal restraints offer little hope for making new changes. Although attitudes of faculty members are usually positive in regard to meeting the needs of older students, they may not press for institutional changes. Too often, faculty find themselves overburdened with routine responsibilities and are reluctant to engage administrators in political confrontations over the needs of what constitutes a small minority of the student population.

What is needed are more interwoven services within programs that simultaneously connect issues for both groups. That is, being female and being disabled should not be separate concerns; a woman of disability should not have to go to a disability resource service to address only her disability access needs, and then receive a referral to a women's center when she discusses how lack of access affects her as a female. Within the disability programs, there should be curriculum and support groups specifically addressing sexism and women's issues in addition to information and referrals to nondisabled women's campus groups. Women's centers must address the problem of disableism within their diversity programs and provide support groups that include women with disabilities, in addition to giving information and referral to disability resource centers. Curricula of women's studies programs should include coursework in disability from the perspective of disabled women as a credible minority group with the same seriousness of purpose as their course offerings on women of color and sexual minority women. Rehabilitation and disability studies programs should address issues of sexism in their required courses, develop seminars that focus on women's concerns, and cross-list them with women's studies in catalogs and registration materials.

All three services (continuing education, women's centers, and disability resource services) have yet to consider the interacting concerns of the increasing numbers of "special students" who are members of more than one minority group. Too often an older, disabled, lesbian student who has been battered goes to the women's center to meet her "woman needs," to the disability office to meet her "disability needs," and to the continuing education office where her "reentry needs" are discussed. Other student services such as the mental health clinic and the career and job placement office rarely have staff who comprehend the complexities of interacting stereotypes. Rarely can they relate both personally and professionally with the increasing multiple minority diversity of students. An increase in student service integration and interoffice communication is especially critical because older women and women of disability already have schedule burdens that reduce their time and energy for seeking out isolated, separate services that may be some distance from each other on campus.

College administrations must also realize that with the increasing multiple minority complexities of the "special student population," there are now women on campus who are over age forty and *also* have disabilities. As continuing education, women's programs, and disability services recognize the intersecting problems of sexism, ageism, and disableism, it is important for the college administration to expand recruitment of role models on campus. Not only must there be more students recruited who are female and older or disabled, but also campus staff, faculty, and administrators who represent membership in these minority communities must be hired. The college must focus on the still-larger community picture: when committees come on campus to evaluate the college for accreditation progress for new or existing programs, advisors with expertise in older women's and disability issues and concomitant problems of sexism, ageism, and disableism should be included.

CONCLUSION: IMPLICATIONS FOR FURTHER STUDY

The concerns of both older women and women with disabilities as they experience their undergraduate college years have been the major focus of this chapter. Older and disabled women have diverse and unique needs and circumstances, yet they share two characteristics (aging and disability are inevitable for both) that set them apart from other minority groups. All women of color and all lesbians will age and be vulnerable to disability resulting from the unpredictability of accidents and illness; however, the possibility of a heterosexual, white, disabled, older woman becoming a lesbian of color overnight is quite remote. Because of the unavoidability of aging and disability, society has deep-seated anxiety and negative feelings about women who defy the youthful beauty standard by appearing in public (the campus included) with wrinkles and wheelchairs. Only in recent history have colleges admitted these women in appreciable numbers. This is also the first generation of women in American history whose longevity has extended activity levels for those attending college who would have not have survived earlier accidents or illness.

Their longevity has created interesting dilemmas for the legal, medical, and economic systems in terms of supporting and funding these "survivors" and for the professors who teach them. Older and disabled women cope with continuous frustrations from the "cumulative burdens" they have brought to the campus in addition to the barriers and lack of access they find when they arrive. Campus personnel, having dealt previously with traditional students (i.e., young, white, nondisabled males), are unprepared for the challenge that these women will present to them. Pathbreaking technology, methodologies, and literature to assist both campus personnel and these new student populations to cope with the challenges they present to each other are only beginning to appear. Empirical studies addressing the interacting components of ageism, disableism, and sexism as experienced on the college campus by nondisabled older women, disabled younger women, and older women of disability are needed. Researchers from the fields of women's studies, gerontology, and rehabilitation/disabilities studies have yet to integrate or unite to the degree needed to produce this multidimensional work.

REFERENCES

Altman, B. M. (1985). Disabled women in the social structure. In S. E. Browne, D. Connors, & N. Stern (Eds.), *With the power of each breath: A disabled women's anthology* (pp. 69-75). San Francisco: Cleis Press.

Asch, A., & Fine, M. (1988). Introduction: Beyond pedestals. In M. Fine & A. Asch (Eds.), *Women with disabilities: Essays in psychology, culture, and politics* (pp. 1-37). Philadelphia: Temple University Press.

Atkins, B. J. (1982). Women as members of special populations in rehabilitation. In *Women and rehabilitation of disabled persons: Women as members of special populations in rehabilitation* (Report of the Mary E. Switzer Memorial Seminar No. 6, chap. 3).

Barker, J. T. (1982). Women as leaders in the field of rehabilitation. *Journal of Rehabilitation, 48*(1), 9-18, 68-70.

Beutell, N., & O'Hara, M. (1987). Coping with role conflict among returning students: Professional versus nonprofessional women. *Journal of College Student Personnel, 28*(2), 141-145.

Bowe, F. (1984). *Disabled women in America* (Statistical report drawn from Census Bureau data). Washington, D.C.: President's Committee on Employment of the Handicapped.

Care that kills. (1986, November/December). *Disability Rag*, pp. 9-10.

Cleave-Hogg, D. (1990). *Learning perspectives of older students enrolled full-time in a regular undergraduate program.* Paper presented at the Fifth Adult Development Symposium of the Society for Research in Adult Development, Cambridge, Mass.

Connors, D. (1985). Disability, sexism and the social order. In S. E. Browne, D. Connors, & N. Stern (Eds.), *With the power of each breath: A disabled women's anthology* (pp. 92-107). San Francisco: Cleis Press.

Danek, M. M., & Lawrence, R. E. (1985). Women in rehabilitation: An analysis of state agency services to disabled women. *Journal of Applied Rehabilitation Counseling, 16*(1), 16-18.

Davis, M. (1989). Gender and sexual development of women with mental retardation. *Disability Studies Quarterly, 9*(3), 19-20.

Deegan, M. J., & Brooks, N. A. (1985). Introduction: Women and disability: The double handicap. In M. J. Deegan & N. A. Brooks (Eds.), *Women and disability: The double handicap* (pp. 1-5). New Brunswick, N.J.: Transaction Books.

Doress, P. B., Siegal, D. L., Midlife and Older Women Book Project, & Boston Women's Health Book Collective. (1987). *Ourselves, growing older: Women aging with knowledge and power.* New York: Simon & Schuster.

Durham, H. (1986, June). *The war on the disabled: Adding insult to injury.* Paper presented at the Conference of National Women's Studies Association, University of Illinois, Urbana-Champaign.

Fine, M., & Asch, A. (1985). Disabled women: Sexism without the pedestal. In M. J. Deegan & N. A. Brooks (Eds.), *Women and disability: The double handicap* (pp. 6-22). New Brunswick, N.J.: Transaction Books.

Gibson, J. W., & Durano, M. I. (1989). *Aging and developmental disabilities: A beginning bibliography* (CDMRC Paper No. 8901). Seattle: University of Washington, School of Social Work and Child Development and Mental Retardation Center.

Giesen, C. (1989). Aging and attractiveness: Marriage makes a difference. *International Journal of Aging and Human Development, 29*(2), 83-94.

Giesen, C. (1990, July). *Self-initiated change.* Paper presented at the 5th Adult Development Symposium, Cambridge, Mass.

Giesen, C. (1991, March). *Adversity and diversity: Advantaged and disadvantaged women coping with challenge.* Paper presented at the 16th National Conference of the Association for Women in Psychology, Hartford, Conn.

Giesen, C. (in press). Self-initiated change: The dialectic of continuing development. In M. Commons, C. Goldberg, & J. Demick (Eds.), *Clinical approaches to adult development.* New York: Ablex.

Grambs, J. (1989). *Women over forty: Visions and realities.* New York: Springer.

Grothaus, R. S. (1985). Abuse of women with disabilities. In S. E. Browne, D. Connors, & N. Stern (Eds.), *With the power of each breath: A disabled women's anthology* (pp. 124-128). San Francisco: Cleis Press.

Hannaford, S. (1985). *Living outside inside: A disabled woman's experience toward a social and political perspective.* Berkeley: Canterbury Press.

Hiemstra, R. (1985). The older adult's learning projects. In D. B. Lumsden (Ed.), *The older adult as learner* (p. 165). New York: Hemisphere Publishing.

Holcomb, L. P. (1984). Disabled women: A new issue in education. *Journal of Rehabilitation, 50*(1), 18-22, 70.

Holcomb, L. P. (1990). *The interaction of issues of disability and aging* (Annotated Bibliography and Position Paper Draft). Seattle: Seattle Women's Commission Project on Ageism and Disableism.

Holcomb, L. P. (1991, March). *Covert oppression, minority groups, and women with disabilities.* Paper presented at the 16th National Conference of the Association for Women in Psychology, Hartford, Conn.

Holcomb, L. P., & Chai, A. Y. (1988, June). *Facing age with disability, facing disability with age.* Panel presentation at the National Women's Studies Association Conference, University of Minnesota, Minneapolis.

Hollingsworth, D. K., & Mastroberti, C. J. (1983). Women, work, and disability. *Personnel and Guidance Journal, 61*(10), 587-591.

Hopkins-Best, M., Murphy, S., & Yurcisin, A. (1988). *Reaching the hidden majority: A leader's guide to career preparation for disabled women and girls.* Cranston, R.I.: Carroll Press.

Hopkins-Best, M., Wiinamaki, M., & Yurcisin, A. (1985). Career education for college women with disabilities. *Journal of College Student Personnel, 26*(3), 220-223.

Imdieke, M. (1988, Spring). The economic status of disabled women. *Womyn's Braille Press Newsletter,* p. 5.

Kinderknecht, C. H. (1989). Aging women and long-term care: Truth and consequences. *Journal of Women & Aging, 1*(4), 71-92.

Kriegsman, K. H., & Bregman, S. (1985). Women with disabilities at midlife. *Rehabilitation Counseling Bulletin, 29*(2), 112-122.

Kroeger, S. A., & Pazandak, C. H. (1990, August). Women with disabilities and the college experience: Report of a study. In S. M. Bruyere (Chair), *Higher education experiences of women with disabilities.* Symposium presented at the Annual Convention of the American Psychological Association, Boston, Mass.

Kutza, E. A. (1985). Benefits for the disabled: How beneficial for women? In M. J. Deegan & N. A. Brooks (Eds.), *Women and disability:*

The double handicap (pp. 68-86). New Brunswick, N.J.: Transaction Books.

Leavitt, R. (1989 . Married women returning to college: A study of their personal and family adjustments. *Smith College Studies in Social Work, 59*(3), 301-315.

Lederer, L. (1991, March/April). Finding common ground: Advocates for seniors and for people with disabilities forge coalitions. *The OWL Observer*, pp. 1-3.

Lesh, K., & Marshall, C. (1984). Rehabilitation: Focus on disabled women as a special population. *Journal of Applied Rehabilitation Counseling, 15*(1), 18-21.

Lumsden, D. B. (Ed.). (1985). *The older adult as learner.* New York: Hemisphere Publishing.

Marshall, C. A. (1990, August). Career guidance and women with disabilities in higher education. In S. M. Bruyere (Chair), *Higher education experiences of women with disabilities.* Symposium presented at the Annual Convention of the American Psychological Association, Boston, Mass.

Matthews, G. F. (1983). *Voices from the shadows: Women with disabilities speak out.* Toronto: Women's Educational Press.

Merriam, S., & Lumsden, D. B. (1985). Educational needs and interests of older learners. In D. B. Lumsden (Ed.), *The older adult as learner* (p. 51). New York: Hemisphere Publishing.

Mudrick, N. R. (1987). Differences in receipt of rehabilitation by impaired midlife men and women. *Rehabilitation Psychology, 32*(1), 17-28.

Munson, R. G. (1987). *Aging and developmental disabilities* (CDMRC Position Paper No. 8701). Seattle: University of Washington, Child Development and Mental Retardation Center.

Myers, T. (1991, Summer). My experience at blind school, part 2. *Womyn's Braille Press Newsletter*, pp. 12-18.

O'Toole, C. J. (1990, Fall). Violence and sexual assault plague many disabled women. *Womyn's Braille Press Newsletter*, pp. 24-27.

O'Toole, J. C., & Weeks, C. (1978). *What happens after school?: A study of disabled women and education* (Contract No. 300-77-0535). Washington, D.C.: U.S. Department of Health, Education, and Welfare.

Owen, M. J. (1988, July). Survival notes at 50-plus. *Gray Panthers Disability Task Force Newsletter*, pp. 1-3.

Palmore, E. (1990). *Ageism: Negative and positive.* New York: Springer.

Peterson, R., & Pelarski, J. (1974, Spring). The deaf woman as wife and mother: Two views. *Gallaudet Today*, pp. 20-23.

Phillips, E. (1986). *Women and girls with disabilities: An introductory teaching packet.* Brooklyn: Organization for Equal Education of the Sexes, Inc.

Porcino, J. (1983). *Growing older, getting better: A handbook for women in the second half of life.* Reading, Mass.: Addison-Wesley.

Roff, L., & Atherton, C. (1989). *Promoting successful aging.* Chicago: Nelson-Hall.

Russo, N. F., & Jansen, M. A. (1988). Women, work, and disability: Opportunities and challenges. In M. Fine & A. Asch (Eds.), *Women with disabilities: Essays in psychology, culture, and politics* (pp. 229-244). Philadelphia: Temple University Press.

Saviola, M. E. (1981). Personal reflections on physically disabled women and dependency. *Professional Psychology, 12*(1), 112-117.

Saxton, M. (1988). *The Project on Women and Disability first year report: 1988.* Boston: The Project on Women and Disability.

Simon, B. L. (1988). Never-married old women and disability: A majority experience. In M. Fine & A. Asch (Eds.), *Women with disabilities: Essays in psychology, culture, and politics* (pp. 215-225). Philadelphia: Temple University Press.

Simons, C. (1991, September). The new integration. *Habilitation: Disabilities Research & Information Coalition,* pp. 8-9, 14.

Sommers, T., & Shields, L. (1987). *Women take care: The consequences of caregiving in today's society.* Gainesville, Fla.: Triad.

Swift, J., Colvin, C., & Mills, D. (1987). Displaced homemakers: Adults returning to college with different characteristics and needs. *Journal of College Student Personnel, 28*(4), 343-350.

Trieschmann, R. B. (1987). *Aging with a disability.* New York: Demos Publications.

Vash, C. L. (1982). Employment issues for women with disabilities. *Rehabilitation Literature, 43*(7/8), 198-207.

Women and Disability Awareness Project. (1984). *Building community: A manual exploring issues of women and disability.* New York: Educational Equity Concepts, Inc.

Teaching the Psychology of Women

Ann Marie Orza
Jane W. Torrey

The field of psychology of women had to begin with teaching. Until there were courses, there was little need to write books that organized the information available about women. Courses gave psychologists a place in the curriculum and the professional task of furthering research. They also attracted students, women especially, to aspire to a future in psychology of women. The same could be said of women's studies in most other academic disciplines as well as of academia generally, as women's studies has blurred the boundaries between disciplines. Two decades of experience with feminist psychology have produced radically new perspectives both on psychology as a whole and on the methodology of teaching. This chapter examines these effects as experienced by two feminist psychologists.

Historical Overview

For more than two decades feminist psychologists have been struggling to compensate for the neglect of women by traditional psychology. A key event in the development of the new "psychology of women" was a paper delivered in 1968 by Naomi Weisstein, "'Kinder, Kuche, Kirche' as Scientific Law: Psychology Constructs the Female" (Weisstein, 1970). She quoted assertions about women, still found in texts today, which reflect the traditional, obviously male, perspective: Bettelheim's "Women . . . want first and foremost to be womanly companions of men and to be mothers" and Erikson's "somatic design harbors an 'inner space' destined to bear the offspring of chosen men, and with it, a biological, psychological, and ethical commitment to take care of human infancy" (p. 206). Weisstein showed that these views and many other common assumptions and conclusions about women, far from being supported, were actually contradicted by much of the available evidence. Her thesis was that "present psychology is less than worthless in contributing to a vision which could truly liberate—men as well as women" (p. 208).

The traditional underrating of women and neglect of their concerns in psychology curricula reflected an assumption that women and their issues were peripheral to the science. As recently as 1976 the first author was allowed to offer a course in psychology of women only in summer and evenings because the subject was regarded as "exotic." Publication of relevant textbooks had begun only a few years earlier. Bardwick's (1971) pioneering textbook, *The Psychology of Women*, was organized around a traditional idea of gender differences as biological, but texts with broader focus progressed rapidly as new research findings on women became increasingly available. Matlin (1987) listed nine new general books on the subject between 1974 and 1976. Paludi (1990) listed fifteen more texts since 1987, including several new editions. As the texts proliferated, research and theory were also progressing. Bem published "The Measurement of Psychological Androgyny" in 1974, and, as more and more varied research on gender appeared, the American Psychological Association in 1973 officially recognized the subject by adding the "Division of the Psychology of Women." Further research and writing have made possible the proliferation of texts and of the material summarized in them.

By 1977 Tavris and Offir (1977) dared to highlight the political nature of the trend by calling their text *The Longest War*, thus exposing themselves to the possibility of backlash charges like those later called "reverse discrimination" or a narrow "political correctness." They also addressed the "oldest mystery": "Why are people inclined to emphasize the sexual differences between men and women instead of their similarities?" (p. vii). However, they were still forced, like others, to dwell on those differences because so many of the traditional data relating to the psychology of women had focused on difference. By the 1980s some texts began to state unequivocally that "It is no longer possible to ignore or deny the fact that the sexes are unequally valued and unequally rewarded" (Stockard & Johnson, 1980, p. xv). Without apology those authors continue: "We have now advanced beyond the stage of simply documenting sexism and are increasingly in a position to explore the social mechanisms which tend to reproduce and sustain it" (p. xv). In the 1980s academics were openly insisting on the relevance of political values to psychology by acknowledging that the inequality built into our culture and its institutions both teaches and forces women to accept without challenge an inferior situation and a damaging self-image.

Although the psychology of women is widely taught today, it has yet to become part of the "canon" of the discipline. There has been little revision of other texts to reflect the increasing research on women. The common insertion of "boxes" into outdated material isolates the subject and fails to show its relevance, that is, how it modifies or contradicts existing male-oriented conclusions. The principle of "separate but unequal" also prevails in curriculum requirements, so that a psychology major can usually graduate having studied only psychology based on males. Furthermore, in the 1990s, with the declining economy serving as the excuse, the psychology of women is again being questioned, and various political tactics are being used to discredit both its teaching and its research. Its introduction of political considerations is described as a violation of scientific objectivity, and where its research methods focus on real life as opposed to laboratory situations, it is underrated as "soft" science. There is even pressure to introduce a psychology of men (which might be a tautology in light of the traditional bias toward men in the supposedly objective science), thus seeming to consign women to the status of "guest in men's studies" (Spender, 1981, p. 28). Even the language used is derided as "politically correct," as if male-oriented language were not itself a manifestation of pervasive politics. These attacks on the academic legitimacy of women's studies force feminists to spend time and labor resisting them, but the effort may be worthwhile to the extent that it requires the defenders to understand for themselves the profound implications of gender balancing for the very nature of the discipline and to examine some of the implicit assumptions that underlie resistance to change. These theoretical considerations need to be understood in order to give substance and direction to the new scholarship on women.

Theoretical Implications of a Feminist Psychology

The term "psychology of women" implied a new focus for the old psychology. It did not seem to imply any fundamental change in the discipline. However, McIntosh (1983) warned us when we first began to introduce the study of women into our curricula that we would have to do more than "add women and stir"; that taking women seriously as subjects of research, first, by examining the reasons why women had been neglected in our disciplines, and, ultimately, by showing how traditional assumptions selectively ignored the kind of information that could be derived from the study of women, would lead us to recognize the need to "re-vision" the whole framework of scholarship. The psychology of women has indeed made it possible to identify assumptions underlying our science that have contributed to the near exclusion of the whole subject of gender, not to mention class and race, as factors in the understanding of humans and their interrelations. In this respect the psychology of women course must be expected to differ in its fundamental assumptions from many other psychology courses and to take into account possible future trends both in society and in psychology.

The inadequacy and bias in our traditional scientific methods have become more visible through the serious study of women in psychological research, in therapy, and in feminist social action. Gilligan (1982) studied Kohlberg's research on moral development, based entirely on male subjects, and showed that the effects of "gender" could be understood as the difference between a "justice" model and a "caring" model of morality. Kohlberg's conclusion that "justice" was the more "mature" way of thinking toward which people progressed, based on his finding that men progressed that way, was not borne out when women were the subjects. His methodology had limited all differences to a purely quantitative comparison with the male-based standard and also excluded consideration of the emotional development in the moral thinking that showed in Gilligan's study.

Miller's (1976) gender analysis of husbands and wives in therapy led her to conclude that human ties are a basic element in human psychology, and, especially that "'doing for others' . . . is a fundamental organizing principle in women's lives" (p. 82). She argues that the social construction of masculinity as strong, independent, and purely rational has tended to deprive men of insight into their own inadequacies, as well as into their interpersonal and emotional needs, and that women's subordinate position has made it easier for them to confront these issues in themselves. In a conference address Miller (1991) illustrated how a woman could find more relief for her anxiety through conversation with another woman, who recognized and responded to her feelings, than in conversation with a husband who responded only by proposing a rational approach to the problem and then changing the subject. The two women found mutual solace, whereas the couple remained alienated from each other and themselves. Miller proposed the term "feelingthoughts" for the kind of thing the women communicated. That she had to grope for a new term to label a familiar phenomenon reflects the fact that psychology itself has assumed our culture's unbridgeable gap between thought and feeling, at the same time valuing thought (reason) over feeling (emotion). It was these same assumptions that marred Kohlberg's interpretation of women. Miller proposed that women's traditional "weaknesses," their sensitivity to emotion and their need for ties with others, were strengths both in self-understanding and in approaching the needs of a future society.

The study by Belenky et al. (1986) that examined intellectual development in women concluded, among other things, that women, because they take a more personal approach to thinking, are especially able to understand the constructivist insight that "All knowledge is constructed, and the knower is an intimate part of the known" (p. 137). These authors speak of "connected knowing," or "finding connections between what women are trying to understand and their own experience" (p. 141). They found that "Women tend not to rely as readily . . . on hypothetico-deductive inquiry, as they do on examining the basic assumptions . . . in which a problem is cast" (p. 139). Possibly this is because women are so often exposed to reasoning based on assumptions different from their own.

Teaching the psychology of women has also forced us to examine social phenomena with obvious psychological implications that had been ignored in male-oriented psychology. Rape, wife battery, and sexual harassment were issues not much addressed until the women's movement called attention to them.

Psychologists trying to understand the gendered nature both of these male behaviors and of women's responses to them, were forced to the realization that the power relations between the sexes were an indispensable key to the underlying psychology. It was not possible to understand these things simply in terms of factors contained within individuals, ignoring the power relations involved.

These insights from the new psychology of women therefore have begun something like a "paradigm shift" in the field of psychology. Kuhn (1962) argued that large breakthroughs in science do not come about through the accumulation of evidence that has gradually modified theory to make it accord with data. Revolutionary progress, he said, occurs by shifts in a framework of assumptions that underlie any and all hypotheses, the basic "paradigm" of the discipline. Psychology has traditionally been based on a "nature-nature" paradigm, an assumption that behavior is to be explained entirely in terms of two sets of factors, both of which work as internal characteristics of individuals—some traits that are inherited biologically and others that are acquired through exposure to the world. It is implicitly assumed that all determiners of behavior are stable characteristics of the individual, incorporated in the body of the person. Learning is *taking in* knowledge, rules, or behavior tendencies shaped by the outside world. But the environment is assumed not to influence behavior unless it has already been made part of the individual through *prior* experience. Motivation is also conceived as an interior engine deriving energy from biological needs modified through personal past experiences. Therefore present or new environmental conditions cannot be considered direct causes of behavior. If a person acts helpless, it cannot be simply because she knows that no help is available, but must be because she has a neurotic attitude that she has learned. Motivation is further said to function only on behalf of the individual's own personal needs, so that altruism, which means working on behalf of others, is inconceivable. Where the apparent goal seems to meet only the needs of another individual, such as the common female behavior of caring for an infant, it must be somehow explained away as satisfying some *individual* need such as a "maternal drive" within the caregiver.

Having assumed that all important factors in behavior are part of the autonomous individual, psychology has proceeded to try to understand and evaluate each person in terms of herm-self (sic). "Maturity" has been interpreted as requiring the development of autonomy, self-direction from within the individual. "Identity" has meant simply knowing oneself, an attitude toward self alone. "Mental health" is said to require a high degree of self-esteem. The highest valued level of development, called "individuation" or "self-actualization," has been regarded as determined from within.

Because we have accepted the white middle-class male as a norm of humanity and studied the world from his viewpoint, it has been easier to ignore a hidden assumption in the practice of explaining behavior on the basis of individual characteristics: that the individuals have the power to act on their own behalf. It is an assumption much better suited to explain powerful people than weak people, to understand masters rather than slaves. Actually, the majority of people on earth usually act according to the needs of someone else: husbands, masters, employers or other superiors, or those of a group such as family or community. They make relatively few choices on their own behalf. They are seldom autonomous or self-directed. Most of their behavior is dictated by their circumstances, their position in the structure of society. It is true that they have often been "nurtured" or trained to accept the authority of others over themselves as individuals, but that influence often has only the effect of making them accept their situation more submissively. It is more often the realistic understanding of their own powerlessness to do otherwise that determines their behavior. Another person, not trained to submit or to be helpless, would have to do the same thing in the same situation of powerlessness, as when they are suddenly imprisoned, enslaved, married, or moved into any new and subordinate situation in life. Present circumstance can have a direct effect on behavior not necessarily mediated through individual need or past learning. Circumstances can make us do things against our biological urges or even survival, against all our training, against all our personality development and motivation. Responses to torture or a gun in the back are not attributable either to nature or to nurture. Widows in India (even today) may immolate themselves no matter what they wish or believe because of the real, external fact that there is no longer a place for them in their society. Battered wives may stay unwillingly in their abuser's home because they know he will kill them or their children if they try to leave. Teenage mothers may be forced by their situation to drop out of school and go on welfare no matter what their previous training or ambition. The individual psychology paradigm that serves fairly well in understanding the white middle-class males of the world becomes less adequate in understanding people whose "choices" are determined by circumstances like these.

Even individual identity is not an individual matter. Identity can exist only in relation to others. One cannot understand what it is to be a woman without knowing what "men" are even as the meaning of being black depends on knowledge of whites. Fanon (1967) reports that growing up black in Martinique did not prepare him for the new black identity he discovered immediately on arriving in France and interacting with white Frenchmen. Fanon noted that "Beyond phylogeny and ontogeny there is sociogeny" (p. 11). The social circumstances in which we live determine our behavior directly as well as through their influence on our development. The institutionalized sexism and racism of our society are as much parts of each individual personality as of the society as a whole. Weisstein (1970) had foreseen this essential insight for any liberating psychology of gender: "Until psychologists realize that it is they who are limiting discovery of human potential by their . . . assumption that people move in a context-free ether, with only their innate dispositions and their individual traits determining what they will do . . . psychology will have nothing of substance to offer" (p. 220) because "it is obvious that a study of human behavior requires . . . a study of the social contexts within which people move, the expectations as to how they will behave, and the authority which tells them who they are and what they are supposed to do" (p. 218). It follows that the traditional laboratory experiment in psychology is an unlikely place to discover the most important truths about the human being.

Some understanding of the fact that human nature is inherently social does have a history within psychology. Freud derived personality from the relations between family members even as he thought in individual terms. Sullivan (1964) asserted that there was no such thing as individual personality. All personality dynamics are interpersonal, that is, they have meaning only in relation to other individuals. Adler (1927) argued that humans could have survived as a species only by gathering together, so that social interest must have been enhanced by natural selection of those who lived socially. In this sense "social concern" for other people must have become an innate characteristic of humans.

Fromm (1962), influenced by Marx, recognized the way in which the specific sociocultural context, including the physical, legal, and economic forces that impinge on individuals in a particular historical era, are incorporated into human *nature*, that is to say, that human behavior could not be understood apart from that context. Jung (1976) recognized the social nature of the human in his concept of a collective unconscious. Without accepting his implication of traits inherited genetically by all individuals from "primitive man," we can find in the archetype a representation of the fact that an unconscious cultural component in our personality exists without necessarily ever having been explicitly articulated or intentionally taught. Even what we think of as external circumstance includes more than the ideas people acquire consciously through perception and logical deduction. The ways of society are known and understood in many less conscious or explicit ways that often include emotions and evaluations. Much of culture takes the form of myths, symbols, word meanings, thought patterns, and feelings that do not originate in us as individuals or derive from our personal experience. They are shared by others in our particular society so that they become for us unspoken assumptions that go with membership in that society and are taken for granted in all our interactions. They are internal in that they are acquired, but without anyone explicitly teaching them and without the knowers even being aware of them. Fromm (1962) calls them the "social unconscious," because their function is not personal but societal in that "each society determines which thoughts and feelings shall be permitted to arrive at the level of awareness and which have to remain unconscious . . . contents which a given society cannot permit its members to be aware of if the society with its specific contradictions is to operate successfully" (p. 88). Just as individual defense mechanisms protect the ego, the social unconscious rationalizes and defends the social order, including its faults, contradictions, and injustices.

The male bias of psychology and other supposedly objective sciences is an example of the implicit cultural mythology of masculinity in our society. Berger and Luckmann (1967) have illustrated how the perception of reality in sociology is "socially constructed," that is, made to support the social order of which the sociologist is a part. Often implicit cultural mythology contradicts more conscious values, as when racist attitudes coexist with abstract beliefs in equality and brother-sisterhood. Sometimes when values conflict, the underlying mythology is papered over with more acceptable representations, as when attitudes that condone misogyny and wife abuse are represented as "family values," rape is interpreted as due to natural sexual drives that are part of normal "manhood," racism was once called "the Southern way of life," and support for war is called "patriotism." These words operate like ego defenses such as rationalization, imposing the patriarchal values of "manhood" or masculinity on our understanding of behavior that would look very different from another point of view.

The study of women has also opened our eyes to the fact that autonomy and separateness are not necessarily the ideal of personal integrity. Many, including Miller (1976), Gilligan (1982), and McIntosh (1983), among others, have pointed out the value of collective thinking and feeling in the woman's world and invited men to help themselves as well as others by participating in a cooperative mutuality rather than competitive individuality. The feminist valorization of empathy and interpersonal connections suggests the need for a healthy change in the structure of the family and the larger society to create circumstances more friendly to a better structure of individual personality. Recognizing the social roots of behavior has had the effect of highlighting some contradictions between reality and many of our values. It has become obvious that the social order today involves grave injustice to women and many others. It follows, as all who begin to study women or other less powerful people discover, that change in people as individuals, their conflicts and their prejudices, cannot be dealt with adequately on the individual level with therapy or even education. The solution will come only when there are changes in the society and culture of which people, including parents, therapists, educators, are a part. The personal, in other words, is political, and vice versa.

The psychological implications of even seemingly biological factors such as menstruation, pregnancy, childbirth, sexual arousal, and menopause cannot be understood apart from society and culture. The mythology of "raging hormonal imbalances"; the religious doctrine that "life," including human rights, begins for an individual at fertilization; the view of contractions in labor as pain that is punishment for sin; terminology that describes the obstetrician, not the mother, as "delivering the child"; the notion that "clitoral orgasm" is childish, to be abandoned in maturity for a passive "vaginal orgasm"; and the diagnosis of "involutional melancholia" all represent the imposition of social meaning to shape psychological response to physical processes. The meanings in these cases are all patriarchal, that is, they assign control to men and consign women to passivity at the mercy of men, biology, or both. The same may be said of biological development, prenatal, infantile, childhood, adolescent, adult, and elderly. At every stage the psychological implications depend as much upon the social meanings assigned to gender as directly to anatomical or physiological change.

The insight that so much of human psychology cannot be understood except in the context of society and culture creates cognitive dissonance with our ideas of human freedom and fulfillment. The fact that so many of us are thwarted by the social circumstances of our gender, race, class, religion, ethnic background, sexual orientation, or disabilities is readily perceived as unnecessary, discriminatory, and unjust. The clear implication of this new psychology is that action for interpersonal and social change is part and parcel of any program for individual change. Values become integral even to a scientific psychology of human beings.

These new approaches suggested by the psychology of women not only indicate the future of the science; they have also inspired a range of new pedagogical techniques for conveying these new insights and material to students of all ages. The present authors share some devices and ideas they have found useful.

PEDAGOGICAL IMPLICATIONS AND TECHNIQUES

Cultural Diversity

Perhaps the most important task confronting women's studies (and all other studies) at this moment in history is to convey the fact that an individual's psychological makeup cannot be understood except in the context of the particular roles he or she plays in the particular culture and community to which he or she belongs as well as in the wider national context. It follows that just as gender status must be taken into account to explain the psychology of women, so also must class, race, and ethnicity be considered in understanding humans of either sex who do not belong to the category of middle-class white male psychologists, whose work has formed and informed the science. As students of the psychology of "women," we are confronted with the reality that there are women, and then there are women. Teachers and researchers in the psychology of women share the goal of including and understanding not only both sexes but also the great variety of people who also differ from the middle-class European male in race, class, or ethnicity. Women of different nations, subgroups in a nation, different cultures, subcultures, and classes have different statuses, circumstances, and powers relative to men in their own groups and relative to women and men in other groups they encounter. But the practical difficulty we meet first in trying to incorporate the diversity of women into our courses is the same we met before in trying to give information about any women: just as psychologists traditionally formed their theories and research around (white, middle-class) men, so when they finally turned their attention to women, they assumed the white middle-class woman. The psychological literature still provides few data that we can be sure truthfully represent other kinds of women. Hence textbooks have all they can do to fill a single chapter on the African American woman, and even less is known about other groups of women. However, until these deficiencies are repaired, there are some makeshift ways in which we can compensate for them even with white middle-class students, who are usually just as ignorant of other women as are the teacher and the textbook. For example, one may assign to each student the task of reading whatever she can find about women in some culture other than white middle-class and considering for herself whether she would expect the psychology textbook's assertions to apply in the same way to them. The second author has asked for a short oral report from each student about their chosen group to make the class aware of the fact that women's circumstances vary widely around the world. Her experience is that a number of students decide to devote their term papers to their chosen group. A limitation with this method is that the reports, whether written or oral, often do not focus on psychological issues very specifically because students are eager to share what they have learned, and what they find is seldom explicitly psychological. Most students, then, will need help in seeing the psychological implications. However, the exercise does give greater cultural breadth to the course than is found in the professional literature, and the discussion often leads to possible psychological implications. An excellent and extremely varied source of information about third world women is the journal WIN, *Women's International Network News*, available from the editor, Fran P. Hosken at 187 Grant Street, Lexington, MA 02173. It reprints excerpts and articles from broadly international sources as well as tables of contents of longer documents. It may be that the most useful advice we can give is to refer the reader to Paludi's (1990) manual of resources for teaching the psychology of women. It seems to contain everything we ever wanted to know, including handbooks, anthologies, bibliographies, abstracts, and indices. It lists research centers and publishers that specialize in women. Pedagogical information includes discussion techniques, audiovisuals, course syllabi, and readings. Everything is organized by topic with all possible attention to inclusiveness and diversity. The authors wish it had been available when they first began to teach the course. A revised version is already in preparation.

When the class itself includes members of culturally different groups, it may sometimes be possible to make use of their personal experience and attitudes, for example, by having students from the groups in question consider the extent to which the "psychology of women" represented in their textbook really applies to the particular cultural groups to which they belong. It can be very useful to have them share their opinions with the rest of the class. However, there are several important cautions for the white middle-class teacher. First, she needs to remember that minority students are individuals, and their beliefs and feelings are extremely various. They often do not want to speak for their group as a whole. In addition, many African American women are tired of being expected to bear the burden of telling white women what it is like to be black. They find it difficult to believe that whites are so ignorant of racism. White middle-class women actually do need the help of other women to appreciate the realities of race and class discrimination, but they must also accept responsibility for broadening their own background.

Second, groups have different priorities. For example, African American and Puerto Rican women know from the experiences of their groups with forced sterilization that reproductive freedom can mean freedom to *have* babies, so discussions of the issue should not focus exclusively on the freedom *not* to have them.

Third, groups have different attitudes. Women struggling to defend the right to legal abortions have a tendency not to address the reservations that many women have about the morality of ending a pregnancy. Abortions have different meanings in different cultures. Homosexuality also may be viewed quite differently by various ethnic groups. This can create serious conflicts unless great care is taken to help students from any group understand the cultural meaning of another's viewpoint.

Matlin's Themes for Re-visioning Gender Differences

As McIntosh foresaw, examining a discipline from the perspective of women does more than add new material; it changes the way one interprets familiar data. The first author has found Matlin's (1987) four themes in the feminist interpretation of sex difference literature useful in demonstrating this fact. First, the psychological differences found are actually very small. What Unger (1979) calls the "illusion of sex differences" stems from the great importance of gender in shaping individual identities and interactions in real life. Second, the differences that exist are found to be attributable more to the responses of other people to the individual than to any internal factors stemming from either nature or nurture. Gould's "X—A fabulous child's story" (1979) illustrates this theme by imagining the consequences of raising a child without letting anyone know its sex. Matlin's third theme is that women are invisible in many important areas, so that the fact that women have accomplished and contributed a great deal to society remains unknown. A film, *The American Woman: Portraits of Courage*, made for the bicentennial, is an effective tool in highlighting the omissions (available from the University of Illinois, 1325 South Oak Street, Champagne, IL 61820).

Finally, Matlin points out the neglect of within-sex variability, which is usually much more significant than the between-sex variation.

Consciousness-Raising

Matlin's third theme, the overwhelmingly androcentric orientation of almost everyone's education, means that few enter their first feminist course with much awareness that anything has been excluded. The first author has found it very useful, therefore, to start by trying to raise students' consciousness of the bias in all disciplines with a test of their knowledge about female figures in history, science, and culture. She asks them to identify women like those named in Table 9-1 or to match names with accomplishments.

Ways of Knowing

Teaching psychology of women makes it necessary to confront women's "ways of knowing," not only because the students are mainly women but because to understand women, people of either sex must be able to see things as women see them. Belenky et al. (1986) conceive of knowledge as a product constructed by psychological activity and thus dependent on properties of the individual knower. They find a "higher level" of knowing in knowledge constructed in terms of women's personalities. Whereas men are trained to idealize logic and exclude emotion, women tend to construct knowledge in a way that includes the affective elements. Miller's (1991) term "feelingthoughts" helps define the content of empathic communication. The idea of "themata" in Murray's Thematic Apperception Test combines need (feeling) with press (knowledge of circumstance). It is probably no accident that "intuitive" knowledge has been considered feminine. Intuition is *immediate* (i.e., direct, not mediated) knowledge, unmediated by intellectual procedures such as logic and "objective" observation. Feelings are not constructed by intellectual procedures; they present themselves without such mediation. But this is not to say they cannot be communicated. We can see sadness in the face and movements of another person; we can hear joy in a tone of voice; we can express feeling in poetry. Observations of this kind have been shown to be just as reliable

TABLE 9-1
Consciousness Raising Exercise: Identifying Important Women

Isabelle Allende	Contemporary Chilean novelist
Kate Chopin	American feminist novelist
Tsitsi Dangarembga	Zimbabwean novelist
Angela Davis	African American philosopher and rights activist
Indira Ghandi	Former prime minister of India
Charlotte Perkins Gilman	American economist
Nadine Gordimer	South African novelist
Frida Kahlo	Mexican surrealist painter
Maxine Hong Kingston	Asian American author
Christine Ladd-Franklin	American mathematician and psychologist
Susanne Langer	American philosopher
Sybil Ludington	16-year-old patriot who rode twice as far as Paul Revere to save Danbury, Connecticut from the British
Rosa Luxemburg	Socialist writer and activist
Wilma Mankiller	Chief of the Cherokee Nation
Golda Meier	Prime minister of Israel
Murasaki	Classic Japanese novelist
Gloria Naylor	African American novelist
Alice Paul	Feminist activist, founder of the Women's Party
Christine de Pisan	Medieval French feminist author
Hortense Powdermaker	American anthropologist
Nawal El Saadawi	Egyptian feminist author
Sakajaweea	Native American guide to Lewis and Clark Expedition
Sojourner Truth	Ex-slave itinerant preacher
Marina Tsvetaeva	Russian poet
Margaret Floy Washburn	American psychologist, President of APA
Ida B. Wells	Antilynching crusader, a founder of NAACP

(i.e., "objective") as those that try to exclude affect on the assumption that it is incompatible with objectivity. Teachers of the psychology of women have devised various ways of introducing feelingknowledge into their material.

One way is to appeal to students' personal experience. Before there was much research on women this was helpful to fill in the empty spaces in procedural knowledge in a science that had never studied women except as deviants from a norm. But personal experience always contains both feelings and values. It cannot pretend to be *im*personal, and thus is not obliged to pretend neutrality. What is good and what is deplorable are not separated from what is.

One way both authors have tried to include the personal is to assign readings in fiction, drama, and even biography. Reaching into representations of individuals' lives makes it possible to deal with "feelingthoughts" or "themata" in a way that "scientific" thinking often precludes. Unlike psychological case reports, most fiction retains all the value, affect, and emotion of people's original experience instead of filtering its facts through abstract concepts. Fiction also allows us to consider circumstances and cultures other than those represented in the classroom.

Use of Fiction and Drama

Psychological issues are often better highlighted in artistic literature, such as novels and plays, than in psychological case studies. For one thing, most artistic literature includes more women characters, deals more directly with interpersonal relations, and is more likely to consider social circumstance and cultural context. Imaginative writers are less likely to be influenced by male-biased psychological theory. They can deal more directly with "feelingthoughts" because their art is allowed, even expected, to focus on emotions in their natural contexts where they are not separated from reason. Selection of authors who are not middle-class white males reduces the effects of patriarchal "scientific" assumptions and stereotyping. A few examples from the authors' experience will also illustrate the potential of this kind of supplementary reading for bringing diversity into a psychology course. Instructors will, of course, choose works according to the particular groups and issues that seem most relevant in their situation.

Hurston, Zora Neale. (1978). *Their eyes were watching God.* Urbana, Ill.: University of Illinois Press. This popular novel has the advantage that, despite its setting in the poor rural black Florida of a few generations ago, it illustrates many of the same problems facing relatively affluent women in maintaining their individual identity while married. Janie finds herself merely used for her husbands' purposes in two marriages and finally escapes into an egalitarian marriage where she can be herself. One difficulty, however, was that the circumstances of her life and society were so different from those of Torrey's students, that they had some trouble identifying with her or understanding her life. In retrospect, Torrey thinks she should have more explicitly compared Janie's position as the mayor's wife with that of the wives of prominent men more like those with whom many students were familiar.

Larsen, Nella. (1986). *Quicksand* and *Passing.* New Brunswick, N.J.: Rutgers University Press. Torrey chose these two short novels because the central character in each is a middle-class black woman with whom students can identify more easily than with Hurston's Janie. In *Quicksand,* Nella's problems with the sexist society are similar to those of white students, but at the same time are modified and exacerbated by the addition of racism. Her sexuality is repressed by an anxiety concerning sex, which is exaggerated by the black middle-class need to counter the sexual aspects of racial stereotypes. In white society the racist imputation of "primitive" sexuality exaggerates her feeling of being more a sex *object* than a human *subject. Passing* shows the same anxiety about sexuality for black women, at the same time illustrating the implications of community membership, black or white, for light-skinned women, namely, the fact that race is more than a matter of external color but includes personal and social identity.

Morrison, Toni. (1970). *The bluest eye.* New York: Washington Square Press. An interesting interaction between sex and race in this novel revolves around the meanings of beauty for black women. Both the central character and her mother are obsessed with what are for them unattainable white standards of beauty, vividly portrayed in the response of some poor black girls to one of their number who has light skin, long hair, and nice clothes. The story also illustrates some implications of class because the central characters belong to a marginal urban "underclass," where few opportunities exist for what even they would consider a "decent" lifestyle.

Atwood, Margaret. (1986). *The handmaid's tale.* New York: Random House. Orza has found that Atwood's novel works well as a class assignment because it takes past and current racist and misogynist practices to their logical and horrifying conclusions in the state of Gilead, where female fertility has become so rare that those who still have it are enslaved for breeding purposes alone and deprived of all other humanity. The story narrates the thoughts of a young woman much like students today, who had once danced in a high school gymnasium and dreamed of romance and marriage. The final section, the futuristic "Historical Notes on the Handmaid's Tale" from the University of Denay (Denial), makes clear that in that institution men are still allowed to pontificate and make lewd jokes at women's expense. This should challenge students to realize that if they do nothing these practices will never end.

Atwood, Margaret. (1979). *Life before man.* New York: Fawcett Popular Library. Torrey has used another Atwood novel to raise questions about gender roles in love and marriage. It describes a love triangle involving a wife, who earns the family living and controls her husband; the husband, who keeps house and pursues his artistic goals; and a woman paleontologist who tries to escape to a prehistoric world where there were no men. Despite the role reversals all three in many ways conform to expectations for their own sex. In addition, issues of class and ethnicity interact with gender in the psychological makeup of all the characters.

We have not tried the following works as class assignments, but our experience suggests that they might be useful, especially to expand diversity.

Sarton, May. (1976). *As we are now.* New York: Norton. Not many novels are about the decrepit, those who are "feeble with old age." This one tells it like it is all too likely to be. Few students of any age will have imagined, let alone considered, the real possibility of ending their lives in the living hell in which Miss Stevens finds herself caught or the desperate measures she takes to effect her escape. Young heterosexuals, especially, will not have contemplated a situation in which a kind of physical love for another woman could be so necessary. It seems as though students could nevertheless identify with Miss Stevens and appreciate her responses.

Dangarembga, Tsitsi. (1988). *Nervous conditions*. Seattle: Seal Press. This apparently autobiographical novel is written by a woman from rural Zimbabwe. It is especially useful because it illustrates the interaction of the gender implications of two different patriarchal cultures in the lives of three women who live both in a traditional Shona context and in an English Christian one. The meanings of sex for status and manners in the two cultures create conflicts in their mutual understandings, in their motivations, and in the responses they encounter from men. The title of the novel is taken from Frantz Fanon: "The condition of native is a nervous condition," meaning that the psychology of the individual, including pathological symptoms, reflects and stems from the social context, especially position in the hierarchy of power under colonialism.

Kingston, Maxine Hong. (1977). *The woman warrior*. New York: Vintage Books. Tan, Amy. (1993). *The Joy Luck Club*. New York: Ivy Books. These two works bring students closer to a culture that is not only more ancient but also more alien to that of the white middle class than that of other American groups. Gender seems to be more fundamental to status and identity among the Chinese as well as among their American descendants. Because of the cultural differences effort will be needed to help most students recognize what similarities do exist between this culture and their own with respect to gender. But they will have no trouble perceiving that "other" women are indeed different, yet in some ways similar to themselves.

Brown, Rita Mae. (1988). *The Rubyfruit jungle*. New York: Bantam. Students will enjoy the rollicking good fun with which a devil-may-care lesbian girl confronts the straight and the homophobic in the world around her—if they are not too homophobic themselves. In the latter case they may not enjoy all of the humor, but they will get a glimpse of another side of the sexual orientation barrier and learn that life in that hidden world isn't necessarily all gloom, doom, and evil.

Flagg, Fannie. (1987). *Fried green tomatoes at the Whistle Stop Café*. New York: McGraw. Homophobia is probably less an obstacle to sympathy with the very committed lesbian couple who are central to this funny-but-serious tale. The narrator and other characters are also older women who illustrate not only some of the problems of various ages, but also the ways women—in this case mostly working-class women—cope with them.

Sarton, May. (1970). *Kinds of love*. New York: Norton. This novel explores at length loves within and between different ages and classes, including young, heterosexual love of the kind with which many students are familiar. Although it is longer than the ideal for collateral reading, it addresses issues of sex, age, and class in situations that are relevant to the psychology of women.

CONCLUSION

The most important inference we can derive from teaching the psychology of women is that in order to do it effectively we need to re-vision psychology as a whole. We must learn to see people as functioning organs of their society, serving to some extent *its* purposes as well as their own. In other words, we must stop thinking of society as simply a collection of human individuals.

This new perspective poses a problem in teaching students who have been accustomed to psychology's more traditional focus on the individual. We will encounter at least three kinds of resistance. First, students will respond to many of our insights as "more sociology than psychology." Second, they will accuse us of a bias toward women. Third, and more important, they will think we violate scientific objectivity by introducing political considerations.

As for the introduction of "sociology" into our courses, it is the very social nature of human beings that blurs the distinction between the disciplines. Because the whole category of women is largely a social construct, we cannot understand individual women if we try to define them entirely through biology. Learning about the long process of gender development should help students understand this reality, but having them examine their own personal experiences of being forced by social circumstances to act against their will should be even more convincing. Literary readings like those we have suggested are powerful persuaders that not only gender but also race, class, and age may determine individuals' decisions and actions—often against their own best interests.

As for our apparent bias toward women, it goes beyond the fact that women are our subject matter. Traditional psychology pretends to be unbiased, but we have found so many ways in which it reflects a bias toward men that even a slight leveling of the balance is bound to be perceived as a bias in the other direction. Just pointing to the gender implications of existing research and theory will appear to some as antimale prejudice. Nevertheless it is essential that we give students a realistic perspective on the antifemale bias in much of existing psychological research. Matlin's themes provide a valuable guide to such an examination.

As for the third kind of resistance, we will have to give serious attention in a course on psychology of women to political factors in the social order even though they are rarely dealt with in laboratory research. We cannot escape politics if we are to understand the psychology of women because our particular society is a hierarchical one in which males hold most of the power. Their law and order defends itself with an ideology structured so as to maintain the status quo, just as rationalizations and repressions defend the structure of the ego. Our society teaches us to regard human beings as autonomous individuals directed by biological nature together with internalized social rules and thus necessarily motivated entirely by self-interest. This assumption limits our science to the study of those who are powerful enough to *be* autonomous and to behave in their own interest. It also has the further effect of making the social and political hierarchy seem natural and inevitable. It is this notion of individual self-determination that imposes on less powerful people the responsibility for their own subordination. It forces them to seek solutions only within themselves and to blame themselves if they feel forced to submit to others. By ignoring and thus repressing the political factor of power in interpersonal behavior, psychology contributes to maintaining the social structure as it is. If we ask students to examine the circumstances of women in "real life" (or in its literary representation), it will be hard for them to ignore the role of power in psychological analysis. When we find women more sensitive than men to social relationships and more ready to act in the interests of people other than themselves, we have another clue to the necessity of seeking some of our understanding and solutions in sociopolitical factors rather than always in individual personalities. Our students must learn to accept the fact that traditional "objective" psychology is also political in that it defends the existing powers by persuading less powerful people that they must devote their efforts to changing themselves and leave the social order, which is the real source of their problems, unchanged.

REFERENCES

Adler, A. (1927). *The practice and theory of individual psychology.* New York: Harcourt, Brace & World.

Bardwick, J. M. (1971). *Psychology of women: A study of biocultural conflicts.* New York: Harper & Row.

Belenky, M. F., Clinchy, B. M., Goldberger, N. R., & Tarule, J. M. (1986). *Women's ways of knowing: The development of self, voice, and mind.* New York: Basic Books.

Bem, S. L. (1974). The measurement of psychological androgyny. *Journal of Consulting and Clinical Psychology, 42,* 155-162.

Berger, P., & Luckmann, T. (1967). *The social construction of reality.* Garden City, N.Y.: Anchor Books.

Gilligan, C. (1982). *In a different voice.* Cambridge, Mass.: Harvard University Press.

Gould, L. (1979). X—A fabulous child's story. In J. W. Mazow (Ed.), *The woman who lost her names: Selected writing by American Jewish women.* San Francisco, Calif.: Harper.

Fanon, F. (1967). *Black skin, white masks.* New York: Grove.

Fromm, E. (1962). *Beyond the chains of illusion: My encounter with Marx and Freud.* New York: Simon & Shuster.

Jung, C. G. (1976). The concept of the collective unconscious. In J. Campbell (Ed.), *The portable Jung* (pp. 59-69). New York: Penguin Books.

Kuhn, T. (1962). *The structure of scientific revolutions.* Chicago: University of Chicago Press.

McIntosh, J. (1983). *Interactive phases of curricular re-vision: A Feminist perspective* (Working Paper No. 124). Wellesley, Mass.: Wellesley College Center for Research on Women.

Matlin, M. W. (1987). *The psychology of women.* New York: Holt, Rinehart & Winston.

Miller, J. B. (1976). *Toward a new psychology of women.* Boston, Mass.: Beacon Press.

Miller, J. B. (1991, March). *Women's psychological development: Connections, disconnections, and violations.* Paper presented at the meeting of the Association for Women in Psychology, Hartford, Conn.

Paludi, M. A. (1990). *Exploring/teaching the psychology of women: A manual of resources.* Albany, N.Y.: State University of New York Press.

Spender, D. (Ed.) (1981). *Men's studies modified: The impact of feminism on the academic disciplines*. Oxford: Pergamon Press.

Stockard, J., & Johnson, M. M. (1980). *Sex roles: Sex inequality and sex role development*. Englewood Cliffs, N.J.: Prentice Hall.

Sullivan, H. A. (1964). *The fusion of psychiatry and social science*. New York: Norton.

Tavris, C., & Offir, C. (1977). *The longest war: Sex differences in perspective*. New York: Harcourt Brace Jovanovich.

Unger, R. K. (1979). Toward a redefinition of sex and gender. *American Psychologist, 31*, 1085-1094.

Weisstein, N. (1970). "Kinder, kuche, kirche" as scientific law: Psychology constructs the female. In R. Morgan (Ed.), *Sisterhood is powerful: An anthology of writings from the women's liberation movement* (pp. 205-220). New York: Vintage Books.

CONCLUSION

Reading this book, one is struck by the fact that there remain so many real gaps in our knowledge about the psychology of women despite twenty years of feminist research, practice, and theory. That women are both similar to and different from each other is obvious; yet psychology has paid much more attention to the "theme" than to the "variations." It is the editors' hope that this volume will draw attention to the many issues that have not yet been adequately addressed. Each chapter suggests ideas for research and applications, and readers will find many avenues to explore.

Two main themes seem to run through the chapters. First, the insistence of the male-dominated professions that women are "emotional" and unstable has negatively affected women's lives. The complaints of those who are "emotional" are easy to dismiss and ignore. Those who dismiss also have the power to decide to what we should pay attention. Thus women's depression, rather than our anger, becomes the focus of therapists' concern. Sexual harassment, rape, battering, racism, classism, heterosexism, women's less frequent referral for rehabilitation benefits, exclusion of women from medical research and leadership positions in religious life, lack of opportunity for mentoring and professional advancement, lack of day care services, inaccessible workplaces and public spaces, and the fact that information about the psychology of women is "boxed" and segregated from the rest of the text are legitimate causes of anger. Yet women are not supposed to be angry. The dismissal of women's complaints is a form of social control. If we're not "really" angry, there's no need to change things. If we're not "really" sick, we can be given psychotropic medications so that physicians can attend to those with "real" health problems.

Second, the invisibility of women and women's issues is another form of social control. Women students sit invisible in the classroom and listen to lectures about white men—their literature, their history, their psychology. The absence of women subjects in medical trials renders our physiology invisible. Two women in a restaurant are asked by a man if they're alone; is one of them invisible? Invisible—lesbians in a gynecologist's office, elderly women and disabled women anywhere. If they ignore us, will we go away?

Becoming visible is empowering. To be empowered does not mean we have to adopt the masculine norm of autonomy as the most worthy approach to life. We can join together in friendship and political coalitions with other women—those similar to us and those different from us—to celebrate our relational values, our connections, and our concern for others.

Stereotypes about women and the invisibility of some of our sisters and most of our issues have had deleterious effects on women's physical and mental health, our roles in society, and our ability to cause change. The social sciences and humanities, which have operated from an androcentric perspective, are poor, restricted illusions. There remains much to be learned before we can adequately describe, let alone remedy, the human condition. The authors and editors of this book are looking ahead to a nonsexist, nonracist, inclusive psychology. If we've inspired you to take steps that will lead toward that end, we've reached our goal.

CONTRIBUTORS

Rosalie J. Ackerman is a clinical neuropsychologist at the Timken Mercy Medical Center in Canton, Ohio. She has written extensively on neuropsychological issues, coauthored neuropsychological assessment batteries, and developed rehabilitation software for brain-injured patients.

Martha E. Banks is a clinical neuropsychologist at the Veterans Administration Medical Center in Brecksville, Ohio. She has written extensively on neuropsychological issues, coauthored neuropsychological assessment batteries, and developed rehabilitation software for brain-injured patients.

Sudha Choldin is a psychotherapist in private practice in Edmonton and teaches at the Women's Resource Centre at the University of Alberta. She was born and raised in India.

Joan C. Chrisler is associate professor of psychology at Connecticut College in New London, Connecticut. She has published extensively on women's health issues, particularly on eating and weight and on psychosocial aspects of the menstrual cycle.

Carolyn A. Corbett is assistant professor of psychology at Gallaudet University in Washington, D.C. Her research has focused on the mental health concerns of the deaf African American community.

Darlene C. DeFour is associate professor of psychology at Hunter College in New York City. Her research has focused on the impact of networks and mentors on the career development of black graduate students and professionals.

Carol B. Giesen is associate professor of psychology at St. Mary's College in St. Mary's City, Maryland. Her research has focused on the cognitive and affective changes that women experience following transitional life events.

Alyce Huston Hemstreet is a psychiatric clinical nurse specialist and APRN in private practice and associated with Lawrence and Memorial Hospital in New London, Connecticut. She is a frequent speaker on health psychology issues and is a Fellow of the American Academy of Pain Management.

Lillian P. Holcomb is a clinical psychologist in private practice in Hilo, Hawaii, and has taught at the University of Hawaii. A woman with multiple disabilities herself, Dr. Holcomb has both personal and professional interest in social justice and political advocacy for women with disabilities.

Gwat-Yong Lie is associate professor of social work at Arizona State University in Tempe, Arizona. Her research has focused on child abuse, partner abuse, and cultural diversity issues.

Jean H. Orost is a licensed psychologist and a Protestant minister. She is currently director of Christian education in a community church and adjunct professor of psychology at Eckerd College in Saint Petersburg, Florida.

Ann Marie Orza is professor of psychology at Eastern Connecticut State University in Willimantic, Connecticut. Her research has focused on gender issues, particularly working mothers, and she is producer and host of a local television program called "What About Women?"

Michele A. Paludi is the founder of Michele Paludi and Associates, consultants in sexual harassment. She has published extensively on all aspects of women's career development and has served as an expert witness in sexual harassment cases.

Suzanna Rose is associate professor of psychology and women's studies and director of the Lesbian and Gay Research Project at the University of Missouri in St. Louis. Her research has focused on personal relationships, particularly friendship, romance, sexuality, and professional networks.

Rachel Josefowitz Siegel is a clinical social worker in private practice in Ithaca, New York. Her professional interests are currently focused on older women and Jewish women.

Geraldine Butts Stahly is associate professor of psychology at California State University in San Bernardino, California. She is an applied social psychologist, and her research has focused on victimology and family violence.

Jane W. Torrey is professor emerita of psychology at Connecticut College and now lives in Jaffrey, New Hampshire. Her early research was in the field of psycholinguistics; more recently she has written about racism and sexism in women's lives.

INDEX